THE
"SUMMA THEOLOGICA"
OF
ST. THOMAS AQUINAS

PART I.
QQ. L.—LXXIV.

(3)

LITERALLY TRANSLATED BY
FATHERS OF THE ENGLISH DOMINICAN
PROVINCE

NEW IMPRESSION

LONDON
BURNS OATES & WASHBOURNE LTD
PUBLISHERS TO THE HOLY SEE

LETTER FROM THE CARDINAL SECRETARY OF STATE.

THE VATICAN,
February 24th, 1912.

To the Very Reverend Father Humbert Everest, O.P., Prior Provincial of the English Dominican Province.

REVEREND FATHER,

I am desired to inform you that the Holy Father has been pleased to express his gratitude on receiving from you the first volume of the *Summa* of St. Thomas Aquinas, which, with the assistance of your beloved brethren of the English Province, you have most wisely determined to translate into your mother-tongue. I say 'most wisely,' because to translate into the language of one's country the immortal works of St. Thomas is to give to its people a great treasure of human and Divine knowledge, and to afford those who are desirous of obtaining it, not only the best method of reasoning in unfolding and elucidating sacred truths, but also the most efficacious means of combating heresies. Therefore, without doubt, you have undertaken a task worthy of religious men—worthy of the sons of St. Dominic.

The Venerable Pontiff, in graciously accepting your gift, returns you most cordial thanks, and earnestly prays that your task may have a successful result and produce abundant fruit. In token of his appreciation, he most lovingly imparts to you and your fellow-workers the Apostolic Benediction.

And for myself I extend to you the right hand of fellowship, and thank you for the special volume of the translation which you presented to me.

I remain, Rev. Father,
Yours devotedly,
R. CARD. MERRY DEL VAL.

LETTER FROM THE MASTER-GENERAL OF THE FRIAR PREACHERS.

COLLEGIO ANGELICO,
ROMA, *May 21st*, 1911.

To the English Translators of the ' Summa Theologica ' of St. Thomas.

VERY REV. AND DEAR FATHERS,

In translating into English the *Summa Theologica* of St. Thomas, you undertake a work which will bring profit to the Church and honour to the Dominican Order, and which, I hope, will be acceptable even to the laity; for what was said of the great doctor by his contemporaries is true for all time—that everybody can gather fruit from his writings, which are within the grasp of all. As a matter of fact, St. Thomas appeals to the light of reason, not in order to weaken the ground of faith, which is the Divine Reason, infinitely surpassing the reason of man, but, on the contrary, in order to increase the merit of faith by making us adhere more firmly to His revelation. For we see thereby how reasonable is our submission, how salutary it is to the mind, how profitable for our guidance, how joyful to the heart.

May your work contribute to this end! Thus it will be a sermon, preached through the press, by reason of its diffusion and duration more fruitful than that preached by word of mouth.

I bless you in our Holy Father, St. Dominic, and ask the help of your prayers for the Order and for myself.

FR. HYACINTH M. CORMIER, O.P.,
Master-General.

CONTENTS

TREATISE ON THE ANGELS

QUESTION		PAGE
L.	OF THE SUBSTANCE OF THE ANGELS ABSOLUTELY CONSIDERED	3
LI.	OF THE ANGELS IN COMPARISON WITH BODIES	17
LII.	OF THE ANGELS IN RELATION TO PLACE	26
LIII.	OF THE LOCAL MOVEMENT OF THE ANGELS	31
LIV.	OF THE KNOWLEDGE OF THE ANGELS	41
LV.	OF THE MEDIUM OF THE ANGELIC KNOWLEDGE	51
LVI.	OF THE ANGELS' KNOWLEDGE OF IMMATERIAL THINGS	59
LVII.	OF THE ANGELS' KNOWLEDGE OF MATERIAL THINGS	67
LVIII.	OF THE MODE OF THE ANGELIC KNOWLEDGE	80
LIX.	THE WILL OF THE ANGELS	95
LX	OF THE LOVE OR DILECTION OF THE ANGELS	105
LXI.	OF THE PRODUCTION OF THE ANGELS IN THE ORDER OF NATURAL BEING	117
LXII.	OF THE PERFECTION OF THE ANGELS IN THE ORDER OF GRACE AND OF GLORY	124
LXIII.	THE MALICE OF THE ANGELS WITH REGARD TO SIN	143
LXIV.	THE PUNISHMENT OF THE DEMONS	164

TREATISE ON THE WORK OF THE SIX DAYS

LXV.	THE WORK OF CREATION OF CORPOREAL CREATURES	179
LXVI.	ON THE ORDER OF CREATION TOWARDS DISTINCTION	191
LXVII.	ON THE WORK OF DISTINCTION IN ITSELF	206
LXVIII.	ON THE WORK OF THE SECOND DAY	217
LXIX.	ON THE WORK OF THE THIRD DAY	230
LXX.	OF THE WORK OF ADORNMENT, AS REGARDS THE FOURTH DAY	238
LXXI.	ON THE WORK OF THE FIFTH DAY	249
LXXII.	ON THE WORK OF THE SIXTH DAY	253
LXXIII.	ON THE THINGS THAT BELONG TO THE SEVENTH DAY	257
LXXIV.	ON ALL THE SEVEN DAYS IN COMMON	264

TREATISE ON THE ANGELS

THE "SUMMA THEOLOGICA"

FIRST PART.
TREATISE ON THE ANGELS.

QUESTION L.
OF THE SUBSTANCE OF THE ANGELS ABSOLUTELY CONSIDERED.
(*In Five Articles.*)

NEXT we consider the distinction of corporeal and spiritual creatures: firstly, the purely spiritual creature which in Holy Scripture is called angel; secondly, the creature wholly corporeal; thirdly, the composite creature, corporeal and spiritual, which is man.

Concerning the angels, we consider first what belongs to their substance; secondly, what belongs to their intellect; thirdly, what belongs to their will; fourthly, what belongs to their creation.

Their substance we consider absolutely, and in relation to corporeal things.

Concerning their substance absolutely considered, there are five points of inquiry: (1) Whether there is any entirely spiritual creature, altogether incorporeal? (2) Supposing that an angel is such, we ask whether it is composed of matter and form? (3) We ask concerning their number. (4) Of their difference from each other. (5) Of their immortality or incorruptibility.

First Article.

WHETHER AN ANGEL IS ALTOGETHER INCORPOREAL?

We proceed thus to the First Article:—

Objection 1. It would seem that an angel is not entirely incorporeal. For what is incorporeal only as regards ourselves, and not in relation to God, is not absolutely incorporeal. But Damascene says (*De Fid. Orth.* ii.) that *an angel is said to be incorporeal and immaterial as regards us, but compared to God it is corporeal and material.* Therefore *he is not simply incorporeal.*

Obj. 2. Further, nothing is moved except a body, as the Philosopher says (*Phys.* vi., text. 32). But Damascene says (*De Fid. Orth.* ii.) that *an angel is an ever movable intellectual substance.* Therefore an angel is a corporeal substance.

Obj. 3. Further, Ambrose says (*De Spir. Sanct.* i. 7): *Every creature is limited within its own nature.* But to be limited belongs to bodies. Therefore, every creature is corporeal. Now angels are God's creatures, as appears from Ps. cxlviii. 2: *Praise ye the Lord, all His angels;* and, farther on (*verse* 4), *For He spoke, and they were made; He commanded, and they were created.* Therefore angels are corporeal.

On the contrary, It is said (Ps. ciii. 4): *Who makes His angels spirits.*

I answer that, There must be some incorporeal creatures. For what is principally intended by God in creatures is good, and this consists in assimilation to God Himself. And the perfect assimilation of an effect to a cause is accomplished when the effect imitates the cause according to that whereby the cause produces the effect; as heat makes heat. Now, God produces the creature by His intellect and will (Q. XIV., A. 8; Q. XIX., A. 4). Hence the perfection of the universe requires that there should be intellectual creatures. Now intelligence cannot be the action of a body, nor of any corporeal faculty; for every body is limited to *here* and *now*. Hence the perfection of the universe requires the existence of an incorporeal creature.

The ancients, however, not properly realizing the force of intelligence, and failing to make a proper distinction between sense and intellect, thought that nothing existed in the world but what could be apprehended by sense and imagination. And because bodies alone fall under imagination, they supposed that no being existed except bodies, as the Philosopher observes (*Phys.* iv., text. 52, 57). Thence came the error of the Sadducees, who said there was no spirit (Acts xxiii. 8).

But the very fact that intellect is above sense is a reasonable proof that there are some incorporeal things comprehensible by the intellect alone.

Reply Obj. 1. Incorporeal substances rank between God and corporeal creatures. Now the medium compared to one extreme appears to be the other extreme, as what is tepid compared to heat seems to be cold; and thus it is said that the angels, compared to God, are material and corporeal, not, however, as if anything corporeal existed in them.

Reply Obj. 2. Movement is there taken in the sense in which it is applied to intelligence and will. Therefore an angel is called an ever mobile substance, because he is ever actually intelligent, and not as if he were sometimes actually and sometimes potentially, as we are. Hence it is clear that the objection rests on an equivocation.

Reply Obj. 3. To be circumscribed by local limits belongs to bodies only; whereas to be circumscribed by essential limits belongs to all creatures, both corporeal and spiritual. Hence Ambrose says (*ibid.*) that *although some things are not contained in corporeal place, still they are none the less circumscribed by their substance.*

Second Article.

WHETHER AN ANGEL IS COMPOSED OF MATTER AND FORM?

We proceed thus to the Second Article:—

Objection 1. It would seem that an angel is composed of matter and form. For everything which is contained under any genus is composed of the genus, and of the difference which added to the genus makes the species. But the genus comes from the matter, and the difference from the form (*Metaph.* xiii., text. 6). Therefore everything which is in a genus is composed of matter and form. But an angel is in the genus of substance. Therefore he is composed of matter and form.

Obj. 2. Further, wherever the properties of matter exist, there is matter. Now the properties of matter are to receive and to substand; whence Boëthius says (*De Trin.*) that *a simple form cannot be a subject:* and the above properties are found in the angel. Therefore an angel is composed of matter and form.

Obj. 3. Further, form is act. So what is form only is pure act. But an angel is not pure act, for this belongs to God alone. Therefore an angel is not form only, but has a form in matter.

Obj. 4. Further, form is properly limited and perfected by matter. So the form which is not in matter is an infinite form. But the form of an angel is not infinite, for every creature is finite. Therefore the form of an angel is in matter.

On the contrary, Dionysius says (*Div. Nom.* iv.): *The first creatures are understood to be as immaterial as they are incorporeal.*

I answer that, Some assert that the angels are composed of matter and form; which opinion Avicebron endeavoured to establish in his book of the *Fount of Life.* For he supposes that whatever things are distinguished by the intellect are really distinct. Now as regards incorporeal substance, the intellect apprehends that which distinguishes it from corporeal substance, and that which it has in common with it. Hence he concludes that what distinguishes incorporeal from corporeal substance is a kind of form to it, and whatever is subject to this distinguishing form, as it were something common, is its matter. Therefore, he asserts, the universal matter of spiritual and corporeal things is the same; so that it must be understood that the form of incorporeal substance is impressed in the matter of spiritual things, in the same way as the form of quantity is impressed in the matter of corporeal things.

But one glance is enough to show that there cannot be one matter of spiritual and of corporeal things. For it is not possible that a spiritual and a corporeal form should be received into the same part of matter, otherwise one and the same thing would be corporeal and spiritual. Hence it would follow that one part of matter receives the corporeal form, and another receives the spiritual form. Matter, however, is not divisible into parts except as regarded under quantity; and without quantity substance is indivisible, as Aristotle says (*Phys.* 1., text. 15). Therefore it would follow that the matter of spiritual things is subject to quantity; which cannot be. Therefore it is impossible that corporeal and spiritual things should have the same matter.

It is, further, impossible for an intellectual substance to have any kind of matter. For the operation belonging to anything is according to the mode of its substance. Now to understand is an altogether immaterial operation, as appears from its object, whence any act receives its species and nature. For a thing is understood according to its degree of immateriality; because forms that exist in matter are individual forms which the intellect cannot apprehend as such. Hence it must be that every intellectual substance is altogether immaterial.

But things distinguished by the intellect are not necessarily distinguished in reality; because the intellect does not apprehend things according to their mode, but according to its own mode. Hence material things which are below our intellect exist in our intellect in a simpler mode than they exist in themselves. Angelic substances, on the other hand, are above our intellect; and hence our intellect cannot attain to apprehend them, as they are in themselves, but by its own mode, according as it apprehends composite things; and in this way also it apprehends God (Q. III.).

Reply Obj. 1. It is difference which constitutes the species. Now everything is constituted in a species according as it is determined to some special grade of being because *the species of things are like numbers,* which differ by the addition and subtraction of unity, as the Philosopher says (*Metaph.* viii., text. 10). But in material things there is one thing which determines to a special grade, and that is the form; and another thing which is determined, and this is the matter; and hence from the latter the *genus* is derived, and from the former the *difference.* Whereas in immaterial things there is no separate determinator and thing determined; each thing by its own self holds a determinate grade in being; and therefore in them *genus* and *difference* are not derived from different things, but from one and the same. Nevertheless, this differs in our mode of conception; for, inasmuch as our intellect considers it as indeterminate, it derives the idea of their *genus;* and inasmuch as it considers it determinately, it derives the idea of their difference.

Reply Obj. 2. This reason is given in the book on the *Fount of Life,* and it would be cogent, supposing that the receptive mode of the intellect and of matter were the same. But this is clearly false. For matter receives the form, that thereby it may be constituted in some species, either of air, or of fire, or of something else. But the intellect does not receive the form in the same way; otherwise the opinion of Empedocles (*De Anima* i. 5, text. 26) would be true, to the effect that we know earth by earth, and fire by fire. But the intelligible form is in the intellect according to the very nature of a form; for as such is it so known by the intellect. Hence such a way of receiving is not that of matter, but of an immaterial substance.

Reply Obj. 3. Although there is no composition of matter and form in an angel, yet there is act and potentiality.

And this can be made evident if we consider the nature of material things, which contain a twofold composition. The first is that of form and matter, whereby the nature is constituted. Such a composite nature is not its own existence; but existence is its act. Hence the nature itself is related to its own existence as potentiality to act. Therefore if there be no matter, and supposing that the form itself subsists without matter, there nevertheless still remains the relation of the form to its very existence, as of potentiality to act. And such a kind of composition is understood to be in the angels; and this is what some say, that an angel is composed of, *whereby he is,* and *what is,* or *existence,* and *what is,* as Boëthius says. For *what is,* is the form itself subsisting; and the existence itself is whereby the substance is; as the running is whereby the runner runs. But in God *existence* and *what is* are not different, as was explained above (Q. III., A. 4). Hence God alone is pure act.

Reply Obj. 4. Every creature is simply finite, inasmuch as its existence is not absolutely subsisting, but is limited to some nature to which it belongs. But there is nothing against a creature being considered relatively infinite. Material creatures are infinite on the part of matter, but finite in their form, which is limited by the matter which receives it. But immaterial created substances are finite in their being; whereas they are infinite in the sense that their forms are not received in anything else; as if we were to say, for example, that whiteness existing separate is infinite as regards the nature of whiteness, forasmuch as it is not contracted to any one subject; while its *being* is finite as determined to some one special nature.

Whence it is said (*De Causis*, prop. 16) that *intelligence is finite from above,* as receiving its being from above itself, and is *infinite from below,* as not received in any matter.

Third Article.

Whether the angels exist in any great number?

We proceed thus to the Third Article:—

Objection 1. It would seem that the angels are not in great numbers. For number is a species of quantity, and follows the division of a continuous body. But this cannot be in the angels, since they are incorporeal, as was shown above (A. 1). Therefore the angels cannot exist in any great number.

Obj. 2. Further, the more a thing approaches to unity, so much the less is it multiplied, as is evident in numbers. But among other created natures the angelic nature approaches nearest to God. Therefore since God is supremely one, it seems that there is the least possible number in the angelic nature.

Obj. 3. Further, the proper effect of the separate substances seems to be the movements of the heavenly bodies. But the movements of the heavenly bodies fall within some small determined number, which we can apprehend. Therefore the angels are not in greater number than the movements of the heavenly bodies.

Obj. 4. Dionysius says (*Div. Nom.* iv.) that *all intelligible and intellectual substances subsist because of the rays of the divine goodness.* But a ray is only multiplied according to the different things that receive it. Now it cannot be said that their matter is receptive of an intelligible ray, since intellectual substances are immaterial, as was shown above (A. 2). Therefore it seems that the multiplication of intellectual substances can only be according to the requirements of the first bodies—that is, of the heavenly ones, so that in some way the shedding form of the aforesaid rays may be terminated in them; and hence, the same conclusion is to be drawn as before.

On the contrary, It is said (Dan. vii. 10): *Thousands of thousands ministered to Him, and ten thousand times a hundred thousand stood before Him.*

SUBSTANCE OF THE ANGELS Q. 50 Art. 3

I answer that, There have been various opinions with regard to the number of the separate substances. Plato contended that the separate substances are the species of sensible things; as if we were to maintain that human nature is a separate substance of itself: and according to this view it would have to be maintained that the number of the separate substances is the number of the species of sensible things. Aristotle, however, rejects this view (*Metaph.* i., text. 31) because matter is of the very nature of the species of sensible things. Consequently the separate substances cannot be the exemplar species of these sensible things; but have their own fixed natures, which are higher than the natures of sensible things. Nevertheless Aristotle held (*Metaph.* xi., text. 43) that those more perfect natures bear relation to these sensible things, as that of mover and end; and therefore he strove to find out the number of the separate substances according to the number of the first movements.

But since this appears to militate against the teachings of Sacred Scripture, Rabbi Moses the Jew, wishing to bring both into harmony, held that the angels, in so far as they are styled immaterial substances, are multiplied according to the number of heavenly movements or bodies, as Aristotle held (*loc. cit.*); while he contended that in the Scriptures even men bearing a divine message are styled angels; and again, even the powers of natural things, which manifest God's almighty power. It is, however, quite foreign to the custom of the Scriptures for the powers of irrational things to be designated as angels.

Hence it must be said that the angels, even inasmuch as they are immaterial substances, exist in exceeding great number, far beyond all material multitude. This is what Dionysius says (*Cœl. Hier.* xiv.): *There are many blessed armies of the heavenly intelligences, surpassing the weak and limited reckoning of our material numbers.* The reason whereof is this, because, since it is the perfection of the universe that God chiefly intends in the creation of things, the more perfect some things are, in so much greater an excess are they created by God. Now, as in bodies such excess is observed in regard to their magnitude, so in things incorporeal is it observed in regard to their multitude. We see, in fact, that incorruptible bodies, which are the most perfect of bodies, exceed corruptible bodies almost incomparably in magnitude; for the entire sphere of things active and passive is something very small in comparison with the heavenly bodies. Hence it is reasonable to conclude that the immaterial substances as it were incomparably exceed material substances as to multitude.

Reply Obj. 1. In the angels number is not that of discrete quantity, brought about by division of what is continuous, but that which is caused by distinction of forms; according as multitude is reckoned among the transcendentals, as was said above (Q. XXX., A. 3; Q. XI.).

Reply Obj. 2. From the angelic nature being nighest unto God, it must needs have least of multitude in its composition, but not so as to be found in few subjects.

Reply Obj. 3. This is Aristotle's argument (*Metaph.* xii., text. 44), and it would conclude necessarily if the separate substances were made for corporeal substances. For thus the immaterial substances would exist to no purpose, unless some movement from them were to appear in corporeal things. But it is not true that the immaterial substances exist on account of the corporeal, because the end is nobler than the means to the end. Hence Aristotle says (*loc. cit.*) that this is not a necessary argument, but a probable one. He was forced to make use of this argument, since only through sensible things can we come to know intelligible ones.

Reply Obj. 4. This argument comes from the opinion of such as hold that matter is the cause of the distinction of things; but this was refuted above (Q. XLVII., A. 1). Accordingly, the multiplication of the angels is not to be taken according to matter, nor according to bodies, but according to the divine wisdom devising the various orders of immaterial substances.

Fourth Article.

WHETHER THE ANGELS DIFFER IN SPECIES?

We proceed thus to the Fourth Article:—

Objection 1. It would seem that the angels do not differ in species. For since the *difference* is nobler than the *genus*, all things which agree in what is noblest in them, agree likewise in their ultimate constitutive difference; and so they are the same according to species. But all the angels agree in what is noblest in them—that is to say, in intellectuality. Therefore all the angels are of one species.

Obj. 2. Further, more and less do not change a species. But the angels seem to differ only from one another according to more and less—namely, as one is simpler than another, and of keener intellect. Therefore the angels do not differ specifically.

Obj. 3. Further, soul and angel are contra-distinguished mutually from each other. But all souls are of the one species. So therefore are the angels.

Obj. 4. Further, the more perfect a thing is in nature, the more ought it to be multiplied. But this would not be so if there were but one individual under one species. Therefore there are many angels of one species.

On the contrary, In things of one species there is no such thing as *first* and *second* (prius et posterius), as the Philosopher says (*Metaph*. iii., text. 2). But in the angels even of the one order there are first, middle, and last, as Dionysius says (*Hier. Ang.* x.). Therefore the angels are not of the same species.

I answer that, Some have said that all spiritual substances, even souls, are of the one species. Others, again, that all the angels are of the one species, but not souls; while others allege that all the angels of one hierarchy, or even of one order, are of the one species.

But this is impossible. For such things as agree in species but differ in number, agree in form, but are distinguished materially. If, therefore, the angels be not composed of matter and form, as was said above (A. 2), it follows that it is impossible for two angels to be of one species; just as it would be impossible for there to be several whitenesses apart, or several humanities, since whitenesses are not several, except in so far as they are in several substances. And if the angels had matter, not even then could there be several angels of one species. For it would be necessary for matter to be the principle of distinction of one from the other, not, indeed, according to the division of quantity, since they are incorporeal, but according to the diversity of their powers: and such diversity of matter causes diversity not merely of species, but of genus.

Reply Obj. 1. *Difference* is nobler than *genus*, as the determined is more noble than the undetermined, and the proper than the common, but not as one nature is nobler than another; otherwise it would be necessary that all irrational animals be of the same species; or that there should be in them some form which is higher than the sensible soul. Therefore irrational animals differ in species according to the various determined degrees of sensitive nature; and in like manner all the angels differ in species according to the diverse degrees of intellectual nature.

Reply Obj. 2. More and less change the species, not according as they are caused by the intensity or remissness of one form, but according as they are caused by forms of diverse degrees; for instance, if we say that fire is more perfect than air: and in this way the angels are diversified according to more and less.

Reply Obj. 3. The good of the species preponderates over the good of the individual. Hence it is much better for the species to be multiplied in the angels than for individuals to be multiplied in the one species.

Reply Obj. 4. Numerical multiplication, since it can be drawn out infinitely, is not intended by the agent, but only specific multiplication, as was said above (Q. XLVII., A. 3). Hence the perfection of the angelic nature calls for the multiplying of species, but not for the multiplying of individuals in one species.

FIFTH ARTICLE.

WHETHER THE ANGELS ARE INCORRUPTIBLE?

We proceed thus to the Fifth Article:—

Objection 1. It would seem that the angels are not incorruptible; for Damascene, speaking of the angel, says (*De Fide Orth.* ii. 3) that he is *an intellectual substance, partaking of immortality by favour, and not by nature.*

Obj. 2. Further, Plato says in the *Timæus: O gods of gods, whose maker and father am I: You are indeed my works, dissoluble by nature, yet indissoluble because I so will it.* But gods such as these can only be understood to be the angels. Therefore the angels are corruptible by their nature.

Obj. 3. Further, according to Gregory (*Moral.* xvi.), *all things would tend towards nothing, unless the hand of the Almighty preserved them.* But what can be brought to nothing is corruptible. Therefore, since the angels were made by God, it would appear that they are corruptible of their own nature.

On the contrary, Dionysius says (*Div. Nom.* iv.) that the intellectual substances *have unfailing life, being free from all corruption, death, matter, and generation.*

I answer that, It must necessarily be maintained that the angels are incorruptible of their own nature. The reason for this is, that nothing is corrupted except by its form being separated from the matter. Hence, since an angel is a subsisting form, as is clear from what was said above (A. 2), it is impossible for its substance to be corruptible. For what belongs to anything considered in itself can never be separated from it; but what belongs to a thing, considered in relation to something else, can be separated, when that something else is taken away, in view of which it belonged to it. Roundness can never be taken from the circle, because it belongs to it of itself; but a bronze circle can lose roundness, if the bronze be deprived of its circular shape. Now to be belongs to a form considered in itself; for everything is an actual being according to its form: whereas matter is an actual being by the form. Consequently a subject composed of matter and form ceases to be actually when the form is separated from the matter. But if the form subsists in its own being, as happens in the angels, as was said above (A. 2), it cannot lose its being. Therefore, the angel's immateriality is the cause why it is incorruptible by its own nature.

A token of this incorruptibility can be gathered from its intellectual operation; for since everything acts according as it is actual, the operation of a thing indicates its mode of being. Now the species and nature of the operation is understood from the object. But an intelligible object, being above time, is everlasting. Hence every intellectual substance is incorruptible of its own nature.

Reply Obj. 1. Damascene is dealing with perfect immortality, which includes complete immutability; since *every change is a kind of death,* as Augustine says (*Contra Maxim.* iii.). The angels obtain perfect immutability only by favour, as will appear later (Q. LXII.).

Reply Obj. 2. By the expression *gods* Plato understands the heavenly bodies, which he supposed to be made up of elements, and therefore dissoluble of their own nature; yet they are for ever preserved in existence by the Divine will.

Reply Obj. 3. As was observed above (Q. XLIV., A. 1) there is a kind of necessary thing which has a cause of its necessity. Hence it is not repugnant to a necessary or incorruptible being to depend for its existence on another as its cause. Therefore, when it is said that all things, even the angels, would lapse into nothing, unless preserved by God, it is not to be gathered therefrom that there is any principle of corruption in the angels; but that the nature of the angels is dependent upon God as its cause. For a thing is said to be corruptible not merely because God can reduce it to non-existence, by withdrawing His act of preservation; but also because it has some principle of corruption within itself, or some contrariety, or at least the potentiality of matter.

QUESTION LI.

OF THE ANGELS IN COMPARISON WITH BODIES.

(*In Three Articles.*)

WE next inquire about the angels in comparison with corporeal things; and in the first place about their comparison with bodies; secondly, of the angels in comparison with corporeal places; and, thirdly, of their comparison with local movement.

Under the first heading there are three points of inquiry : (1) Whether angels have bodies naturally united to them? (2) Whether they assume bodies? (3) Whether they exercise functions of life in the bodies assumed?

FIRST ARTICLE.

WHETHER THE ANGELS HAVE BODIES NATURALLY UNITED TO THEM?

We proceed thus to the First Article:—

Objection 1. It would seem that angels have bodies naturally united to them. For Origen says (*Peri Archon* i.) : *It is God's attribute alone—that is, it belongs to the Father, the Son, and the Holy Ghost, as a property of nature, that He is understood to exist without any material substance and without any companionship of corporeal addition.* Bernard likewise says (*Hom. vi. super Cant.*) : *Let us assign incorporeity to God alone even as we do immortality, whose nature alone, neither for its own sake nor on account of anything else, needs the help of any corporeal organ. But it is clear that every created spirit needs corporeal assistance.* Augustine also says (*Gen. ad lit.* iii.) :

The demons are called animals of the atmosphere because their nature is akin to that of aerial bodies. But the nature of demons and angels is the same. Therefore angels have bodies naturally united to them.

Obj. 2. Further, Gregory (*Hom.* x. *in Ev.*) calls an angel a rational animal. But every animal is composed of body and soul. Therefore angels have bodies naturally united to them.

Obj. 3. Further, life is more perfect in the angels than in souls. But the soul not only lives, but gives life to the body. Therefore the angels animate bodies which are naturally united to them.

On the contrary, Dionysius says (*Div. Nom.* iv.) that *the angels are understood to be incorporeal.*

I answer that, The angels have not bodies naturally united to them. For whatever belongs to any nature as an accident is not found universally in that nature: thus, for instance, to have wings, because it is not of the essence of an animal, does not belong to every animal. Now since to understand is not the act of a body, nor of any corporeal energy, as will be shown later (Q. LXXV., A. 2), it follows that to have a body united to it is not of the nature of an intellectual substance, as such; but it is accidental to some intellectual substance on account of something else. Even so it belongs to the human soul to be united to a body, because it is imperfect and exists potentially in the genus of intellectual substances, not having the fulness of knowledge in its own nature, but acquiring it from sensible things through the bodily senses, as will be explained later on (Q. LXXXIV., A. 6; Q. LXXXIX., A. 1). Now whenever we find something imperfect in any genus we must presuppose something perfect in that genus. Therefore in the intellectual nature there are some perfectly intellectual substances, which do not need to acquire knowledge from sensible things. Consequently not all intellectual substances are united to bodies; but some are quite separated from bodies, and these we call angels.

Reply Obj. 1. As was said above (Q. L., A. 1) it was the

opinion of some that every being is a body; and consequently some seem to have thought that there were no incorporeal substances existing except as united to bodies; so much so that some even held that God was the soul of the world, as Augustine tells us (*De Civ. Dei* vii.). As this is contrary to Catholic Faith, which asserts that God is exalted above all things, according to Psalm viii. 2 : *Thy magnificence is exalted beyond the heavens;* Origen, while refusing to say such a thing of God, followed the above opinion of others regarding the other substances; being deceived here as he was also in many other points, by following the opinions of the ancient philosophers. Bernard's expression can be explained, that the created spirit needs some bodily instrument, which is not naturally united to it, but assumed for some purpose, as will be explained (A. 2). Augustine speaks, not as asserting the fact, but merely using the opinion of the Platonists, who maintained that there are some aerial animals, which they termed demons.

Reply Obj. 2. Gregory calls the angel a rational animal metaphorically, on account of the likeness to the rational nature.

Reply Obj. 3. To give life effectively is a perfection simply speaking; hence it belongs to God, as is said (1 Kings ii. 6) : *The Lord killeth, and maketh alive.* But to give life formally belongs to a substance which is part of some nature, and which has not within itself the full nature of the species. Hence an intellectual substance which is not united to a body is more perfect than one which is united to a body.

SECOND ARTICLE.

WHETHER ANGELS ASSUME BODIES ?

We proceed thus to the Second Article :—

Objection 1. It would seem that angels do not assume bodies. For there is nothing superfluous in the work of an angel, as there is nothing of the kind in the work of nature. But it would be superfluous for the angels to assume bodies, because an angel has no need for a body, since his own power exceeds all bodily power. Therefore an angel does not assume a body.

Obj. 2. Further, every assumption is terminated in some union; because to assume implies a taking to oneself (*ad se sumere*). But a body is not united to an angel as to a form, as stated (A. 1); while in so far as it is united to the angel as to a mover, it is not said to be assumed, otherwise it would follow that all bodies moved by the angels are assumed by them. Therefore the angels do not assume bodies.

Obj. 3. Further, angels do not assume bodies from the earth or water, or they could not suddenly disappear; nor again from fire, otherwise they would burn whatever things they touched; nor again from air, because air is without shape or colour. Therefore the angels do not assume bodies.

On the contrary, Augustine says (*De Civ. Dei* xvi.) that angels appeared to Abraham under assumed bodies.

I answer that, Some have maintained that the angels never assume bodies, but that all that we read in Scripture of apparitions of angels happened in prophetic vision— that is, according to imagination. But this is contrary to the intent of Scripture; for whatever is beheld in imaginary vision is only in the beholder's imagination, and consequently is not seen by everybody. Yet Divine Scripture from time to time introduces angels so apparent as to be seen commonly by all; just as the angels who appeared to Abraham were seen by him and by his whole family, by Lot, and by the citizens of Sodom; in like manner the angel who appeared to Tobias was seen by all present. From all this it is clearly shown that such apparitions were beheld by bodily vision, whereby the object seen exists outside the person beholding it, and can accordingly be seen by all. Now by such vision only a body can be beheld. Consequently, since the angels are not bodies, nor have they bodies naturally united with them, as is clear from what has been said (A. 1; Q. L., A. 1), it follows that they sometimes assume bodies.

Reply Obj. 1. Angels need an assumed body, not for themselves, but on our account; that by conversing familiarly with men they may give evidence of that intellectual companionship which men expect to have with them in the life to come. Moreover that angels assumed bodies under the Old Law was a figurative indication that the Word of God would take a human body; because all the apparitions in the Old Testament were ordained to that one whereby the Son of God appeared in the flesh.

Reply Obj. 2. The body assumed is united to the angel not as its form, nor merely as its mover, but as its mover represented by the assumed movable body. For as in the Sacred Scripture the properties of intelligible things are set forth by the likenesses of things sensible, in the same way by Divine power sensible bodies are so fashioned by angels as fittingly to represent the intelligible properties of an angel. And this is what we mean by an angel assuming a body.

Reply Obj. 3. Although air as long as it is in a state of rarefaction has neither shape nor colour, yet when condensed it can both be shaped and coloured as appears in the clouds. Even so the angels assume bodies of air, condensing it by Divine power in so far as is needful for forming the assumed body.

THIRD ARTICLE.

WHETHER THE ANGELS EXERCISE FUNCTIONS OF LIFE IN THE BODIES ASSUMED?

We proceed thus to the Third Article:—

Objection 1. It would seem that the angels exercise functions of life in assumed bodies. For pretence is unbecoming in angels of truth. But it would be pretence if the body assumed by them, which seems to live and to exercise vital functions, did not possess these functions. Therefore the angels exercise functions of life in the assumed body.

Obj. 2. Further, in the works of the angels there is

nothing without a purpose. But eyes, nostrils, and the other instruments of the senses, would be fashioned without a purpose in the body assumed by the angel, if he perceived nothing by their means. Consequently, the angel perceives by the assumed body ; and this is the most special function of life.

Obj. 3. Further, to move hither and thither is one of the functions of life, as the Philosopher says (*De Anima* ii.). But the angels are manifestly seen to move in their assumed bodies. For it is said (Gen. xviii. 16) that *Abraham walked with* the angels, who had appeared to him, *bringing them on the way;* and when Tobias said to the angel (Tob. v. 7, 8) : *Knowest thou the way that leadeth to the city of the Medes?* he answered : *I know it; and I have often walked through all the ways thereof.* Therefore the angels often exercise functions of life in assumed bodies.

Obj. 4. Further, speech is the function of a living subject, for it is produced by the voice, while the voice itself is a sound conveyed from the mouth. But it is evident from many passages of Sacred Scripture that angels spoke in assumed bodies. Therefore in their assumed bodies they exercise functions of life.

Obj. 5. Further, eating is a purely animal function. Hence the Lord after His Resurrection ate with His disciples in proof of having resumed life (Luke xxiv.). Now when angels appeared in their assumed bodies they ate, and Abraham offered them food, after having previously adored them as God (Gen. xviii.). Therefore the angels exercise functions of life in assumed bodies.

Obj. 6. Further, to beget offspring is a vital act. But this has befallen the angels in their assumed bodies; for it is related : *After the sons of God went in to the daughters of men, and they brought forth children, these are the mighty men of old, men of renown* (Gen. vi. 4). Consequently the angels exercised vital functions in their assumed bodies.

On the contrary, The bodies assumed by angels have no life, as was stated in the previous article (*ad* 3). Therefore they cannot exercise functions of life through assumed bodies.

I answer that, Some functions of living subjects have something in common with other operations; just as speech, which is the function of a living creature, agrees with other sounds of inanimate things, in so far as it is sound; and walking agrees with other movements, in so far as it is movement. Consequently vital functions can be performed in assumed bodies by the angels, as to that which is common in such operations; but not as to that which is special to living subjects; because, according to the Philosopher (*De Somn. et Vig.* i.), *that which has the faculty has the action*. Hence nothing can have a function of life except what has life, which is the potential principle of such action.

Reply Obj. 1. As it is in no wise contrary to truth for intelligible things to be set forth in Scripture under sensible figures, since it is not said for the purpose of maintaining that intelligible things are sensible, but in order that properties of intelligible things may be understood according to similitude through sensible figures; so it is not contrary to the truth of the holy angels that through their assumed bodies they appear to be living men, although they really are not. For the bodies are assumed merely for this purpose, that the spiritual properties and works of the angels may be manifested by the properties of man and of his works. This could not so fittingly be done if they were to assume true men; because the properties of such men would lead us to men, and not to angels.

Reply Obj. 2. Sensation is entirely a vital function. Consequently it can in no way be said that the angels perceive through the organs of their assumed bodies. Yet such bodies are not fashioned in vain; for they are not fashioned for the purpose of sensation through them, but to this end, that by such bodily organs the spiritual powers of the angels may be made manifest; just as by the eye the power of the angel's knowledge is pointed out, and other powers by the other members, as Dionysius teaches (*Cœl. Hier.*).

Reply Obj. 3. Movement coming from a united mover is a proper function of life; but the bodies assumed by the angels are not thus moved, since the angels are not their forms. Yet the angels are moved accidentally, when such bodies are moved, since they are in them as movers are in the moved; and they are here in such a way as not to be elsewhere, which cannot be said of God. Accordingly, although God is not moved when the things are moved in which He exists, since He is everywhere; yet the angels are moved accidentally according to the movement of the bodies assumed. But they are not moved according to the movement of the heavenly bodies, even though they be in them as the movers in the things moved, because the heavenly bodies do not change place in their entirety; nor for the spirit which moves the world is there any fixed locality according to any restricted part of the world's substance, which now is in the east, and now in the west, but according to a fixed quarter; because *the moving energy is always in the east,* as stated in *Phys.* viii., text. 84.

Reply Obj. 4. Properly speaking, the angels do not talk through their assumed bodies; yet there is a semblance of speech, in so far as they fashion sounds in the air like to human voices.

Reply Obj. 5. Properly speaking, the angels cannot be said to eat, because eating involves the taking of food convertible into the substance of the eater.

Although after the Resurrection food was not converted into the substance of Christ's body, but resolved into pre-existing matter; nevertheless Christ had a body of such a true nature that food could be changed into it; hence it was a true eating. But the food taken by angels was neither changed into the assumed body, nor was the body of such a nature that food could be changed into it; consequently, it was not a true eating, but figurative of spiritual eating. This is what the angel said to Tobias: *When I was with you, I seemed indeed to eat and to drink; but I use an invisible meat and drink* (Tob. xii. 19).

Abraham offered them food, deeming them to be men, in

whom, nevertheless, he worshipped God, as God is wont to be in the prophets, as Augustine says (*De Civ. Dei* xvi.).

Reply Obj. 6. As Augustine says (*De Civ. Dei* xv.) : *Many persons affirm that they have had the experience, or have heard from such as have experienced it, that the Satyrs and Fauns, whom the common folk call incubi, have often presented themselves before women, and have sought and procured intercourse with them. Hence it is folly to deny it. But God's holy angels could not fall in such fashion before the deluge. Hence by the sons of God are to be understood the sons of Seth, who were good; while by the daughters of men the Scripture designates those who sprang from the race of Cain. Nor is it to be wondered at that giants should be born of them; for they were not all giants, albeit there were many more before than after the deluge.* Still if some are occasionally begotten from demons, it is not from the seed of such demons, nor from their assumed bodies, but from the seed of men taken for the purpose; as when the demon assumes first the form of a woman, and afterwards of a man; just as they take the seed of other things for other generating purposes, as Augustine says (*De Trin.* iii.), so that the person born is not the child of a demon, but of a man.

QUESTION LII.

OF THE ANGELS IN RELATION TO PLACE.
(In Three Articles.)

WE now inquire into the place of the angels. Touching this there are three subjects of inquiry: (1) Is the angel in a place? (2) Can he be in several places at once? (3) Can several angels be in the same place?

FIRST ARTICLE.

WHETHER AN ANGEL IS IN A PLACE?

We proceed thus to the First Article:—

Objection 1. It would seem that an angel is not in a place. For Boëthius says (*De Hebd.*): *The common opinion of the learned is that things incorporeal are not in a place.* And again, Aristotle observes (*Phys.* iv., text. 48, 57) that *it is not everything existing which is in a place, but only a movable body.* But an angel is not a body, as was shown above (Q. L.). Therefore an angel is not in a place.

Obj. 2. Further, place is a *quantity having position.* But everything which is in a place has some position. Now to have a position cannot befit an angel, since his substance is devoid of quantity, the proper difference of which is to have a position. Therefore an angel is not in a place.

Obj. 3. Further, to be in a place is to be measured and to be contained by such place, as is evident from the Philosopher (*ibid.*, text. 14, 119). But an angel can neither be measured nor contained by a place, because the container is more formal than the contained; as air with regard to water (*ibid.*, text. 35, 49). Therefore an angel is not in a place.

On the contrary, It is said in the Collect* : *Let Thy holy angels who dwell herein, keep us in peace.*

I answer that, It is befitting an angel to be in a place; yet an angel and a body are said to be in a place in quite a different sense. A body is said to be in a place in such a way that it is applied to such place according to the contact of dimensive quantity; but there is no such quantity in the angels, for theirs is a virtual one. Consequently an angel is said to be in a corporeal place by application of the angelic power in any manner whatever to any place.

Accordingly there is no need for saying that an angel can be deemed commensurate with a place, or that he occupies a space in the continuous; for this is proper to a located body which is endowed with dimensive quantity. In similar fashion it is not necessary on this account for the angel to be contained by a place; because an incorporeal substance virtually contains the thing with which it comes into contact, and is not contained by it : for the soul is in the body as containing it, not as contained by it. In the same way an angel is said to be in a place which is corporeal, not as the thing contained, but as somehow containing it.

And hereby we have the answers to the objections.

SECOND ARTICLE.

WHETHER AN ANGEL CAN BE IN SEVERAL PLACES AT ONCE ?

We proceed thus to the Second Article :—

Objection 1. It would seem that an angel can be in several places at once. For an angel is not less endowed with power than the soul. But the soul is in several places at once, for it is entirely in every part of the body, as Augustine says (*De Trin.* vi.). Therefore an angel can be in several places at once.

Obj. 2. Further, an angel is in the body which he assumes ; and, since the body which he assumes is continuous, it would appear that he is in every part thereof. But accord-

* Prayer at Compline, Dominican Breviary.

ing to its various parts there are various places. Therefore the angel is at one time in various places.

Obj. 3. Further, Damascene says (*De Fid. Orth.* ii.) that *where the angel operates, there he is*. But occasionally he operates in several places at one time, as is evident from the angel destroying Sodom (Gen. xix. 25). Therefore an angel can be in several places at the one time.

On the contrary, Damascene says (*ibid.*) that *while the angels are in heaven, they are not on earth*.

I answer that, An angel's power and nature are finite, whereas the Divine power and essence, which is the universal cause of all things, is infinite : consequently God through His power touches all things, and is not merely present in some places, but is everywhere. Now since the angel's power is finite, it does not extend to all things, but to one determined thing. For whatever is compared with one power must be compared therewith as one determined thing. Consequently since all being is compared as one thing to God's universal power, so is one particular being compared as one with the angelic power. Hence, since the angel is in a place by the application of his power to the place, it follows that he is not everywhere, nor in several places, but in only one place.

Some, however, have been deceived in this matter. For some who were unable to go beyond the reach of their imaginations supposed the indivisibility of the angel to be like that of a point; consequently they thought that an angel could be only in a place which is a point. But they were manifestly deceived, because a point is something indivisible, yet having its situation; whereas the angel is indivisible, and beyond the genus of quantity and situation. Consequently there is no occasion for determining in his regard one indivisible place as to situation : any place which is either divisible or indivisible, great or small suffices, according as of his own free-will he applies his power to a great or to a small body. So the entire body to which he is applied by his power, corresponds as one place to him.

Neither, if any angel moves the heavens, is it necessary for him to be everywhere. First of all, because his power is applied only to what is first moved by him. Now there is one part of the heavens in which there is movement first of all, namely, the part to the east : hence the Philosopher (*Phys.* viii., text. 84) attributes the power of the heavenly mover to the part which is in the east. Secondly, because philosophers do not hold that one separate substance moves all the spheres immediately. Hence it need not be everywhere.

So, then, it is evident that to be in a place appertains quite differently to a body, to an angel, and to God. For a body is in a place in a circumscribed fashion, since it is measured by the place. An angel, however, is not there in a circumscribed fashion, since he is not measured by the place, but definitively, because he is in one place in such a manner that he is not in another. But God is neither circumscriptively nor definitely there, because He is everywhere.

From this we can easily gather an answer to the objections : because the entire subject to which the angelic power is immediately applied, is reputed as one place, even though it be continuous.

Third Article.

Whether several angels can be at the same time in the same place?

We proceed thus to the Third Article:—

Objection 1. It would seem that several angels can be at the same time in the same place. For several bodies cannot be at the same time in the same place, because they fill the place. But angels do not fill a place, because only a body fills a place, so that it be not empty, as appears from the Philosopher (*Phys.* iv., text. 52, 58). Therefore several angels can be in the one place.

Obj. 2. Further, there is a greater difference between an angel and a body than there is between two angels. But an angel and a body are at the one time in the one place :

because there is no place which is not filled with a sensible body, as we find proved in *Physics* iv., text. 58. Much more, then, can two angels be in the same place.

Obj. 3. Further, the soul is in every part of the body, according to Augustine (*De Trin.* vi.). But demons, although they do not obsess souls, do obsess bodies occasionally; and thus the soul and the demon are at the one time in the same place: and consequently for the same reason all other spiritual substances.

On the contrary, There are not two souls in the same body. Therefore for a like reason there are not two angels in the same place.

I answer that, There are not two angels in the same place. The reason of this is because it is impossible for two complete causes to be the causes immediately of one and the same thing. This is evident in every class of causes: for there is one proximate form of one thing, and there is one proximate mover, although there may be several remote movers. Nor can it be objected that several individuals may row a boat, since no one of them is a perfect mover, because no one man's strength is sufficient for moving the boat; while all together are as one mover, in so far as their united strengths all combine in producing the one movement. Hence, since the angel is said to be in one place by the fact that his power touches the place immediately by way of a perfect container, as was said (A. 1), there can be but one angel in one place.

Reply Obj. 1. Several angels are not hindered from being in the same place because of their filling the place; but for another reason, as has been said.

Reply Obj. 2. An angel and a body are not in a place in the same way; hence the conclusion does not follow.

Reply Obj. 3. Not even a demon and a soul are compared to a body according to the same relation of causality; since the soul is its form, while the demon is not. Hence the inference does not follow.

QUESTION LIII.

OF THE LOCAL MOVEMENT OF THE ANGELS.

(*In Three Articles.*)

WE must next consider the local movement of the angels; under which heading there are three points of inquiry: (1) Whether an angel can be moved locally? (2) Whether in passing from place to place he passes through intervening space? (3) Whether the angel's movement is in time or instantaneous?

FIRST ARTICLE.

WHETHER AN ANGEL CAN BE MOVED LOCALLY?

We proceed thus to the First Article:—

Objection 1. It seems that an angel cannot be moved locally. For, as the Philosopher proves (*Phys.* vi., text. 32, 86), *nothing which is devoid of parts is moved;* because, while it is in the term *wherefrom*, it is not moved; nor while it is in the term *whereto*, for it is then already moved; consequently it remains that everything which is moved, while it is being moved, is partly in the term *wherefrom* and partly in the term *whereto*. But an angel is without parts. Therefore an angel cannot be moved locally.

Obj. 2. Further, movement is *the act of an imperfect being*, as the Philosopher says (*Phys.* iii., text. 14). But a beatified angel is not imperfect. Consequently a beatified angel is not moved locally.

Obj. 3. Further, movement is simply because of want. But the holy angels have no want. Therefore the holy angels are not moved locally.

On the contrary, It is the same thing for a beatified angel to be moved as for a beatified soul to be moved. But it must necessarily be said that a blessed soul is moved locally, because it is an article of faith that Christ's soul descended into Hell. Therefore a beatified angel is moved locally.

I answer that, A beatified angel can be moved locally. As, however, to be in a place belongs equivocally to a body and to an angel, so likewise does local movement. For a body is in a place in so far as it is contained under the place, and is commensurate with the place. Hence it is necessary for local movement of a body to be commensurate with the place, and according to its exigency. Hence it is that the continuity of movement is according to the continuity of magnitude; and according to priority and posteriority in magnitude is the priority and posteriority of local movement, as the Philosopher says (*Phys.* iv., text. 99). But an angel is not in a place as commensurate and contained, but rather as containing it. Hence it is not necessary for the local movement of an angel to be commensurate with the place, nor for it to be according to the exigency of the place, so as to have continuity therefrom; but it is a non-continuous movement. For since the angel is in a place only by virtual contact, as was said above (Q. LII., A. 1), it follows necessarily that the movement of an angel in a place is nothing else than the various contacts of various places successively, and not at once; because an angel cannot be in several places at one time, as was said above (Q. LII., A. 2). Nor is it necessary for these contacts to be continuous. Nevertheless a certain kind of continuity can be found in such contacts. Because, as was said above (*ibid.*, A. 1), there is nothing to hinder us from assigning a divisible place to an angel according to virtual contact; just as a divisible place is assigned to a body by contact of magnitude. Hence as a body successively, and not all at once, quits the place in which it was before, and thence arises continuity in its local movement; so likewise an angel can successively quit the divisible place in which he was before, and so his movement will be continuous. And he can all at once quit the whole place, and in the same instant apply himself to the whole of another place, and thus his movement will not be continuous.

Reply. Obj. 1. This argument fails of its purpose for a twofold reason. First of all, because Aristotle's demonstration deals with what is indivisible according to quantity, to which responds a place necessarily indivisible. And this cannot be said of an angel.

Secondly, because Aristotle's demonstration deals with movement which is continuous. For if the movement were not continuous, it might be said that a thing is moved while it is in the term *wherefrom*, and while it is in the term *whereto*: because the very succession of *wheres*, regarding the same thing, would be called movement: hence, in whichever of those *wheres* the thing might be, it could be said to be moved. But the continuity of movement prevents this; because nothing which is continuous is in its term, as is clear, because the line is not in the point. Therefore it is necessary for the thing moved to be not totally in either of the terms while it is being moved; but partly in the one, and partly in the other. Therefore, according as the angel's movement is not continuous, Aristotle's demonstration does not hold good. But according as the angel's movement is held to be continuous, it can be so granted, that, while an angel is in movement, he is partly in the term *wherefrom*, and partly in the term *whereto* (yet so that such partiality be not referred to the angel's substance, but to the place); because at the outset of his continuous movement the angel is in the whole divisible place from which he begins to be moved; but while he is actually in movement, he is in part of the first place which he quits, and in part of the second place which he occupies. This very fact that he can occupy the parts of two places appertains to the angel from this, that he can occupy a divisible place by applying his power; as a body does by application of magnitude. Hence it follows regarding a body which is movable according to place, that it is divisible according to magnitude; but regarding an angel, that his power can be applied to something which is divisible.

Reply Obj. 2. The movement of that which is in potentiality is the act of an imperfect agent. But the movement which is by application of energy is the act of one in act: because energy implies actuality.

Reply Obj. 3. The movement of that which is in potentiality is on account of its own need: but the movement of what is in act is not for any need of its own, but for another's need. In this way, because of our need, the angel is moved locally, according to Heb. i. 14: *They are all* ministering spirits, sent to minister for them who receive the inheritance of salvation.*

Second Article.

WHETHER AN ANGEL PASSES THROUGH INTERMEDIATE SPACE?

We proceed thus to the Second Article:—

Objection 1. It would seem that an angel does not pass through intermediate space. For everything that passes through a middle space first travels along a place of its own dimensions, before passing through a greater. But the place responding to an angel, who is indivisible, is confined to a point. Therefore if the angel passes through middle space, he must reckon infinite points in his movement: which is not possible.

Obj. 2. Further, an angel is of simpler substance than the soul. But our soul by taking thought can pass from one extreme to another without going through the middle: for I can think of France and afterwards of Syria, without ever thinking of Italy, which stands between them. Therefore much more can an angel pass from one extreme to another without going through the middle.

On the contrary, If the angel be moved from one place to another, then, when he is in the term *whither,* he is no longer in motion, but is changed. But a process of changing precedes every actual change: consequently he was being moved while existing in some place. But he was not moved so long as he was in the term *whence.* Therefore, he was

* Vulg., *Are they not all* . . .?

moved while he was in mid-space : and so it was necessary for him to pass through intervening space.

I answer that, As was observed above in the preceding article, the local motion of an angel can be continuous, and non-continuous. If it be continuous, the angel cannot pass from one extreme to another, without passing through the mid space; because, as is said by the Philosopher (*Phys.* v., text. 22; vi., text. 77), *The middle is that into which a thing which is continually moved comes, before arriving at the last into which it is moved;* because the order of first and last in continuous movement, is according to the order of first and last in magnitude, as he says (*Phys.* iv., text. 99).

But if an angel's movement be not continuous, it is possible for him to pass from one extreme to another without going through the middle : which is evident thus. Between the two extreme limits there are infinite intermediate places ; whether the places be taken as divisible or as indivisible. This is clearly evident with regard to places which are indivisible ; because between every two points that are infinite intermediate points, since no two points follow one another without a middle, as is proved in *Phys.* vi., text. 1. And the same must of necessity be said of divisible places : and this is shown from the continuous movement of a body. For a body is not moved from place to place except in time. But in the whole time which measures the movement of a body, there are not two *nows* in which the body moved is not in one place and in another ; for if it were in one and the same place in two *nows,* it would follow that it would be at rest there; since to be at rest is nothing else than to be in the same place now and previously. Therefore, since there are infinite *nows* between the first and the last *now* of the time which measures the movement, there must be infinite places between the first from which the movement begins, and the last where the movement ceases. This again is made evident from sensible experience. Let there be a body of a palm's length, and let there be a plane measuring two palms, along which it travels; it is evident that the first place from which the movement starts is that of the one palm; and the place wherein the movement ends is that of the other palm. Now it is clear that when it begins to move, it gradually quits the first palm and enters the second. According, then, as the magnitude of the palm is divided, even so are the intermediate places multiplied; because every distinct point in the magnitude of the first palm is the beginning of a place, and a distinct point in the magnitude of the other palm is the limit of the same. Accordingly, since magnitude is infinitely divisible, and the points in every magnitude are likewise infinite in potentiality, it follows that between every two places there are infinite intermediate places.

Now a movable body only exhausts the infinity of the intermediate places by the continuity of its movement; because, as the intermediate places are infinite in potentiality, so likewise must there be reckoned some infinitudes in movement which is continuous. Consequently, if the movement be not continuous, then all the parts of the movement will be actually numbered. If, therefore, any movable body be moved, but not by continuous movement, it follows, either that it does not pass through all the intermediate places, or else that it actually numbers infinite places: which is not possible. Accordingly, then, as the angel's movement is not continuous, he does not pass through all intermediate places.

Now, the actual passing from one extreme to the other, without going through the mid-space, is quite in keeping with an angel's nature; but not with that of a body, because a body is measured by and contained under a place; hence it is bound to follow the laws of place in its movement. But an angel's substance is not subject to place as contained thereby, but is above it as containing it: hence it is under his control to apply himself to a place just as he wills, either through or without the intervening place.

Reply Obj. 1. The place of an angel is not taken as equal to him according to magnitude, but according to contact of power: and so the angel's place can be divisible, and is not always a mere point. Yet even the intermediate divisible

LOCAL MOVEMENT OF ANGELS

places are infinite, as was said above: but they are consumed by the continuity of the movement, as is evident from the foregoing.

Reply Obj. 2. While an angel is moved locally, his essence is applied to various places : but the soul's essence is not applied to the things thought of, but rather the things thought of are in it. So there is no comparison.

Reply Obj. 3. In continuous movement the actual change is not a part of the movement, but its conclusion : hence movement must precede change. Accordingly such movement is through the mid-space. But in movement which is not continuous, the change is a part, as a unit is a part of number : hence the succession of the various places, even without the mid-space, constitutes such movement.

THIRD ARTICLE.

WHETHER THE MOVEMENT OF AN ANGEL IS INSTANTANEOUS?

We proceed thus to the Third Article :—

Objection 1. It would seem that an angel's movement is instantaneous. For the greater the power of the mover, and the less the moved resist the mover, the more rapid is the movement. But the power of an angel moving himself exceeds beyond all proportion the power which moves a body. Now the proportion of velocities is reckoned according to the lessening of the time. But between one length of time and any other length of time there is proportion. If therefore a body be moved in time, an angel is moved in an instant.

Obj. 2. Further, the angel's movement is simpler than any bodily change. But some bodily change is effected in an instant, such as illumination; both because the subject is not illuminated successively, as it gets hot successively ; and because a ray does not reach sooner what is near than what is remote. Much more therefore is the angel's movement instantaneous.

Obj. 3. Further, if an angel be moved from place to place in time, it is manifest that in the last instant of such time he is in the term *whereto*: but in the whole of the preceding time, he is either in the place immediately preceding, which is taken as the term *wherefrom*; or else he is partly in the one, and partly in the other. But if he be partly in the one and partly in the other, it follows that he is divisible; which is impossible. Therefore during the whole of the preceding time he is in the term *wherefrom*. Therefore he rests there: since to be at rest is to be in the same place now and previously, as was said (A. 2). Therefore it follows that he is not moved except in the last instant of time.

On the contrary, In every change there is a before and after. Now the before and after of movement is reckoned by time. Consequently every movement, even of an angel, is in time, since there is a before and after in it.

I answer that, Some have maintained that the local movement of an angel is instantaneous. They said that when an angel is moved from place to place, during the whole of the preceding time he is in the term *wherefrom*; but in the last instant of such time he is in the term *whereto*. Nor is there any need for a medium between the terms, just as there is no medium between time and the limit of time. But there is a mid-time between two *nows* of time: hence they say that a last *now* cannot be assigned in which it was in the term *wherefrom*, just as in illumination, and in the substantial generation of fire, there is no last instant to be assigned in which the air was dark, or in which the matter was under the privation of the form of fire: but a last time can be assigned, so that in the last instant of such time there is light in the air, or the form of fire in the matter. And so illumination and substantial generation are called instantaneous movements.

But this does not hold good in the present case; and it is shown thus. It is of the nature of rest that the subject in repose be not otherwise disposed now than it was before: and therefore in every *now* of time which measures rest, the subject reposing is in the same *where* in the first, in the middle, and in the last *now*. On the other hand, it is of the very nature of movement for the subject moved to be other-

LOCAL MOVEMENT OF ANGELS Q. 53. ART. 3

wise now than it was before: and therefore in every *now* of time which measures movement, the movable subject is in various dispositions; hence in the last *now* it must have a different form from what it had before. So it is evident that to rest during the whole time in some (disposition), for instance, in whiteness, is to be in it in every instant of such time. Hence it is not possible for anything to rest in one term during the whole of the preceding time, and afterwards in the last instant of that time to be in the other term. But this is possible in movement: because to be moved in any whole time, is not to be in the same disposition in every instant of that time. Therefore all instantaneous changes of the kind are terms of a continuous movement: just as generation is the term of the alteration of matter, and illumination is the term of the local movement of the illuminating body. Now the local movement of an angel is not the term of any other continuous movement, but is of itself, depending upon no other movement. Consequently it is impossible to say that he is in any place during the whole time, and that in the last *now* he is in another place: but some *now* must be assigned in which he was last in the preceding place. But where there are many *nows* succeeding one another, there is necessarily time; since time is nothing else than the reckoning of before and after in movement. It remains, then, that the movement of an angel is in time. It is in continuous time if his movement be continuous, and in non-continuous time if his movement be non-continuous; for, as was said (A.1), his movement can be of either kind, since the continuity of time comes of the continuity of movement, as the Philosopher says (*Phys.* iv., text. 99).

But that time, whether it be continuous or not, is not the same as the time which measures the movement of the heavens, and whereby all corporeal things are measured, which have their changeableness from the movement of the heavens; because the angel's movement does not depend upon the movement of the heavens.

Reply Obj. 1. If the time of the angel's movement be not continuous, but a kind of succession of *nows*, it will have no proportion to the time which measures the movement of corporeal things, which is continuous; since it is not of the same nature. If, however, it be continuous, it is indeed proportionable, not, indeed, because of the proportion of the mover and the movable, but on account of the proportion of the magnitudes in which the movement exists. Besides, the swiftness of the angel's movement is not measured by the quantity of his power, but according to the determination of his will.

Reply Obj. 2. Illumination is the term of a movement; and is an alteration, not a local movement, as though the light were understood to be moved to what is near, before being moved to what is remote. But the angel's movement is local, and, besides, it is not the term of movement; hence there is no comparison.

Reply Obj. 3. This objection is based on continuous time. But the same time of an angel's movement can be non-continuous. So an angel can be in one place in one instant, and in another place in the next instant, without any time intervening. If the time of the angel's movement be continuous, he is changed through infinite places throughout the whole time which precedes the last *now;* as was already shown (A. 2). Nevertheless he is partly in one of the continuous places, and partly in another, not because his substance is susceptible of parts, but because his power is applied to a part of the first place and to a part of the second, as was said above (A. 2).

QUESTION LIV.

OF THE KNOWLEDGE OF THE ANGELS.

(*In Five Articles.*)

AFTER considering what belongs to the angel's substance, we now proceed to his knowledge. This investigation will be fourfold. In the first place inquiry must be made into his power of knowledge : secondly, into his medium of knowledge : thirdly, into the objects known : and fourthly, into the manner whereby he knows them.

Under the first heading there are five points of inquiry : (1) Is the angel's understanding his substance? (2) Is his being his understanding? (3) Is his substance his power of intelligence? (4) Is there in the angels an active and a passive intellect? (5) Is there in them any other power of knowledge besides the intellect?

FIRST ARTICLE.

WHETHER AN ANGEL'S ACT OF UNDERSTANDING IS HIS SUBSTANCE?

We proceed thus to the First Article:—

Objection 1. It would seem that the angel's act of understanding is his substance. For the angel is both higher and simpler than the active intellect of a soul. But the substance of the active intellect is its own action; as is evident from Aristotle (*De Anima* iii.) and from his Commentator.* Therefore much more is the angel's substance his action,— that is his act of understanding.

Obj. 2. Further, the Philosopher says (*Metaph.* xii., text. 39) that *the action of the intellect is life.* But *since in living*

* Averroes, A D 1126-1198.

things to live is to be, as he says (*De Anima* II., text. 37), it seems that life is essence. Therefore the action of the intellect is the essence of an angel who understands.

Obj. 3. Further, if the extremes be one, then the middle does not differ from them; because extreme is farther from extreme than the middle is. But in an angel the intellect and the object understood are the same, at least in so far as he understands his own essence. Therefore the act of understanding, which is between the intellect and the thing understood, is one with the substance of the angel who understands.

On the contrary, The action of anything differs more from its substance than does its existence. But no creature's existence is its substance, for this belongs to God only, as is evident from what was said above (Q. III., A. 4). Therefore neither the action of an angel, nor of any other creature, is its substance.

I answer that, It is impossible for the action of an angel, or of any other creature, to be its own substance. For an action is properly the actuality of a power; just as existence is the actuality of a substance, or of an essence. Now it is impossible for anything which is not a pure act, but which has some admixture of potentiality, to be its own actuality: because actuality is opposed to potentiality. But God alone is pure act. Hence only in God is His substance the same as His existence and His action.

Besides, if an angel's act of understanding were his substance, it would be necessary for it to be subsisting. Now a subsisting act of intelligence can be but one; just as an abstract thing that subsists. Consequently an angel's substance would neither be distinguished from God's substance, which is His very act of understanding subsisting in itself, nor from the substance of another angel.

Also, if the angel were his own act of understanding, there could then be no degrees of understanding more or less perfectly; for this comes about through the diverse participation of the act of understanding.

Reply Obj. 1. When the active intellect is said to be its

own action, such predication is not essential, but concomitant, because, since its very nature consists in act, instantly, so far as lies in itself, action accompanies it: which cannot be said of the passive intellect, for this has no actions until after it has been reduced to act.

Reply Obj. 2. The relation between *life* and *to live* is not the same as that between *essence* and *to be;* but rather as that between *a race* and *to run,* one of which signifies the act in the abstract, and the other in the concrete. Hence it does not follow, if *to live* is *to be,* that *life* is *essence.* Although life is sometimes put for the essence, as Augustine says (*De Trin.* x.), *Memory and understanding and will are one essence, one life:* yet it is not taken in this sense by the Philosopher, when he says that *the act of the intellect is life.*

Reply Obj. 3. The action which is transient, passing to some extrinsic object, is really a medium between the agent and the subject receiving the action. The action which remains within the agent, is not really a medium between the agent and the object, but only according to the manner of expression; for it really follows the union of the object with the agent. For the act of understanding is brought about by the union of the object understood with the one who understands it, as an effect which differs from both.

SECOND ARTICLE.

WHETHER IN THE ANGEL TO UNDERSTAND IS TO EXIST?

We proceed thus to the Second Article:—

Objection 1. It would seem that in the angel to understand is to exist. For in living things to live is to be, as the Philosopher says (*De Anima* II., text. 37). But to *understand is in a sense to live* (*ibid.*). Therefore in the angel to understand is to exist.

Obj. 2. Further, cause bears the same relation to cause, as effect to effect. But the form whereby the angel exists is the same as the form by which he understands at least himself. Therefore in the angel to understand is to exist.

On the contrary, The angel's act of understanding is his

movement, as is clear from Dionysius (*Div. Nom.* iv.). But to exist is not movement. Therefore in the angel to be is not to understand.

I answer that, The action of the angel, as also the action of any creature, is not his existence. For as it is said (*Metaph.* ix., text. 16), there is a twofold class of action; one which passes out to something beyond, and causes passion in it, as burning and cutting; and another which does not pass outwards, but which remains within the agent, as to feel, to understand, to will; by such actions nothing outside is changed, but the whole action takes place within the agent. It is quite clear regarding the first kind of action that it cannot be the agent's very existence: because the agent's existence is signified as within him, while such an action denotes something as issuing from the agent into the thing done. But the second action of its own nature has infinity, either simple or relative. As an example of simple infinity, we have the act *to understand,* of which the object is *the true;* and the act *to will,* of which the object is *the good;* each of which is convertible with being; and so, to understand and to will, of themselves, bear relation to all things, and each receives its species from its object. But the act of sensation is relatively infinite, for it bears relation to all sensible things; as sight does to all things visible. Now the being of every creature is restricted to one in genus and species; God's being alone is simply infinite, comprehending all things in itself, as Dionysius says (*Div. Nom.* v.). Hence the Divine nature alone is its own act of understanding and its own act of will.

Reply Obj. 1. Life is sometimes taken for the existence of the living subject: sometimes also for a vital operation, that is, for one whereby something is shown to be living. In this way the Philosopher says that to understand is, in a sense, to live: for there he distinguishes the various grades of living things according to the various functions of life.

Reply Obj. 2. The essence of an angel is the reason of his entire existence, but not the reason of his whole act of understanding, since he cannot understand everything by his essence. Consequently in its own specific nature as such an essence, it is compared to the existence of the angel, whereas to his act of understanding it is compared as included in the idea of a more universal object, namely, truth and being. Thus it is evident, that, although the form is the same, yet it is not the principle of existence and of understanding according to the same formality. On this account it does not follow that in the angel *to be* is the same as *to understand*.

THIRD ARTICLE.

WHETHER AN ANGEL'S POWER OF INTELLIGENCE IS HIS ESSENCE?

We proceed thus to the Third Article:—

Objection 1. It would seem that in an angel the power or faculty of understanding is not different from his essence. For, *mind* and *intellect* express the power of understanding. But in many passages of his writings, Dionysius styles angels *intellects* and *minds*. Therefore the angel is his own power of intelligence.

Obj. 2. Further, if the angel's power of intelligence be anything besides his essence, then it must needs be an accident; for that which is besides the essence of anything, we call its accident. But *a simple form cannot be a subject,* as Boethius states (*De Trin.* 1.). Thus an angel would not be a simple form, which is contrary to what has been previously said (Q. L., A. 2).

Obj. 3. Further, Augustine (*Confess.* xii.) says, that God made the angelic nature *nigh unto Himself,* while He made primary matter *nigh unto nothing;* from this it would seem that the angel is of a simpler nature than primary matter, as being closer to God. But primary matter is its own power. Therefore much more is an angel his own power of intelligence.

On the contrary, Dionysius says (*Cœl. Hier.* xi.) that *the angels are divided into substance, power, and operation.* Therefore substance, power, and operation, are all distinct in them.

I answer that, Neither in an angel nor in any creature, is the power or operative faculty the same as its essence: which is made evident thus. Since every power is ordained to an act, then according to the diversity of acts must be the diversity of powers; and on this account it is said that each proper act responds to its proper power. But in every creature the essence differs from the existence, and is compared to it as potentiality is to act, as is evident from what has been already said (Q. XLIV., A. 1). Now the act to which the operative power is compared is operation. But in the angel to understand is not the same as to exist, nor is any operation in him, nor in any other created thing, the same as his existence. Hence the angel's essence is not his power of intelligence: nor is the essence of any creature its power of operation.

Reply Obj. 1. An angel is called *intellect* and *mind,* because all his knowledge is intellectual: whereas the knowledge of a soul is partly intellectual and partly sensitive.

Reply Obj. 2. A simple form which is pure act cannot be the subject of accident, because subject is compared to accident as potentiality is to act. God alone is such a form: and of such is Boethius speaking there. But a simple form which is not its own existence, but is compared to it as potentiality is to act, can be the subject of accident; and especially of such incident as follows the species : for such accident belongs to the form;—whereas an accident which belongs to the individual, and which does not belong to the whole species, results from the matter, which is the principle of individuation. And such a simple form is an angel.

Reply Obj. 3. The power of matter is a potentiality in regard to substantial being itself, whereas the power of operation regards accidental being. Hence there is no comparison.

Fourth Article.
WHETHER THERE IS AN ACTIVE AND A PASSIVE INTELLECT IN AN ANGEL?

We proceed thus to the Fourth Article:—

Objection 1. It would seem that there is both an active and a passive intellect in an angel. The Philosopher says (*De Anima* iii., text. 17) that, *in the soul, just as in every nature, there is something whereby it can become all things, and there is something whereby it can make all things.* But an angel is a kind of nature. Therefore there is an active and a passive intellect in an angel.

Obj. 2. Further, the proper function of the passive intellect is to receive; whereas to enlighten is the proper function of the active intellect, as is made clear in *De Anima* iii. (text. 2, 3, 18). But an angel receives enlightenment from a higher angel, and enlightens a lower one. Therefore there is in him an active and a passive intellect.

On the contrary, The distinction of active and passive intellect in us is in relation to the phantasms, which are compared to the passive intellect as colours to the sight; but to the active intellect as colours to the light, as is clear from *De Anima* iii. (text. 18). But this is not so in the angel. Therefore there is no active and passive intellect in the angel.

I answer that, The necessity for admitting a passive intellect in us is derived from the fact that we understand sometimes only in potentiality, and not actually. Hence there must exist some power, which, previous to the act of understanding, is in potentiality to intelligible things, but which becomes actuated in their regard when it apprehends them, and still more when it reflects upon them. This is the power which is denominated the passive intellect. The necessity for admitting an active intellect is due to this,— that the natures of the material things which we understand do not exist outside the soul, as immaterial and actually intelligible, but are only intelligible in potentiality so long as they are outside the soul. Consequently it is necessary that there should be some power capable of rendering such natures actually intelligible: and this power in us is called the active intellect.

But each of these necessities is absent from the angels. They are neither sometimes understanding only in potentiality, with regard to such things as they naturally apprehend; nor, again, are their intelligible objects intelligible in potentiality, but they are actually such; for they first and principally understand immaterial things, as will appear later (QQ. LXXXIV., A. 7, and LXXXV., A. 1). Therefore there cannot be an active and a passive intellect in them, except equivocally.

Reply Obj. 1. As the words themselves show, the Philosopher understands those two things to be in every nature in which there chances to be generation or making. Knowledge, however, is not generated in the angels, but is present naturally. Hence there is no need for admitting an active and a passive intellect in them.

Reply Obj. 2. It is the function of the active intellect to enlighten, not another intellect, but things which are intelligible in potentiality, in so far as by abstraction it makes them to be actually intelligible. It belongs to the passive intellect to be in potentiality with regard to things which are naturally capable of being known, and sometimes to apprehend them actually. Hence for one angel to enlighten another does not belong to the notion of an active intellect: neither does it belong to the passive intellect for the angel to be enlightened with regard to supernatural mysteries, to the knowledge of which he is sometimes in potentiality. But if anyone wishes to call these by the names of active and passive intellect, he will then be speaking equivocally; and it is not about names that we need trouble.

Fifth Article.

WHETHER THERE IS ONLY INTELLECTUAL KNOWLEDGE IN THE ANGELS?

We proceed thus to the Fifth Article:—

Objection 1. It would seem that the knowledge of the angels is not exclusively intellectual. For Augustine says (*De Civ. Dei* viii.) that in the angels there is *life which understands and feels*. Therefore there is a sensitive faculty in them as well.

Obj. 2. Further, Isidore says (*De Summo Bono*) that the angels have learnt many things by experience. But experience comes of many remembrances, as stated in *Metaph.* i. 1. Consequently they have likewise a power of memory.

Obj. 3. Further, Dionysius says (*Div. Nom.* iv.) that there is a sort of *perverted phantasy* in the demons. But phantasy belongs to the imaginative faculty. Therefore the power of the imagination is in the demons; and for the same reason it is in the angels, since they are of the same nature.

On the contrary, Gregory says (Hom. 29 *in Ev*.), that *man senses in common with the brutes, and understands with the angels*.

I answer that, In our soul there are certain powers whose operations are exercised by corporeal organs; such powers are acts of sundry parts of the body, as sight of the eye, and hearing of the ear. There are some other powers of the soul whose operations are not performed through bodily organs, as intellect and will: these are not acts of any parts of the body. Now the angels have no bodies naturally joined to them, as is manifest from what has been said already (Q. LI., A. 1). Hence of the soul's powers only intellect and will can belong to them.

The Commentator (*Metaph.* xii.) says the same thing, namely, that the separated substances are divided into intellect and will. And it is in keeping with the order of the universe for the highest intellectual creature to be entirely intelligent; and not in part, as is our soul. For this reason the angels are called *intellects* and *minds*, as was said above (A. 3 *ad* 1).

A twofold answer can be returned to the contrary objections. First, it may be replied that those authorities are speaking according to the opinion of such men as contended that angels and demons have bodies naturally united to them. Augustine often makes use of this opinion in his books, although he does not mean to assert it; hence he says (*De Civ. Dei* xxi.) that *such an inquiry does not call for much labour.* Secondly, it may be said that such authorities and the like are to be understood as by way of similitude. Because, since sense has a sure apprehension of its proper sensible object, it is a common usage of speech, when we understand something for certain, to say that we *sense* it. And hence it is that we use the word *sentence.* Experience can be attributed to the angels according to the likeness of the things known, although not by likeness of the faculty knowing them. We have experience when we know single objects through the senses : the angels likewise know single objects, as we shall show (Q. LVII., A. 2), yet not through the senses. But memory can be allowed in the angels, according as Augustine (*De Trin.* x.) puts it in the mind; although it cannot belong to them in so far as it is a part of the sensitive soul. In like fashion *a perverted phantasy* is attributed to demons, since they have a false practical estimate of what is the true good; while deception in us comes properly from the phantasy, whereby we sometimes hold fast to images of things as to the things themselves, as is manifest in sleepers and lunatics.

QUESTION LV.

OF THE MEDIUM OF THE ANGELIC KNOWLEDGE.

(*In Three Articles.*)

NEXT in order, the question arises as to the medium of the angelic knowledge. Under this heading there are three points of inquiry : (1) Do the angels know everything by their substance, or by some species ? (2) If by species, is it by connatural species, or is it by such as they have derived from things? (3) Do the higher angels know by more universal species than the lower angels ?

FIRST ARTICLE.

WHETHER THE ANGELS KNOW ALL THINGS BY THEIR SUBSTANCE ?

We proceed thus to the First Article:—

Objection 1. It would seem that the angels know all things by their substance. For Dionysius says (*Div. Nom.* vii.) that *the angels, according to the proper nature of a mind, know the things which are happening upon earth.* But the angel's nature is his essence. Therefore the angel knows things by his essence.

Obj. 2. Further, according to the Philosopher (*Metaph.* xii., text. 51; *De Anima* iii., text. 15), *in things which are without matter, the intellect is the same as the object understood.* But the object understood is the same as the one who understands it, as regards that whereby it is understood. Therefore in things without matter, such as the angels, the medium whereby the object is understood is the very substance of the one understanding it.

Obj. 3. Further, everything which is contained in another is there according to the mode of the container. But an angel has an intellectual nature. Therefore whatever is in him is there in an intelligible mode. But all things are in him: because the lower orders of beings are essentially in the higher, while the higher are in the lower participatively: and therefore Dionysius says (*Div. Nom.* iv.) that God *enfolds the whole in the whole,* i.e. all in all. Therefore the angel knows all things in his substance.

On the contrary, Dionysius says (*ibid.*) that *the angels are enlightened by the forms of things.* Therefore they know by the forms of things, and not by their own substance.

I reply that, The medium through which the intellect understands, is compared to the intellect understanding it as its form, because it is by the form that the agent acts. Now in order that the faculty may be perfectly completed by the form, it is necessary for all things to which the faculty extends to be contained under the form. Hence it is that in things which are corruptible, the form does not perfectly complete the potentiality of the matter: because the potentiality of the matter extends to more things than are contained under this or that form. But the intellective power of the angel extends to understanding all things: because the object of the intellect is universal being or universal truth. The angel's essence, however, does not comprise all things in itself, since it is an essence restricted to a genus and species. This is proper to the Divine essence, which is infinite, simply and perfectly to comprise all things in Itself. Therefore God alone knows all things by His essence. But an angel cannot know all things by his essence; and his intellect must be perfected by some species in order to know things.

Reply Obj. 1. When it is said that the angel knows things according to his own nature, the words *according to* do not determine the medium of such knowledge, since the medium is the similitude of the thing known; but they denote the knowing power, which belongs to the angel of his own nature.

Reply Obj. 2. As the sense in act is the sensible in act, as stated in *De Anima* ii., text. 53, not so that the sensitive power is the sensible object's likeness contained in the sense, but because one thing is made from both as from act and potentiality : so likewise the intellect in act is said to be the thing understood in act, not that the substance of the intellect is itself the similitude by which it understands, but because that similitude is its form. Now, it is precisely the same thing to say *in things which are without matter, the intellect is the same thing as the object understood,* as to say that *the intellect in act is the thing understood in act;* for a thing is actually understood, precisely because it is immaterial.

Reply Obj. 3. The things which are beneath the angel, and those which are above him, are in a measure in his substance, not indeed perfectly, nor according to their own proper formality—because the angel's essence, as being finite, is distinguished by its own formality from other things—but according to some common formality. Yet all things are perfectly and according to their own formality in God's essence, as in the first and universal operative power, from which proceeds whatever is proper or common to anything. Therefore God has a proper knowledge of all things by His own essence : and this the angel has not, but only a common knowledge.

Second Article.

WHETHER THE ANGELS UNDERSTAND BY SPECIES DRAWN FROM THINGS?

We proceed thus to the Second Article:—

Objection 1. It would seem that the angels understand by species drawn from things. For everything understood is apprehended by some likeness within him who understands it. But the likeness of the thing existing in another is there either by way of an exemplar, so that the likeness is the cause of the thing; or else by way of an image, so that it is caused by such thing. All knowledge, then, of the person understanding must either be the cause of the object understood, or else caused by it. Now the angel's knowledge is not the cause of existing things; that belongs to the Divine knowledge alone. Therefore it is necessary for the species, by which the angelic mind understands, to be derived from things.

Obj. 2. Further, the angelic light is stronger than the light of the active intellect of the soul. But the light of the active intellect abstracts intelligible species from phantasms. Therefore the light of the angelic mind can also abstract species from sensible things. So there is nothing to hinder us from saying that the angel understands through species drawn from things.

Obj. 3. Further, the species in the intellect are indifferent to what is present or distant, except in so far as they are taken from sensible objects. Therefore, if the angel does not understand by species drawn from things, his knowledge would be indifferent as to things present and distant; and so he would be moved locally to no purpose.

On the contrary, Dionysius says (*Div. Nom.* vii.) that the *angels do not gather their Divine knowledge from things divisible or sensible.*

I answer that, The species whereby the angels understand are not drawn from things, but are connatural to them. For we must observe that there is a similarity between the distinction and order of spiritual substances and the distinction and order of corporeal substances. The highest bodies have in their nature a potentiality which is fully perfected by the form; whereas in the lower bodies the potentiality of matter is not entirely perfected by the form, but receives from some agent, now one form, now another. In like fashion also the lower intellectual substances—that is to say, human souls—have a power of understanding which is not naturally complete, but is successively completed in them by their drawing intelligible species from things. But in the higher spiritual substances—that is, the angels—the power of understanding is naturally complete by intelligible species, in so far as they have such species connatural to them, so as to understand all things which they can know naturally.

ANGELIC KNOWLEDGE Q. 55 Art. 2

The same is evident from the manner of existence of such substances. The lower spiritual substances—that is, souls—have a nature akin to a body, in so far as they are the forms of bodies: and consequently from their very mode of existence it behoves them to seek their intelligible perfection from bodies, and through bodies; otherwise they would be united with bodies to no purpose. On the other hand, the higher substances—that is, the angels—are utterly free from bodies, and subsist immaterially and in their own intelligible nature; consequently they attain their intelligible perfection through an intelligible outpouring, whereby they received from God the species of things known, together with their intellectual nature. Hence Augustine says (*Gen. ad lit.* ii. 8): *The other things which are lower than the angels are so created that they first receive existence in the knowledge of the rational creature, and then in their own nature.*

Reply Obj. 1. There are images of creatures in the angel's mind, not, indeed, derived from creatures, but from God, Who is the cause of creatures, and in Whom the likenesses of creatures first exist. Hence Augustine says (*ibid.*) that, *As the type, according to which the creature is fashioned, is in the Word of God before the creature which is fashioned, so the knowledge of the same type exists first in the intellectual creature, and is afterwards the very fashioning of the creature.*

Reply Obj. 2. To go from one extreme to the other it is necessary to pass through the middle. Now the nature of a form in the imagination, which form is without matter but not without material conditions, stands midway between the nature of a form which is in matter, and the nature of a form which is in the intellect by abstraction from matter and from material conditions. Consequently, however powerful the angelic mind might be, it could not reduce material forms to an intelligible condition, except it were first to reduce them to the nature of imagined forms; which is impossible, since the angel has no imagination, as was said above (Q. LIV., A. 5). Even granted that he could abstract intelligible species from material things, yet he would not do so; because he would not need them, for he has connatural intelligible species.

Reply Obj. 3. The angel's knowledge is quite indifferent as to what is near or distant. Nevertheless his local movement is not purposeless on that account: for he is not moved to a place for the purpose of acquiring knowledge, but for the purpose of operation.

THIRD ARTICLE.

WHETHER THE HIGHER ANGELS UNDERSTAND BY MORE UNIVERSAL SPECIES THAN THE LOWER ANGELS?

We proceed thus to the Third Article:—

Objection 1. It would seem that the higher angels do not understand by more universal species than the lower angels. For the universal, seemingly, is what is abstracted from particulars. But angels do not understand by species abstracted from things. Therefore it cannot be said that the species of the angelic intellect are more or less universal.

Obj. 2. Further, whatever is known in detail is more perfectly known than what is known generically; because to know anything generically is, in a fashion, midway between potentiality and act. If, therefore, the higher angels know by more universal species than the lower, it follows that the higher have a more imperfect knowledge than the lower; which is not befitting.

Obj. 3. Further, the same cannot be the proper type of many. But if the higher angel knows various things by one universal form, which the lower angel knows by several special forms, it follows that the higher angel uses one universal form for knowing various things. Therefore he will not be able to have a proper knowledge of each; which seems unbecoming.

On the contrary, Dionysius says (*Cœl. Hier.* xii.) that the higher angels have a more universal knowledge than the lower. And in *De Causis* it is said that the higher angels have more universal forms.

ANGELIC KNOWLEDGE Q. 55. ART. 3

I answer that, For this reason are some things of a more exalted nature, because they are nearer to and more like unto the first, which is God. Now in God the whole plenitude of intellectual knowledge is contained in one thing, that is to say, in the Divine essence, by which God knows all things. This plenitude of knowledge is found in created intellects in a lower manner, and less simply. Consequently it is necessary for the lower intelligences to know by many forms what God knows by one, and by so many the more according as the intellect is lower.

Thus the higher the angel is, by so much the fewer species will he be able to apprehend the whole mass of intelligible objects. Therefore his forms must be more universal; each one of them, as it were, extending to more things. An example of this can in some measure be observed in ourselves. For some people there are who cannot grasp an intelligible truth, unless it be explained to them in every part and detail; this comes of their weakness of intellect: while there are others of stronger intellect, who can grasp many things from few.

Reply Obj. 1. It is accidental to the universal to be abstracted from particulars, in so far as the intellect knowing it derives its knowledge from things. But if there be an intellect which does not derive its knowledge from things, the universal which it knows will not be abstracted from things, but in a measure will be pre-existing to them; either according to the order of causality, as the universal ideas of things are in the Word of God; or at least in the order of nature, as the universal ideas of things are in the angelic mind.

Reply Obj. 2. To know anything universally can be taken in two senses. In one way, on the part of the thing known, namely, that only the universal nature of the thing is known. To know a thing thus is something less perfect: for he would have but an imperfect knowledge of a man who only knew him to be an animal. In another way, on the part of the medium of such knowledge. In this way it is more perfect to know a thing in the universal; for the intellect, which by one universal medium can know each of the things which are properly contained in it, is more perfect than one which cannot.

Reply Obj. 3. The same cannot be the proper and adequate type of several things. But if it be eminent, then it can be taken as the proper type and likeness of many. Just as in man, there is a universal prudence with respect to all the acts of the virtues; which can be taken as the proper type and likeness of that prudence which in the lion leads to acts of magnanimity, and in the fox to acts of wariness; and so on of the rest. The Divine essence, on account of Its eminence, is in like fashion taken as the proper type of each thing contained therein: hence each one is likened to It according to its proper type. The same applies to the universal form which is in the mind of the angel, so that, on account of its excellence, many things can be known through it with a proper knowledge.

QUESTION LVI.

OF THE ANGELS' KNOWLEDGE OF IMMATERIAL THINGS.

(*In Three Articles.*)

WE now inquire into the knowledge of the angels with regard to the objects known by them. We shall treat of their knowledge, first, of immaterial things, secondly of things material. Under the first heading there are three points of inquiry: (1) Does an angel know himself? (2) Does one angel know another? (3) Does the angel know God by his own natural principles?

FIRST ARTICLE.

WHETHER AN ANGEL KNOWS HIMSELF?

We proceed thus to the First Article:—

Objection 1. It would seem that an angel does not know himself. For Dionysius says that *the angels do not know their own powers* (*Cœl. Hier.* vi.). But, when the substance is known, the power is known. Therefore an angel does not know his own essence.

Obj. 2. Further, an angel is a single substance, otherwise he would not act, since acts belong to single subsistences. But nothing single is intelligible. Therefore, since the angel possesses only knowledge which is intellectual, no angel can know himself.

Obj. 3. Further, the intellect is moved by the intelligible object: because, as stated in *De Anima* iii. 4, understanding is a kind of passion. But nothing is moved by or is passive to itself; as appears in corporeal things. Therefore the angel cannot understand himself.

On the contrary, Augustine says (*Gen. ad lit.* ii.) that

the angel knew himself when he was established, that is, enlightened by truth.

I answer that, As is evident from what has been previously said (QQ. XIV., A. 2; LIV., A. 2), the object is on a different footing in an immanent, and in a transient, action. In a transient action the object or matter into which the action passes is something separate from the agent, as the thing heated is from what gave it heat, and the building from the builder; whereas in an immanent action, for the action to proceed, the object must be united with the agent; just as the sensible object must be in contact with sense, in order that sense may actually perceive. And the object which is united to a faculty bears the same relation to actions of this kind as does the form which is the principle of action in other agents : for, as heat is the formal principle of heating in the fire, so is the species of the thing seen the formal principle of sight to the eye.

It must, however, be borne in mind that this image of the object exists sometimes only potentially in the knowing faculty; and then there is only knowledge in potentiality; and in order that there may be actual knowledge, it is required that the faculty of knowledge be actuated by the species. But if it always actually possesses the species, it can thereby have actual knowledge without any preceding change or reception. From this it is evident that it is not of the nature of knower, as knowing, to be moved by the object, but as knowing in potentiality. Now, for the form to be the principle of the action, it makes no difference whether it be inherent in something else, or self-subsisting; because heat would give forth heat none the less if it were self-subsisting, than it does by inhering in something else. So therefore, if in the order of intelligible beings there be any subsisting intelligible form, it will understand itself. And since an angel is immaterial, he is a subsisting form; and, consequently, he is actually intelligible. Hence it follows that he understands himself by his form, which is his substance.

KNOWLEDGE OF THE ANGELS Q. 56. ART. 2

Reply Obj. 1. That is the text of the old translation, which is amended in the new one, and runs thus : *furthermore they*, that is to say the angels, *knew their own powers:* instead of which the old translation read—*and furthermore they do not know their own powers.* Although even the letter of the old translation might be kept in this respect, that the angels do not know their own power perfectly; according as it proceeds from the order of the Divine Wisdom, Which to the angels is incomprehensible.

Reply Obj. 2. We have no knowledge of single corporeal things, not because of their particularity, but on account of the matter, which is their principle of individuation. Accordingly, if there be any single things subsisting without matter, as the angels are, there is nothing to prevent them from being actually intelligible.

Reply Obj. 3. It belongs to the intellect, in so far as it is in potentiality, to be moved and to be passive. Hence this does not happen in the angelic intellect, especially as regards the fact that he understands himself. Besides the action of the intellect is not of the same nature as the action found in corporeal things, which passes out into some other matter.

SECOND ARTICLE.

WHETHER ONE ANGEL KNOWS ANOTHER?

We proceed thus to the Second Article:—

Objection 1. It would seem that one angel does not know another. For the Philosopher says (*De Anima* iii., text. 4), that if the human intellect were to have in itself any one of the natures of sensible things, then such a nature existing within it would prevent it from apprehending external things : as likewise, if the pupil of the eye were coloured with some particular colour, it could not see every colour. But as the human intellect is disposed for understanding corporeal things, so is the angelic mind for understanding immaterial things. Therefore, since the angelic intellect has within itself some one determinate nature from the number of such natures, it would seem that it cannot understand other natures.

Obj. 2. Further, it is stated in *De Causis* that *every intelligence knows what is above it, in so far as it is caused by it; and what is beneath it, in so far as it is its cause.* But one angel is not the cause of another. Therefore one angel does not know another.

Obj. 3. Further, one angel cannot be known to another angel by the essence of the one knowing; because all knowledge is effected by way of a likeness. But the essence of the angel knowing is not like the essence of the angel known, except generically; as is clear from what has been said before (QQ. L., A. 4; LV., A. 1 ad 3). Hence, it follows that one angel would not have a particular knowledge of another, but only a general knowledge. In like manner it cannot be said that one angel knows another by the essence of the angel known; because that whereby the intellect understands is something within the intellect; whereas the Trinity alone can penetrate the mind. Again, it cannot be said that one angel knows the other by a species; because that species would not differ from the angel understood, since each is immaterial. Therefore in no way does it appear that one angel can understand another.

Obj. 4. Further, if one angel did understand another, this would be either by an innate species; and so it would follow that, if God were now to create another angel, such an angel could not be known by the existing angels; or else he would have to be known by a species drawn from things; and so it would follow that the higher angels could not know the lower, from whom they receive nothing. Therefore in no way does it seem that one angel knows another.

On the contrary, We read in *De Causis* that *every intelligence knows the things which are not corrupted.*

I answer that, As Augustine says (*Gen. ad lit.* ii.), such things as pre-existed from eternity in the Word of God, came forth from Him in two ways: first, into the angelic mind; and secondly, so as to subsist in their own natures.

They proceeded into the angelic mind in such a way, that God impressed upon the angelic mind the images of the things which He produced in their own natural being. Now in the Word of God from eternity there existed not only the forms of corporeal things, but likewise the forms of all spiritual creatures. So in every one of these spiritual creatures, the forms of all things, both corporeal and spiritual, were impressed by the Word of God; yet so that in every angel there was impressed the form of his own species according to both its natural and its intelligible condition, so that he should subsist in the nature of his species, and understand himself by it; while the forms of other spiritual and corporeal natures were impressed in him only according to their intelligible natures, so that by such impressed species he might know corporeal and spiritual creatures.

Reply Obj. 1. The spiritual natures of the angels are distinguished from one another in a certain order, as was already observed (Q. L., A. 4, *ad* 1, 2). So the nature of an angel does not hinder him from knowing the other angelic natures, since both the higher and lower bear affinity to his nature, the only difference being according to their various degrees of perfection.

Reply Obj. 2. The nature of cause and effect does not lead one angel to know another, except on account of likeness, so far as cause and effect are alike. Therefore if likeness without causality be admitted in the angels, this will suffice for one to know another.

Reply Obj. 3. One angel knows another by the species of such angel existing in his intellect, which differs from the angel whose image it is, not according to material and immaterial nature, but according to natural and intentional existence. The angel is himself a subsisting form in his natural being; but his species in the intellect of another angel is not so, for there it possesses only an intelligible existence. As the form of colour on the wall has a natural existence; but, in the deferent medium, it has only intentional existence.

Reply Obj. 4. God made every creature proportionate to the universe which He determined to make. Therefore had God resolved to make more angels or more natures of things, He would have impressed more intelligible species in the angelic minds; as a builder who, if he had intended to build a larger house, would have made larger foundations. Hence, for God to add a new creature to the universe, means that He would add a new intelligible species to an angel.

THIRD ARTICLE.

WHETHER AN ANGEL KNOWS GOD BY HIS OWN NATURAL PRINCIPLES?

We proceed thus to the Third Article:—

Objection 1. It would seem that the angels cannot know God by their natural principles. For Dionysius says (*Div. Nom.* i.) that God *by His incomprehensible might is placed above all heavenly minds.* Afterwards he adds that, *since He is above all substances, He is remote from all knowledge.*

Obj. 2. Further, God is infinitely above the intellect of an angel. But what is infinitely beyond cannot be reached. Therefore it appears that an angel cannot know God by his natural principles.

Obj. 3. Further, it is written (1 Cor. xiii. 12): *We see now through a glass in a dark manner; but then face to face.* From this it appears that there is a twofold knowledge of God; the one, whereby He is seen in His essence, according to which He is said to be seen face to face; the other whereby He is seen in the mirror of creatures. As was already shown (Q. XII., A. 4), an angel cannot have the former knowledge by his natural principles. Nor does vision through a mirror belong to the angels, since they do not derive their knowledge of God from sensible things, as Dionysius observes (*Div. Nom.* vii.). Therefore the angels cannot know God by their natural powers.

On the contrary, The angels are mightier in knowledge than men. Yet men can know God through their natural principles; according to Rom. i. 19 : *what is known of God is manifest in them*. Therefore much more so can the angels.

I answer that, The angels can have some knowledge of God by their own natural principles. In evidence whereof it must be borne in mind that a thing is known in three ways : first, by the presence of its essence in the knower, as light can be seen in the eye; and so we have said that an angel knows himself;—secondly, by the presence of its similitude in the power which knows it, as a stone is seen by the eye from its image being in the eye;—thirdly, when the image of the object known is not drawn directly from the object itself, but from something else in which it is made to appear, as when we behold a man in a mirror.

To the first-named class that knowledge of God is likened by which He is seen through His essence; and knowledge such as this cannot accrue to any creature from its natural principles, as was said above (Q. XII., A. 4). The third class comprises the knowledge whereby we know God while we are on earth, by His likeness reflected in creatures, according to Rom. 1. 20 : *The invisible things of God are clearly seen, being understood by the things that are made.* Hence, too, we are said to see God in a mirror. But the knowledge, whereby according to his natural principles the angel knows God, stands midway between these two; and is likened to that knowledge whereby a thing is seen through the species abstracted from it. For since God's image is impressed on the very nature of the angel in his essence, the angel knows God in as much as he is the image of God. Yet he does not behold God's essence; because no created likeness is sufficient to represent the Divine essence. Such knowledge then approaches rather to the specular kind; because the angelic nature is itself a kind of mirror representing the Divine image.

Reply Obj. 1. Dionysius is speaking of the knowledge of comprehension, as his words expressly state. In this way God is not known by any created intellect.

Reply Obj. 2. Since an angel's intellect and essence are

infinitely remote from God, it follows that he cannot comprehend Him; nor can he see God's essence through his own nature. Yet it does not follow on that account that he can have no knowledge of Him at all: because, as God is infinitely remote from the angel, so the knowledge which God has of Himself is infinitely above the knowledge which an angel has of Him.

Reply Obj. 3. The knowledge which an angel has of God is midway between these two kinds of knowledge; nevertheless it approaches more to one of them, as was said above.

QUESTION LVII

OF THE ANGELS' KNOWLEDGE OF MATERIAL THINGS.

(*In Five Articles.*)

WE next investigate the material objects which are known by the angels. Under this heading there are five points of inquiry: (1) Whether the angels know the natures of material things? (2) Whether they know single things? (3) Whether they know the future? (4) Whether they know secret thoughts? (5) Whether they know all mysteries of grace?

FIRST ARTICLE.

WHETHER THE ANGELS KNOW MATERIAL THINGS?

We proceed thus to the First Article:—

Objection 1. It would seem that the angels do not know material things. For the object understood is the perfection of him who understands it. But material things cannot be the perfections of angels, since they are beneath them. Therefore the angels do not know material things.

Obj. 2. Further, intellectual vision is only of such things as exist within the soul by their essence, as is said in a gloss.* But material things cannot enter by their essence into man's soul, nor into the angel's mind. Therefore they cannot be known by intellectual vision, but only by imaginary vision, whereby the images of bodies are apprehended, and by sensible vision, which regards bodies in themselves. Now there is neither imaginary nor sensible vision in the angels, but only intellectual. Therefore the angels cannot know material things.

Obj. 3. Further, material things are not actually in-

* On 2 Cor. xii. 2, taken from Augustine (*Gen. ad lit.* xii. 28).

telligible, but are knowable by apprehension of sense and of imagination, which does not exist in angels. Therefore angels do not know material things.

On the contrary, Whatever the lower power can do, the higher can do likewise. But man's intellect, which in the order of nature is inferior to the angel's, can know material things. Therefore much more can the mind of an angel.

I answer that, The established order of things is for higher beings to be more perfect than lower; and for whatever is contained deficiently, partially, and in manifold manner in the lower beings, to be contained in the higher eminently, and in a certain degree of fulness and simplicity. Therefore, in God, as in the highest source of things, all things pre-exist supersubstantially in respect of His simple Being itself, as Dionysius says (*Div. Nom.* i.). But among other creatures the angels are nearest to God, and resemble Him most; hence they share more fully and more perfectly in the Divine goodness, as Dionysius says (*Cœl. Hier.* iv.). Consequently, all material things pre-exist in the angels more simply and less materially even than in themselves, yet in a more manifold manner and less perfectly than in God.

Now whatever exists in any subject, is contained in it after the manner of such subject. But the angels are intellectual beings of their own nature. Therefore, as God knows material things by His essence, so do the angels know them, forasmuch as they are in the angels by their intelligible species.

Reply Obj. 1. The thing understood is the perfection of the one who understands, by reason of the intelligible species which he has in his intellect. And thus the intelligible species which are in the intellect of an angel are perfections and acts in regard to that intellect.

Reply Obj. 2. Sense does not apprehend the essences of things, but only their outward accidents. In like manner neither does the imagination; for it apprehends only the images of bodies. The intellect alone apprehends the essences of things. Hence it is said (*De Anima* iii., text. 26) that the object of the intellect is *what a thing is*, regarding which it does not err; as neither does sense regarding its proper sensible object. So therefore the essences of material things are in the intellect of man and angels, as the thing understood is in him who understands, and not according to their real natures. But some things are in an intellect or in the soul according to both natures; and in either case there is intellectual vision.

Reply Obj. 3. If an angel were to draw his knowledge of material things from the material things themselves, he would require to make them actually intelligible by a process of abstraction. But he does not derive his knowledge of them from the material things themselves; he has knowledge of material things by actually intelligible species of things, which species are connatural to him; just as our intellect has, by species which it makes intelligible by abstraction.

SECOND ARTICLE.

WHETHER AN ANGEL KNOWS SINGULARS?

We proceed thus to the Second Article:—
Objection 1. It would seem that angels do not know singulars. For the Philosopher says (*Post.* i., text. 22): *The sense has for its object singulars, but the intellect, universals.* Now, in the angels there is no power of understanding save the intellectual power, as is evident from what was said above (Q. LIV., A. 5). Consequently they do not know singulars.

Obj. 2. Further, all knowledge comes about by some assimilation of the knower to the object known. But it is not possible for any assimilation to exist between an angel and a singular object, in so far as it is singular; because, as was observed above (Q. L., A. 2), an angel is immaterial, while matter is the principle of singularity. Therefore the angel cannot know singulars.

Obj. 3. Further, if an angel does know singulars, it is either by singular or by universal species. It is not by singular species; because in this way he would require to have an infinite number of species. Nor is it by universal species; since the universal is not the sufficient principle for knowing the singular as such, because singular things are not known in the universal except potentially. Therefore the angel does not know singulars.

On the contrary, No one can guard what he does not know. But angels guard individual men, according to Ps. xc. 11 : *He hath given His angels charge over Thee.* Consequently the angels know singulars.

I answer that, Some have denied to the angels all knowledge of singulars. In the first place this derogates from the Catholic faith, which asserts that these lower things are administered by angels, according to Heb. i. 14 : *They are all ministering spirits.* Now, if they had no knowledge of singulars, they could exercise no provision over what is going on in this world; since acts belong to individuals : and this is against the text of Eccles. v. 5 : *Say not before the angel: There is no providence.* Secondly, it is also contrary to the teachings of philosophy, according to which the angels are stated to be the movers of the heavenly spheres, and to move them according to their knowledge and will.

Consequently others have said that the angel possesses knowledge of singulars, but in their universal causes, to which all particular effects are reduced; as if the astronomer were to foretell a coming eclipse from the dispositions of the movements of the heavens. This opinion does not escape the aforesaid implications; because, to know a singular, merely in its universal causes, is not to know it as singular, that is, as it exists here and now. The astronomer, knowing from computation of the heavenly movements that an eclipse is about to happen, knows it in the universal; yet he does not know it as taking place now, except by the senses. But administration, providence and movement are of singulars, as they are here and now existing.

Therefore it must be said differently, that, as man by his

various powers of knowledge knows all classes of things, apprehending universals and immaterial things by his intellect, and things singular and corporeal by the senses, so an angel knows both by his one mental power. For the order of things runs in this way, that the higher a thing is, so much the more is its power unified and far-reaching: thus in man himself it is manifest that the common sense which is higher than the proper sense, although it is but one faculty, knows everything apprehended by the five outward senses, and some other things which no outer sense knows; for example, the difference between white and sweet. The same is to be observed in other cases. Accordingly, since an angel is above man in the order of nature, it is unreasonable to say that a man knows by any one of his powers something which an angel by his one faculty of knowledge, namely, the intellect, does not know. Hence Aristotle pronounces it ridiculous to say that a discord, which is known to us, should be unknown to God (*De Anima* i., text. 80; *Metaph.*, text. 15).

The manner in which an angel knows singular things can be considered from this, that, as things proceed from God in order that they may subsist in their own natures, so likewise they proceed in order that they may exist in the angelic mind. Now it is clear that there comes forth from God not only whatever belongs to their universal nature, but likewise all that goes to make up their principles of individuation; since He is the cause of the entire substance of the thing, as to both its matter and its form. And for as much as He causes, does He know; for His knowledge is the cause of a thing, as was shown above (Q. XIV., A. 8). Therefore as by His essence, by which He causes all things, God is the likeness of all things, and knows all things, not only as to their universal natures, but also as to their singularity; so through the species imparted to them do the angels know things, not only as to their universal nature, but likewise in their individual conditions, in so far as they are the manifold representations of that one simple essence.

Reply Obj. 1. The Philosopher is speaking of our intellect, which apprehends things only by a process of abstraction; and by such abstraction from material conditions the thing abstracted becomes a universal. Such a manner of understanding is not in keeping with the nature of the angels, as was said above (Q. LV., A. 2, A. 3 *ad* 1), and consequently there is no comparison.

Reply Obj. 2. It is not according to their nature that the angels are likened to material things, as one thing resembles another by agreement in genus, species, or accident; but as the higher bears resemblance to the lower, as the sun does to fire. Even in this way there is in God a resemblance of all things, as to both matter and form, in so far as there pre-exists in Him as in its cause whatever is to be found in things. For the same reason, the species in the angel's intellect, which are images drawn from the Divine essence, are the images of things not only as to their form, but also as to their matter.

Reply Obj. 3. Angels know singulars by universal forms, which nevertheless are the images of things both as to their universal, and as to their individuating principles. How many things can be known by the same species, has been already stated above (Q. LV., A. 3 *ad* 3).

THIRD ARTICLE.

WHETHER ANGELS KNOW THE FUTURE?

We proceed thus to the Third Article:—

Objection 1. It would seem that the angels know future events. For angels are mightier in knowledge than men. But some men know many future events. Therefore much more do the angels.

Obj. 2. Further, the present and the future are differences of time. But the angel's intellect is above time; because, as is said in *De Causis, an intelligence keeps pace with eternity,* that is, æviternity. Therefore, to the angel's mind, past and future are not different, but he knows each indifferently.

KNOWLEDGE OF THE ANGELS Q. 57. ART. 3

Obj. 3. Further, the angel does not understand by species derived from things, but by innate universal species. But universal species refer equally to present, past, and future. Therefore it appears that the angels know indifferently things past, present, and future.

Obj. 4. Further, as a thing is spoken of as distant by reason of time, so is it by reason of place. But angels know things which are distant according to place. Therefore they likewise know things distant according to future time.

On the contrary, Whatever is the exclusive sign of the Divinity, does not belong to the angels. But to know future events is the exclusive sign of the Divinity, according to Isa. xli. 23 : *Show the things that are to come hereafter, and we shall know that ye are gods.* Therefore the angels do not know future events.

I answer that, The future can be known in two ways. First, it can be known in its cause. And thus, future events which proceed necessarily from their causes, are known with sure knowledge; as that the sun will rise to-morrow. But events which proceed from their causes in the majority of cases, are not known for certain, but conjecturally; thus the doctor knows beforehand the health of the patient. This manner of knowing future events exists in the angels, and by so much the more than it does in us, as they understand the causes of things both more universally and more perfectly; thus doctors who penetrate more deeply into the causes of an ailment can pronounce a surer verdict on the future issue thereof. But events which proceed from their causes in the minority of cases are quite unknown; such as casual and chance events.

In another way future events are known in themselves. To know the future in this way belongs to God alone; and not merely to know those events which happen of necessity, or in the majority of cases, but even casual and chance events; for God sees all things in His eternity, which, being simple, is present to all time, and embraces all time. And therefore God's one glance is cast over all things which happen in all time as present before Him; and He beholds all things as they are in themselves, as was said before when dealing with God's knowledge (Q. XIV., A. 13). But the mind of an angel, and every created intellect, fall far short of God's eternity; hence the future as it is in itself cannot be known by any created intellect.

Reply Obj. 1. Men cannot know future things except in their causes, or by God's revelation. The angels know the future in the same way, but much more distinctly.

Reply Obj. 2. Although the angel's intellect is above that time according to which corporeal movements are reckoned, yet there is a time in his mind according to the succession of intelligible concepts; of which Augustine says (*Gen. ad lit.* viii.) that *God moves the spiritual creature according to time.* And thus, since there is succession in the angel's intellect, not all things that happen through all time, are present to the angelic mind.

Reply Obj. 3. Although the species in the intellect of an angel, in so far as they are species, refer equally to things present, past, and future; nevertheless the present, past, and future do not bear the same relations to the species. Present things have a nature according to which they resemble the species in the mind of an angel: and so they can be known thereby. Things which are yet to come have not yet a nature whereby they are likened to such species: consequently, they cannot be known by those species.

Reply Obj. 4. Things distant according to place are already existing in nature; and share in some species, whose image is in the angel; whereas this is not true of future things, as has been stated. Consequently there is no comparison.

FOURTH ARTICLE.

WHETHER ANGELS KNOW SECRET THOUGHTS?

We proceed thus to the Fourth Article:—

Objection 1. It would seem that the angels know secret thoughts. For Gregory (*Moral.* xviii.), explaining Job xxviii. 17: *Gold or crystal cannot equal it,* says that *then,*

KNOWLEDGE OF THE ANGELS Q 57 ART. 4

namely in the bliss of those rising from the dead, *one shall be as evident to another as he is to himself, and when once the mind of each is seen, his conscience will at the same time be penetrated.* But those who rise shall be like the angels, as is stated (Matt. xxii. 30). Therefore an angel can see what is in another's conscience.

Obj. 2. Further, intelligible species bear the same relation to the intellect as shapes do to bodies. But when the body is seen its shape is seen. Therefore, when an intellectual substance is seen, the intelligible species within it is also seen. Consequently, when one angel beholds another, or even a soul, it seems that he can see the thoughts of both.

Obj. 3. Further, the ideas in our intellect resemble the angel more than do the images in our imagination; because the former are actually understood, while the latter are understood only potentially. But the images in our imagination can be known by an angel as corporeal things are known: because the imagination is a corporeal faculty. Therefore it seems that an angel can know the thoughts of the intellect.

On the contrary, What is proper to God does not belong to angels. But it is proper to God to read the secrets of hearts, according to Jer. xvii. 9: *The heart is perverse above all things, and unsearchable; who can know it? I am the Lord, Who search the heart.* Therefore angels do not know the secrets of hearts.

I answer that, A secret thought can be known in two ways: first, in its effect. In this way it can be known not only by an angel, but also by man; and with so much the greater subtlety according as the effect is the more hidden. For thought is sometimes discovered not merely by outward act, but also by change of countenance; and doctors can tell some passions of the soul by the mere pulse. Much more then can angels, or even demons, the more deeply they penetrate these occult bodily modifications. Hence Augustine says (*De divin. dæmon*) that demons *sometimes with the greatest facility learn man's dispositions, not only when expressed by speech, but even when conceived in* thought, when the soul expresses them by certain signs in the body; although (*Retract.* ii. 30) he says *it cannot be asserted how this is done.*

In another way thoughts can be known as they are in the mind, and affections as they are in the will : and thus God alone can know the thoughts of hearts and affections of wills. The reason of this is, because the rational creature is subject to God only, and He alone can work in it Who is its principal object and last end : this will be developed later (Q. LXIII., A. 1; Q. CV., A. 5). Consequently all that is in the will, and all things that depend only on the will, are known to God alone. Now it is evident that it depends entirely on the will for anyone actually to consider anything; because a man who has a habit of knowledge, or any intelligible species, uses them at will. Hence the Apostle says (1 Cor. ii. 11) : *For what man knoweth the things of a man, but the spirit of a man that is in him?*

Reply Obj. 1. In the present life one man's thought is not known by another owing to a twofold hindrance; namely, on account of the grossness of the body, and because the will shuts up its secrets. The first obstacle will be removed at the Resurrection, and does not exist at all in the angels; while the second will remain, and is in the angels now. Nevertheless the brightness of the body will show forth the quality of the soul; as to its amount of grace and of glory. In this way one will be able to see the mind of another.

Reply Obj. 2. Although one angel sees the intelligible species of another, by the fact that the species are proportioned to the rank of these substances according to greater or lesser universality, yet it does not follow that one knows how far another makes use of them by actual consideration.

Reply Obj. 3. The appetite of the brute does not control its act, but follows the impression of some other corporeal or spiritual cause. Since, therefore, the angels know corporeal things and their dispositions, they can thereby know what is passing in the appetite or in the imaginative apprehension of the brute beasts, and even of man, in so far as the sensitive appetite sometimes, through following some bodily impression, influences his conduct, as always happens in brutes. Yet the angels do not necessarily know the movements of the sensitive appetite and the imaginative apprehension of man, in so far as these are moved by the will and reason; because, even the lower part of the soul has some share of reason, as obeying its ruler, as is said in *Ethics* iii. 12. But it does not follow that, if the angel knows what is passing through man's sensitive appetite or imagination, he knows what is in the thought or will: because the intellect or will is not subject to the sensitive appetite or the imagination, but can make various uses of them.

FIFTH ARTICLE.

WHETHER THE ANGELS KNOW THE MYSTERIES OF GRACE?

We proceed thus to the Fifth Article:—

Objection 1. It would seem that the angels know mysteries of grace. For, the mystery of the Incarnation is the most excellent of all mysteries. But the angels knew of it from the beginning; for Augustine (*Gen. ad lit.* v. 19) says: *This mystery was hidden in God through the ages, yet so that it was known to the princes and powers in heavenly places.* And the Apostle says (1 Tim. iii. 16): *That great mystery of godliness appeared unto angels.** Therefore the angels know the mysteries of grace.

Obj. 2. Further, the reasons of all mysteries of grace are contained in the Divine wisdom. But the angels behold God's wisdom, which is His essence. Therefore they know the mysteries of grace.

Obj. 3. Further, the prophets are enlightened by the angels, as is clear from Dionysius (*Cœl. Hier.* iv.). But the prophets knew mysteries of grace, for it is said (Amos iii. 7): *For the Lord God doth nothing without revealing His secret to His servants the prophets.* Therefore angels know the mysteries of grace.

* Vulg *Great is the mystery of godliness, which . . . appeared unto angels.*

On the contrary, No one learns what he knows already. Yet even the highest angels seek out and learn mysteries of grace. For it is stated (*Cœl. Hier.* vii.) that *Sacred Scripture describes some heavenly essences as questioning Jesus, and learning from Him the knowledge of His Divine work for us; and Jesus as teaching them directly:* as is evident in Isa. lxiii. 1, where, on the angels asking, *Who is he who cometh up from Edom?* Jesus answered, *It is I, Who speak justice.* Therefore the angels do not know mysteries of grace.

I answer that, There is a twofold knowledge in the angel. The first is his natural knowledge, according to which he knows things both by his essence, and by innate species. By such knowledge the angels cannot know mysteries of grace. For these mysteries depend upon the pure will of God: and if an angel cannot learn the thoughts of another angel, which depend upon the will of such angel, much less can he ascertain what depends entirely upon God's will. The Apostle reasons in this fashion (1 Cor. ii. 11): *No one knoweth the things of a man,** *but the spirit of a man that is in him. So, the things also that are of God no man knoweth but the Spirit of God.*

There is another knowledge of the angels, which renders them happy; it is the knowledge whereby they see the Word, and things in the Word. By such vision they know mysteries of grace, but not all mysteries: nor do they all know them equally; but just as God wills them to learn by revelation; as the Apostle says (1 Cor. ii. 10): *But to us God hath revealed them through His Spirit;* yet so that the higher angels beholding the Divine wisdom more clearly, learn more and deeper mysteries in the vision of God, which mysteries they communicate to the lower angels by enlightening them. Some of these mysteries they knew from the very beginning of their creation; others they are taught afterwards, as befits their ministrations.

Reply Obj. 1. One can speak in two ways of the mystery of the Incarnation. First of all, in general; and in this way

* Vulg., *What man knoweth the things of a man, but* . . . ?

79 KNOWLEDGE OF THE ANGELS Q. 57. ART. 5

it was revealed to all from the commencement of their beatitude. The reason of this is, that this is a kind of general principle to which all their duties are ordered. For *all are* ministering spirits, sent to minister for them who shall receive the inheritance of salvation* (Heb. i. 14); and this is brought about by the mystery of the Incarnation. Hence it was necessary for all of them to be instructed in this mystery from the very beginning.

We can speak of the mystery of the Incarnation in another way, as to its special conditions. Thus not all the angels were instructed on all points from the beginning; even the higher angels learned these afterwards, as appears from the passage of Dionysius already quoted.

Reply Obj. 2. Although the angels in bliss behold the Divine wisdom, yet they do not comprehend it. So it is not necessary for them to know everything hidden in it.

Reply Obj. 3. Whatever the prophets knew by revelation of the mysteries of grace, was revealed in a more excellent way to the angels. And although God revealed in general to the prophets what He was one day to do regarding the salvation of the human race, still the apostles knew some particulars of the same, which the prophets did not know. Thus we read (Eph. iii. 4, 5) : *As you reading, may understand my knowledge in the mystery of Christ, which in other generations was not known to the sons of men, as it is now revealed to His holy apostles.* Among the prophets also, the later ones knew what the former did not know; according to Ps. cxviii. 100 : *I have had understanding above ancients,* and Gregory says : *The knowledge of Divine things increased as time went on (Homil.* xvi. *in Ezech.).*

* Vulg., *Are they not all.*

QUESTION LVIII.

OF THE MODE OF THE ANGELIC KNOWLEDGE.
(In Seven Articles.)

AFTER the foregoing we have now to treat of the mode of the angelic knowledge, concerning which there are seven points of inquiry: (1) Whether the angel's intellect be sometimes in potentiality, and sometimes in act? (2) Whether the angel can understand many things at the same time? (3) Whether the angel's knowledge is discursive? (4) Whether he understands by composing and dividing? (5) Whether there can be error in the angel's intellect? (6) Whether his knowledge can be styled as morning and evening? (7) Whether the morning and evening knowledge are the same, or do they differ?

FIRST ARTICLE.

WHETHER THE ANGEL'S INTELLECT IS SOMETIMES IN POTENTIALITY, AND SOMETIMES IN ACT?

We proceed thus to the First Article:—

Objection 1. It would seem that the angel's intellect is sometimes in potentiality and sometimes in act. For movement is the act of what is in potentiality, as stated in *Phys.* iii. 6. But the angels' minds are moved by understanding, as Dionysius says (*Div. Nom.* iv.). Therefore the angelic minds are sometimes in potentiality.

Obj. 2. Further, since desire is of a thing not possessed but possible to have, whoever desires to know anything is in potentiality thereto. But it is said (1 Pet. i. 12): *On Whom the angels desire to look.* Therefore the angel's intellect is sometimes in potentiality.

Obj. 3. Further, in the book *De Causis* it is stated that an intelligence understands according to the mode of its substance. But the angel's intelligence has some admixture of potentiality. Therefore it sometimes understands potentially.

On the contrary, Augustine says (*Gen. ad lit.* ii.) : *Since the angels were created, in the eternity of the Word, they enjoy holy and devout contemplation.* Now a contemplating intellect is not in potentiality, but in act. Therefore the intellect of an angel is not in potentiality.

I answer that, As the Philosopher states (*De Anima* iii., text. 8; *Phys.* viii. 32), the intellect is in potentiality in two ways; first, *as before learning or discovering,* that is, before it has the habit of knowledge; secondly, as *when it possesses the habit of knowledge, but does not actually consider.* In the first way an angel's intellect is never in potentiality with regard to the things to which his natural knowledge extends. For, as the higher, namely, the heavenly, bodies have no potentiality to existence, which is not fully actuated, in the same way the heavenly intellects, the angels, have no intelligible potentiality which is not fully completed by connatural intelligible species. But with regard to things divinely revealed to them, there is nothing to hinder them from being in potentiality : because even the heavenly bodies are at times in potentiality to being enlightened by the sun.

In the second way an angel's intellect can be in potentiality with regard to things learnt by natural knowledge; for he is not always actually considering everything that he knows by natural knowledge. But as to the knowledge of the Word, and of the things he beholds in the Word, he is never in this way in potentiality; because he is always actually beholding the Word, and the things he sees in the Word. For the bliss of the angels consists in such vision; and beatitude does not consist in habit, but in act, as the Philosopher says (*Ethics* i. 8).

Reply Obj. 1. Movement is taken there not as the act of something imperfect, that is, of something existing in potentiality, but as the act of something perfect, that is, of one actually existing. In this way understanding and feeling are termed movements, as stated in *De Anima* iii., text. 28).

Reply Obj. 2. Such desire on the part of the angels does not exclude the object desired, but weariness thereof. Or they are said to desire the vision of God with regard to fresh revelations, which they receive from God to fit them for the tasks which they have to perform.

Reply Obj. 3. In the angel's substance there is no potentiality divested of act. In the same way, the angel's intellect is never so in potentiality as to be without act.

SECOND ARTICLE.

WHETHER AN ANGEL CAN UNDERSTAND MANY THINGS AT THE SAME TIME?

We proceed thus to the Second Article:—

Objection 1. It would seem that an angel cannot understand many things at the same time. For the Philosopher says (*Topic.* ii. 4) that *it may happen that we know many things, but understand only one.*

Obj. 2. Further, nothing is understood unless the intellect be informed by an intelligible species; just as the body is formed by shape. But one body cannot be formed into many shapes. Therefore neither can one intellect simultaneously understand various intelligible things.

Obj. 3. Further, to understand is a kind of movement. But no movement terminates in various terms. Therefore many things cannot be understood altogether.

On the contrary, Augustine says (*Gen. ad lit.* iv. 32): *The spiritual faculty of the angelic mind comprehends most easily at the same time all things that it wills.*

I answer that, As unity of term is requisite for unity of movement, so is unity of object required for unity of operation. Now it happens that several things may be taken as several or as one; like the parts of a continuous whole. For if each of the parts be considered severally, they are many: consequently neither by sense nor by intellect are they grasped by one operation, nor all at once. In another way they are taken as forming one in the whole; and so they are grasped both by sense and intellect all at once and by one operation; as long as the entire continuous whole is considered, as is stated in *De anima* iii., text. 23. In this way our intellect understands together both the subject and the predicate, as forming parts of one proposition; and also two things compared together, according as they agree in one point of comparison. From this it is evident that many things, in so far as they are distinct, cannot be understood at once; but in so far as they are comprised under one intelligible concept, they can be understood together. Now everything is actually intelligible according as its image is in the intellect. All things, then, which can be known by one intelligible species, are known as one intelligible object, and therefore are understood simultaneously. But things known by various intelligible species, are apprehended as different intelligible objects.

Consequently, by such knowledge as the angels have of things through the Word, they know all things under one intelligible species, which is the Divine essence. Therefore, as regards such knowledge, they know all things at once: just as in heaven *our thoughts will not be fleeting, going and returning from one thing to another, but we shall survey all our knowledge at the same time by one glance,* as Augustine says (*De Trin.* xv. 16). But by that knowledge wherewith the angels know things by innate species, they can at the one time know all things which can be comprised under one species; but not such as are under various species.

Reply Obj. 1. To understand many things as one, is, so to speak, to understand one thing.

Reply Obj. 2. The intellect is informed by the intelligible species which it has within it. So it can behold at the same time many intelligible objects under one species; as one body can by one shape be likened to many bodies.

To the third objection the answer is the same as to the first.

THIRD ARTICLE.

WHETHER AN ANGEL'S KNOWLEDGE IS DISCURSIVE?

We proceed thus to the Third Article:—

Objection 1. It would seem that the knowledge of an angel is discursive. For the discursive movement of the mind comes from one thing being known through another. But the angels know one thing through another; for they know creatures through the Word. Therefore the intellect of an angel knows by discursive method.

Obj. 2. Further, whatever a lower power can do, the higher can do. But the human intellect can syllogize, and know causes in effects; all of which is the discursive method. Therefore the intellect of the angel, which is higher in the order of nature, can with greater reason do this.

Obj. 3. Further, Isidore (*De sum. bono* i. 10) says that *demons learn many things by experience*. But experimental knowledge is discursive: for, *one experience comes of many remembrances, and one universal from many experiences,* as Aristotle observes (*Poster.* ii., *Metaph.* i.). Therefore an angel's knowledge is discursive.

On the contrary, Dionysius says (*Div. Nom.* vii.) that the *angels do not acquire Divine knowledge from separate discourses, nor are they led to something particular from something common.*

I answer that, As has often been stated (A. 1; Q. LV., A. 1), the angels hold that grade among spiritual substances which the heavenly bodies hold among corporeal substances: for Dionysius calls them *heavenly minds* (*loc. cit.*). Now, the difference between heavenly and earthly bodies is this, that earthly bodies obtain their last perfection by change and movement: while the heavenly bodies have their last perfection at once from their very nature. So, likewise, the lower, namely, the human, intellects obtain their perfection in the knowledge of truth by a kind of movement and discursive intellectual operation; that is to say, as they advance from one known thing to another.

ANGELIC KNOWLEDGE Q. 58. ART. 3

But, if from the knowledge of a known principle they were straightway to perceive as known all its consequent conclusions, then there would be no discursive process at all. Such is the condition of the angels, because in the truths which they know naturally, they at once behold all things whatsoever that can be known in them.

Therefore they are called *intellectual* beings : because even with ourselves the things which are instantly grasped by the mind are said to be understood (*intelligi*); hence *intellect* is defined as the habit of first principles. But human souls which acquire knowledge of truth by the discursive method are called *rational;* and this comes of the feebleness of their intellectual light. For if they possessed the fulness of intellectual light, like the angels, then in the first aspect of principles they would at once comprehend their whole range, by perceiving whatever could be reasoned out from them.

Reply Obj. 1. Discursion expresses movement of a kind. Now all movement is from something before to something after. Hence discursive knowledge comes about according as from something previously known one attains to the knowledge of what is afterwards known, and which was previously unknown. But if in the thing perceived something else be seen at the same time, as an object and its image are seen simultaneously in a mirror, it is not discursive knowledge. And in this way the angels know things in the Word.

Reply Obj. 2. The angels can syllogize, in the sense of knowing a syllogism ; and they see effects in causes, and causes in effects : yet they do not acquire knowledge of an unknown truth in this way, by syllogizing from causes to effect, or from effect to cause.

Reply Obj. 3. Experience is affirmed of angels and demons simply by way of similitude, forasmuch as they know sensible things which are present, yet without any discursion withal.

Fourth Article.

WHETHER THE ANGELS UNDERSTAND BY COMPOSING AND DIVIDING?

We proceed thus to the Fourth Article:—

Objection 1. It would seem that the angels understand by composing and dividing. For, where there is multiplicity of things understood, there is composition of the same, as is said in *De Anima* iii., text. 21. But there is a multitude of things understood in the angelic mind; because angels apprehend different things by various species, and not all at one time. Therefore there is composition and division in the angel's mind.

Obj. 2. Further, negation is far more remote from affirmation than any two opposite natures are; because the first of distinctions is that of affirmation and negation. But the angel knows certain distant natures not by one, but by diverse species, as is evident from what was said (A. 2). Therefore he must know affirmation and negation by diverse species. And so it seems that he understands by composing and dividing.

Obj. 3. Further, speech is a sign of the intellect. But in speaking to men, angels use affirmative and negative expressions, which are signs of composition and of division in the intellect; as is manifest from many passages of Sacred Scripture. Therefore it seems that the angel understands by composing and dividing.

On the contrary, Dionysius says (*Div. Nom.* vii.) that *the intellectual power of the angel shines forth with the clear simplicity of divine concepts*. But a simple intelligence is without composition and division. Therefore the angel understands without composition or division.

I answer that, As in the intellect, when reasoning, the conclusion is compared with the principle, so in the intellect composing and dividing, the predicate is compared with the subject. For if our intellect were to see at once the truth of the conclusion in the principle, it would never understand by discursion and reasoning. In like manner, if the intellect in apprehending the quiddity of the subject were at once to have knowledge of all that can be attributed to, or removed from, the subject, it would never understand by composing and dividing, but only by understanding the essence. Thus it is evident that for the self-same reason our intellect understands by discursion, and by composing and dividing: namely, that in the first apprehension of anything newly apprehended it does not at once grasp all that is virtually contained in it. And this comes from the weakness of the intellectual light within us, as has been said (A. 3). Hence, since the intellectual light is perfect in the angel, for he is a pure and most clear mirror, as Dionysius says (*Div. Nom.* iv.), it follows that as the angel does not understand by reasoning, so neither does he by composing and dividing.

Nevertheless, he understands the composition and the division of enunciations, just as he apprehends the reasoning of syllogisms: for he understands simply, such things as are composite, things movable immovably, and material things immaterially.

Reply Obj. 1. Not every multitude of things understood causes composition, but a multitude of such things understood that one of them is attributed to, or denied of, another. When an angel apprehends the nature of anything, he at the same time understands whatever can be either attributed to it, or denied of it. Hence, in apprehending a nature, he by one simple perception grasps all that we can learn by composing and dividing.

Reply Obj. 2. The various natures of things differ less as to their mode of existing than do affirmation and negation. Yet, as to the way in which they are known, affirmation and negation have something more in common; because directly the truth of an affirmation is known, the falsehood of the opposite negation is known also.

Reply Obj. 3. The fact that angels use affirmative and negative forms of speech, shows that they know both composition and division: yet not that they know by composing and dividing, but by knowing simply the nature of a thing.

FIFTH ARTICLE.

WHETHER THERE CAN BE FALSEHOOD IN THE INTELLECT OF AN ANGEL?

We proceed thus to the Fifth Article:—
Objection 1. It would seem that there can be falsehood in the angel's intellect. For perversity appertains to falsehood. But, as Dionysius says (*Div. Nom.* iv.), there is *a perverted fancy* in the demons. Therefore it seems that there can be falsehood in the intellect of the angels.

Obj. 2. Further, nescience is the cause of estimating falsely. But, as Dionysius says (*Eccl. Hier.* vi.), there can be nescience in the angels. Therefore it seems there can be falsehood in them.

Obj. 3. Further, everything which falls short of the truth of wisdom, and which has a depraved reason, has falsehood or error in its intellect. But Dionysius (*Div. Nom.* vii.) affirms this of the demons. Therefore it seems that there can be error in the minds of the angels.

On the contrary, The Philosopher says (*De Anima* iii., text. 41) that *the intelligence is always true.* Augustine likewise says (QQ. LXXXIII., *qu.* 32) that *nothing but what is true can be the object of intelligence.* Therefore there can be neither deception nor falsehood in the angel's knowledge.

I answer that, The truth of this question depends partly upon what has gone before. For it has been said (A. 4) that an angel understands not by composing and dividing, but by understanding what a thing is. Now the intellect is always true as regards what a thing is, just as the sense regarding its proper object, as is said in *De Anima* iii., text. 26. But by accident, deception and falsehood creep in, when we understand the essence of a thing by some kind of composition, and this happens either when we take the definition of one thing for another, or when the parts of a definition do not hang together, as if we were to accept as the definition of some creature, *a four-footed flying beast,* for there is no such animal. And this comes about in things composite, the definition of which is drawn from diverse elements, one of which is as matter to the other. But there is no room for error in understanding simple quiddities, as is stated in *Metaph.* ix., text. 22; for either they are not grasped at all, and so we know nothing respecting them; or else they are known precisely as they exist.

So therefore, no falsehood, error, or deception can exist of itself in the mind of any angel; yet it does so happen accidentally; but very differently from the way it befalls us. For we sometimes get at the quiddity of a thing by a composing and dividing process, as when, by division and demonstration, we seek out the truth of a definition. Such is not the method of the angels; but through the (knowledge of the) essence of a thing they know everything that can be said regarding it. Now it is quite evident that the quiddity of a thing can be a source of knowledge with regard to everything belonging to such thing, or excluded from it; but not of what may be dependent on God's supernatural ordinance. Consequently, owing to their upright will, from their knowing the nature of every creature, the good angels form no judgments as to the nature of qualities therein, save under the Divine ordinance; hence there can be no error or falsehood in them. But since the minds of demons are utterly perverted from the Divine wisdom, they at times form their opinions of things simply according to the natural conditions of the same. Nor are they ever deceived as to the natural properties of anything; but they can be misled with regard to supernatural matters; for example, on seeing a dead man, they may suppose that he will not rise again, or, on beholding Christ, they may judge Him not to be God.

From all this the answers to the objections on both sides of the question are evident. For the perversity of the demons comes of their not being subject to the Divine wisdom; while nescience is in the angels as regards things knowable, not naturally but supernaturally. It is, furthermore, evident that their understanding of what a thing is, is always true, save accidentally, according as it is, in an undue manner, referred to some composition or division.

SIXTH ARTICLE.

WHETHER THERE IS A "MORNING" AND AN "EVENING" KNOWLEDGE IN THE ANGELS?

We proceed thus to the Sixth Article:—

Objection 1. It would seem that there is neither an evening nor a morning knowledge in the angels; because evening and morning have an admixture of darkness. But there is no darkness in the knowledge of an angel; since there is no error nor falsehood. Therefore the angelic knowledge ought not to be termed morning and evening knowledge.

Obj. 2. Further, between evening and morning the night intervenes; while noonday falls between morning and evening. Consequently, if there be a morning and an evening knowledge in the angels, for the same reason it appears that there ought to be a noonday and a night knowledge.

Obj. 3. Further, knowledge is diversified according to the difference of the objects known: hence the Philosopher says (*De Anima* iii., text. 38), *The sciences are divided just as things are.* But there is a threefold existence of things: to wit, in the Word; in their own natures; and in the angelic knowledge, as Augustine observes (*Gen. ad lit.* ii, 8). If, therefore, a morning and an evening knowledge be admitted in the angels, because of the existence of things in the Word, and in their own nature, then there ought to be admitted a third class of knowledge, on account of the existence of things in the angelic mind.

On the contrary, Augustine (*Gen. ad lit.* iv. 22, 31; *Civ. Dei* xii. 7, 20) divides the knowledge of the angels into morning and evening knowledge.

I answer that, The expression "morning" and "evening" knowledge was devised by Augustine; who interprets the six days wherein God made all things, not as ordinary days measured by the solar circuit, since the sun was only made on the fourth day, but as one day, namely, the day of angelic knowledge as directed to six classes of things. As in the ordinary day, morning is the beginning, and evening the close of day, so, their knowledge of the primordial being of things is called morning knowledge; and this is according as things exist in the Word. But their knowledge of the very being of the thing created, as it stands in its own nature, is termed evening knowledge; because the being of things flows from the Word, as from a kind of primordial principle; and this flow is terminated in the being which they have in themselves.

Reply Obj. 1. Evening and morning in the angelic knowledge are not taken as compared to the admixture of darkness, but as compared to beginning and end. Or else it can be said, as Augustine puts it (*Gen. ad lit.* iv. 23), that there is nothing to prevent us from calling something light in comparison with one thing, and darkness with respect to another. In the same way the life of the faithful and the just is called light in comparison with the wicked, according to Eph. v. 8 : *You were heretofore darkness; but now, light in the Lord:* yet this very life of the faithful, when set in contrast to the life of glory, is termed darkness, according to 2 Pet. i. 19 : *You have the firm prophetic word, whereunto you do well to attend, as to a light that shineth in a dark place.* So the angel's knowledge by which he knows things in their own nature, is day in comparison with ignorance or error; yet it is dark in comparison with the vision of the Word.

Reply Obj. 2. The morning and evening knowledge belong to the day, that is, to the enlightened angels, who are quite apart from the darkness, that is, from the evil spirits. The good angels, while knowing the creature, do not adhere to it, for that would be to turn to darkness and to night; but they refer this back to the praise of God, in Whom, as in their principle, they know all things. Consequently after *evening* there is no night, but *morning;* so that morning is the end of the preceding day, and the beginning of the following, in so far as the angels refer to God's praise their knowledge of the preceding work. Noonday is comprised under the name of day, as the middle between the two extremes. Or else the noon can be referred to their knowledge of God Himself, Who has neither beginning nor end.

Reply Obj. 3. The angels themselves are also creatures. Accordingly the existence of things in the angelic knowledge is comprised under evening knowledge, as also the existence of things in their own nature.

SEVENTH ARTICLE.

WHETHER THE MORNING AND EVENING KNOWLEDGE ARE ONE?

We proceed thus to the Seventh Article:—

Objection 1. It would seem that the morning and the evening knowledge are one. For it is said (Gen. i. 5): *There was evening and morning, one day.* But by the expression *day* the knowledge of the angels is to be understood, as Augustine says *(loc. cit.).* Therefore the morning and the evening knowledge of the angels are one and the same.

Obj. 2. Further, it is impossible for one faculty to have two operations at the same time. But the angels are always using their morning knowledge; because they are always beholding God and things in God, according to Matt. xviii. 10. Therefore, if the evening knowledge were different from the morning, the angel could never exercise his evening knowledge.

Obj. 3. Further, the Apostle says (1 Cor. xiii. 10): *When that which is perfect is come, then that which is in part shall be done away.* But, if the evening knowledge be different from the morning, it is compared to it as the less perfect to the perfect. Therefore the evening knowledge cannot exist together with the morning knowledge.

On the contrary, Augustine says *(Gen. ad lit.* iv. 24)· *There is a vast difference between knowing anything as it*

ANGELIC KNOWLEDGE Q. 58. Art. 7

is in the Word of God, and as it is in its own nature; so that the former belongs to the day, and the latter to the evening.

I answer that, As was observed (A. 6), the evening knowledge is that by which the angels know things in their proper nature. This cannot be understood as if they drew their knowledge from the proper nature of things, so that the preposition *in* denotes the form of a principle; because, as has been already stated (Q. LV., A. 2), the angels do not draw their knowledge from things. It follows, then, that when we say *in their proper nature* we refer to the aspect of the thing known in so far as it is an object of knowledge; that is to say, that the evening knowledge is in the angels in so far as they know the being of things which those things have in their own nature.

Now they know this through a twofold medium, namely, by innate ideas, or by the forms of things existing in the Word. For by beholding the Word, they know not merely the being of things as existing in the Word, but the being as possessed by the things themselves; as God by contemplating Himself sees that being which things have in their own nature. If, therefore, it be called evening knowledge, in so far as when the angels behold the Word, they know the being which things have in their proper nature, then the morning and the evening knowledge are essentially one and the same, and only differ as to the things known. If it be called evening knowledge, in so far as through innate ideas they know the being which things have in their own natures, then the morning and the evening knowledge differ. Thus Augustine seems to understand it when he assigns one as inferior to the other.

Reply Obj. 1. The six days, as Augustine understands them, are taken as the six classes of things known by the angels; so that the day's unit is taken according to the unit of the thing understood; which, nevertheless, can be apprehended by various ways of knowing it.

Reply Obj. 2. There can be two operations of the same faculty at the one time, one of which is referred to the other; as is evident when the will at the same time wills the end and the means to the end; and the intellect at the same instant perceives principles and conclusions through those principles, when it has already acquired knowledge. As Augustine says,* the evening knowledge is referred to the morning knowledge in the angels; hence there is nothing to hinder both from being at the same time in the angels.

Reply Obj. 3. On the coming of what is perfect, the opposite imperfect is done away : just as faith, which is of the things that are not seen, is made void when vision succeeds. But the imperfection of the evening knowledge is not opposed to the perfection of the morning knowledge. For that a thing be known in itself, is not opposite to its being known in its cause. Nor, again, is there any inconsistency in knowing a thing through two mediums, one of which is more perfect and the other less perfect; just as we can have a demonstrative and a probable medium for reaching the same conclusion. In like manner a thing can be known by the angel through the uncreated Word, and through an innate idea.

* *Gen. ad lit.* iv. 24.

QUESTION LIX.

THE WILL OF THE ANGELS.
(In Four Articles.)

IN the next place we must treat of things concerning the will of the angels. In the first place we shall treat of the will itself; secondly, of its movement, which is love. Under the first heading there are four points of inquiry: (1) Whether there is will in the angels? (2) Whether the will of the angel is his nature, or his intellect? (3) Is there free-will in the angels? (4) Is there an irascible and a concupiscible appetite in them?

FIRST ARTICLE.
WHETHER THERE IS WILL IN THE ANGELS?

We proceed thus to the First Article:—

Objection 1. It would seem that there is no will in the angels. For as the Philosopher says (*De Anima* iii., text 42), *The will is in the reason.* But there is no reason in the angels, but something higher than reason. Therefore there is no will in the angels, but something higher than the will.

Obj. 2. Further, the will is comprised under the appetite, as is evident from the Philosopher (*ibid.*). But, appetite argues something imperfect; because it is a desire of something not as yet possessed. Therefore, since there is no imperfection in the angels, especially in the blessed ones, it seems that there is no will in them.

Obj. 3. Further, the Philosopher says (*ibid.*, text. 54) that the will is a mover which is moved; for it is moved by the appetible object understood. Now the angels are immovable, since they are incorporeal. Therefore there is no will in the angels.

On the contrary, Augustine says (*De Trin.* x., 11, 12) that the image of the Trinity is found in the soul according to memory, understanding, and will. But God's image is found not only in the soul of man, but also in the angelic mind, since it also is capable of knowing God. Therefore there is will in the angels.

I answer that, We must necessarily place a will in the angels. In evidence thereof, it must be borne in mind that, since all things flow from the Divine will, all things in their own way are inclined by appetite towards good, but in different ways. Some are inclined to good by their natural inclination, without knowledge, as plants and inanimate bodies. Such inclination towards good is called *a natural appetite*. Others, again, are inclined towards good, but with some knowledge; not that they know the aspect of goodness, but that they apprehend some particular good; as the sense, which knows the sweet, the white, and so on. The inclination which follows this apprehension is called *a sensitive appetite*. Other things, again, have an inclination towards good, but with a knowledge whereby they perceive the aspect of goodness; this belongs to the intellect. This is most perfectly inclined towards what is good; not, indeed, as if it were merely guided by another towards good, like things devoid of knowledge, nor towards some particular good only, as things which have only sensitive knowledge, but as inclined towards good in general. Such inclination is termed *will*. Accordingly, since the angels by their intellect know the universal aspect of goodness, it is manifest that there is a will in them.

Reply Obj. 1. Reason surpasses sense in a different way from that in which intellect surpasses reason. Reason surpasses sense according to the diversity of the objects known; for sense judges of particular objects, while reason judges of universals. Therefore there must be one appetite tending towards good in the abstract, which appetite belongs to reason; and another with a tendency towards particular good, which appetite belongs to sense. But intellect and reason differ as to their manner of knowing; because the intellect knows by simple intuition, while reason knows by a process of discursion from one thing to another. Nevertheless by such discursion reason comes to know what intellect learns without it, namely, the universal. Consequently the object presented to the appetitive faculty on the part of reason and on the part of intellect is the same. Therefore in the angels, who are purely intellectual, there is no appetite higher than the will.

Reply Obj. 2. Although the name of the appetitive part is derived from seeking things not yet possessed, yet the appetitive part reaches out not to these things only, but also to many other things; thus the name of a stone (*lapis*) is derived from injuring the foot (*læsione pedis*), though not this alone belongs to a stone. In the same way the irascible faculty is so denominated from anger (*ira*); though at the same time there are several other passions in it, as hope, daring, and the rest.

Reply Obj. 3. The will is called a mover which is moved, according as to will and to understand are termed movements of a kind; and there is nothing to prevent movement of this kind from existing in the angels, since such movement is the act of a perfect agent, as stated in *De Anima* iii., text. 28.

SECOND ARTICLE.

WHETHER IN THE ANGELS THE WILL DIFFERS FROM THE INTELLECT?

We proceed thus to the Second Article:—

Objection 1. It would seem that in the angels the will does not differ from the intellect and from the nature. For an angel is more simple than a natural body. But a natural body is inclined through its form towards its end, which is its good. Therefore much more so is the angel. Now the angel's form is either the nature in which he subsists, or else it is some species within his intellect. Therefore the angel inclines towards the good through his own nature, or through an intelligible species. But such inclination towards the good belongs to the will. Therefore the will of the angel does not differ from his nature or his intellect.

Obj. 2. Further, the object of the intellect is the true, while the object of the will is the good. Now the good and the true differ, not really but only logically.* Therefore will and intellect are not really different.

Obj. 3. Further, the distinction of common and proper does not differentiate the faculties; for the same power of sight perceives colour and whiteness. But the good and the true seem to be mutually related as common to particular; for the true is a particular good, to wit, of the intellect. Therefore the will, whose object is the good, does not differ from the intellect, whose object is the true.

On the contrary, The will in the angels regards good things only, while their intellect regards both good and bad things, for they know both. Therefore the will of the angels is distinct from their intellect.

I answer that, In the angels the will is a special faculty or power, which is neither their nature nor their intellect. That it is not their nature is manifest from this, that the nature or essence of a thing is completely comprised within it: whatever, then, extends to anything beyond it, is not its essence. Hence we see in natural bodies that the inclination to being does not come from anything superadded to the essence, but from the matter which desires being before possessing it, and from the form which keeps it in such being when once it exists. But the inclination towards something extrinsic comes from something superadded to the essence; as tendency to a place comes from gravity or lightness, while the inclination to make something like itself comes from the active qualities.

Now the will has a natural tendency towards good. Consequently there alone are essence and will identified where all good is contained within the essence of him who wills; that is to say, in God, Who wills nothing beyond Himself except on account of His goodness. This cannot be said

* See above, Q. XVI., A. 4.

THE WILL OF THE ANGELS

of any creature, because infinite goodness is quite foreign to the nature of any created thing. Accordingly, neither the will of the angel, nor that of any creature, can be the same thing as its essence.

In like manner neither can the will be the same thing as the intellect of angel or man. Because knowledge comes about in so far as the object known is within the knower; consequently the intellect extends itself to what is outside it, according as what, in its essence, is outside it is disposed to be somehow within it. On the other hand, the will goes out to what is beyond it, according as by a kind of inclination it tends, in a manner, to what is outside it. Now it belongs to one faculty to have within itself something which is outside it, and to another faculty to tend to what is outside it. Consequently intellect and will must necessarily be different powers in every creature. It is not so with God, for He has within Himself universal being and the universal good. Therefore both intellect and will are His nature.

Reply Obj. 1. A natural body is moved to its own being by its substantial form : while it is inclined to something outside by something additional, as has been said.

Reply Obj. 2. Faculties are not differentiated by any material difference of their objects, but according to their formal distinction, which is taken from the nature of the object as such. Consequently the diversity derived from the notion of good and true suffices for the difference of intellect from will.

Reply Obj. 3. Because the good and the true are really convertible, it follows that the good is apprehended by the intellect as something true; while the true is desired by the will as something good. Nevertheless the diversity of their aspects is sufficient for diversifying the faculties, as was said above (*ad* 2).

Third Article.

WHETHER THERE IS FREE-WILL IN THE ANGELS?

We proceed thus to the Third Article:—

Objection 1. It would seem that there is no free-will in the angels. For the act of free-will is to choose. But there can be no choice with the angels, because choice is *the desire of something after taking counsel,* while counsel is *a kind of inquiry,* as stated in *Ethic.* iii., 3. But the angels' knowledge is not the result of inquiring, for this belongs to the discursiveness of reason. Therefore it appears that there is no free-will in the angels.

Obj. 2. Further, free-will implies indifference to alternatives. But in the angels on the part of their intellect there is no such indifference; because, as was observed already (Q. LVIII., A. 5), their intellect is not deceived as to things which are naturally intelligible to them. Therefore neither on the part of their appetitive faculty can there be free-will.

Obj. 3. Further, the natural endowments of the angels belong to them according to degrees of more or less; because in the higher angels the intellectual nature is more perfect than in the lower. But free-will does not admit of degrees. Therefore there is no free-will in them.

On the contrary, Free-will is part of man's dignity. But the angels' dignity surpasses that of men. Therefore, since free-will is in men, with much more reason is it in the angels.

I answer that, Some things there are which act, not from any previous judgment, but, as it were, moved and made to act by others; just as the arrow is directed to the target by the archer. Others act from some kind of judgment; but not from free-will, such as irrational animals; for the sheep flies from the wolf by a kind of judgment whereby it esteems it to be hurtful to itself : such a judgment is not a free one, but implanted by nature. Only an agent endowed with an intellect can act with a judgment which is free, in so far as it apprehends the common note of good.

ness; from which it can judge this or the other thing to be good. Consequently, wherever there is intellect, there is free-will. It is therefore manifest that just as there is intellect, so is there free-will in the angels, and in a higher degree of perfection than in man.

Reply Obj. 1. The Philosopher is speaking of choice, as it is in man. As a man's estimate in speculative matters differs from an angel's in this, that the one needs not to inquire, while the other does so need; so is it in practical matters. Hence there is choice in the angels, yet not with the inquisitive deliberation of counsel, but by the sudden acceptance of truth.

Reply Obj. 2. As was observed already (A. 2), knowledge is effected by the presence of the known within the knower. Now it is a mark of imperfection in anything not to have within it what it should naturally have. Consequently an angel would not be perfect in his nature, if his intellect were not determined to every truth which he can know naturally. But the act of the appetitive faculty comes of this, that the affection is directed to something outside. Yet the perfection of a thing does not come from everything to which it is inclined, but only from something which is higher than it. Therefore it does not argue imperfection in an angel if his will be not determined with regard to things beneath him; but it would argue imperfection in him, were he to be indeterminate to what is above him.

Reply Obj. 3. Free-will exists in a nobler manner in the higher angels than it does in the lower, as also does the judgment of the intellect. Yet it is true that liberty, in so far as the removal of compulsion is considered, is not susceptible of greater and less degree; because privations and negations are not lessened nor increased directly of themselves; but only by their cause, or through the addition of some qualification.

Fourth Article.

WHETHER THERE IS AN IRASCIBLE AND A CONCUPISCIBLE APPETITE IN THE ANGELS?

We proceed thus to the Fourth Article:—

Objection 1. It would seem that there is an irascible and a concupiscible appetite in the angels. For Dionysius says (*Div. Nom.* iv.) that in the demons there is *unreasonable fury and wild concupiscence.* But demons are of the same nature as angels; for sin has not altered their nature. Therefore there is an irascible and a concupiscible appetite in the angels.

Obj. 2. Further, love and joy are in the concupiscible; while anger, hope, and fear, are in the irascible appetite. But in the Sacred Scriptures these things are attributed both to the good and to the wicked angels. Therefore there is an irascible and a concupiscible appetite in the angels.

Obj. 3. Further, some virtues are said to reside in the irascible appetite and some in the concupiscible: thus charity and temperance appear to be in the concupiscible, while hope and fortitude are in the irascible. But these virtues are in the angels. Therefore there is both a concupiscible and an irascible appetite in the angels.

On the contrary, The Philosopher says (*De Anima* iii., text. 42) that the irascible and concupiscible are in the sensitive part, which does not exist in angels. Consequently there is no irascible or concupiscible appetite in the angels.

I answer that, The intellective appetite is not divided into irascible and concupiscible; only the sensitive appetite is so divided. The reason of this is because, since the faculties are distinguished from one another not according to the material but only by the formal distinction of objects, if to any faculty there respond an object according to some common idea, there will be no distinction of faculties according to the diversity of the particular things contained under that common idea. Just as if the proper object of the power of sight be colour as such, then there are not several powers of sight distinguished according to the difference of black and white: whereas if the proper object of any faculty were white, as white, then the faculty of seeing white would be distinguished from the faculty of seeing black.

Now it is quite evident from what has been said (A. 1; Q. XVI., A. 1), that the object of the intellective appetite, otherwise known as the will, is good according to the common aspect of goodness; nor can there be any appetite except of what is good. Hence, in the intellective part, the appetite is not divided according to the distinction of some particular good things, as the sensitive appetite is divided, which does not crave for what is good according to its common aspect, but for some particular good object. Accordingly, since there exists in the angels only an intellective appetite, their appetite is not distinguished into irascible and concupiscible, but remains undivided; and it is called the will.

Reply Obj. 1. Fury and concupiscence are metaphorically said to be in the demons, as anger is sometimes attributed to God;—on account of the resemblance in the effect.

Reply Obj. 2. Love and joy, in so far as they are passions, are in the concupiscible appetite, but in so far as they express a simple act of the will, they are in the intellective part: in this sense to love is to wish well to anyone; and to be glad is for the will to repose in some good possessed. Universally speaking, none of these things is said of the angels, as by way of passions; as Augustine says (*De Civ. Dei* ix.).

Reply Obj. 3. Charity, as a virtue, is not in the concupiscible appetite, but in the will; because the object of the concupiscible appetite is the good as delectable to the senses. But the Divine goodness, which is the object of charity, is not of any such kind. For the same reason it must be said that hope does not exist in the irascible appetite; because the object of the irascible appetite is something arduous belonging to the sensible order, which the virtue of hope does not regard; since the object of hope is something arduous and divine. Temperance, however, considered as a human virtue, deals with the desires of sensible pleasures, which belong to the concupiscible faculty. Similarly, fortitude regulates daring and fear, which reside in the irascible part. Consequently temperance, in so far as it is a human virtue, resides in the concupiscible part, and fortitude in the irascible. But they do not exist in the angels in this manner. For in them there are no passions of concupiscence, nor of fear and daring, to be regulated by temperance and fortitude. But temperance is predicated of them according as in moderation they display their will in conformity with the Divine will. Fortitude is likewise attributed to them, in so far as they firmly carry out the Divine will. All of this is done by their will, and not by the irascible or concupiscible appetite.

QUESTION LX.

OF THE LOVE OR DILECTION OF THE ANGELS.

(*In Five Articles.*)

THE next subject for our consideration is that act of the will which is love or dilection; because every act of the appetitive faculty comes of love.

Under this heading there are five points of inquiry: (1) Whether there is natural love in the angels? (2) Whether there is in them love of choice? (3) Whether the angel loves himself with natural love or with love of choice? (4) Whether one angel loves another with natural love as he loves himself? (5) Whether the angel loves God more than self with natural love?

FIRST ARTICLE.

WHETHER THERE IS NATURAL LOVE OR DILECTION IN AN ANGEL?

We proceed thus to the First Article:—

Objection 1. It would seem that there is no natural love or dilection in the angels. For, natural love is contradistinguished from intellectual love, as stated by Dionysius (*Div. Nom.* iv.). But an angel's love is intellectual. Therefore it is not natural.

Obj 2. Further, those who love with natural love are more acted upon than active in themselves; for nothing has control over its own nature. Now the angels are not acted upon, but act of themselves; because they possess free-will, as was shown above (Q. LIX., A. 3). Consequently there is no natural love in them.

Obj. 3. Further, every love is either ordinate or inordinate.

Now ordinate love belongs to charity; while inordinate love belongs to wickedness. But neither of these belongs to nature; because charity is above nature, while wickedness is against nature. Therefore there is no natural love in the angels.

On the contrary, Love results from knowledge; for, nothing is loved except it be first known, as Augustine says (*De Trin.* x., 1, 2). But there is natural knowledge in the angels. Therefore there is also natural love.

I answer that, We must necessarily place natural love in the angels. In evidence of this we must bear in mind that what comes first is always sustained in what comes after it. Now nature comes before intellect, because the nature of every subject is its essence. Consequently whatever belongs to nature must be preserved likewise in such subjects as have intellect. But it is common to every nature to have some inclination; and this is its natural appetite or love. This inclination is found to exist differently in different natures; but in each according to its mode. Consequently, in the intellectual nature there is to be found a natural inclination coming from the will; in the sensitive nature, according to the sensitive appetite; but in a nature devoid of knowledge, only according to the tendency of the nature to something. Therefore, since an angel is an intellectual nature, there must be a natural love in his will.

Reply Obj. 1. Intellectual love is contradistinguished from that natural love, which is merely natural, in so far as it belongs to a nature which has not likewise the perfection of either sense or intellect.

Reply Obj. 2. All things in the world are moved to act by something else except the First Agent, Who acts in such a manner that He is in no way moved to act by another; and in Whom, nature and will are the same. So there is nothing unfitting in an angel being moved to act in so far as such natural inclination is implanted in him by the Author of his nature. Yet he is not so moved to act that he does not act himself, because he has free-will.

Reply Obj. 3. As natural knowledge is always true, so

is natural love always well regulated; because natural love is nothing else than the inclination implanted in nature by its Author. To say that a natural inclination is not well regulated, is to derogate from the Author of nature. Yet the rectitude of natural love is different from the rectitude of charity and virtue: because the one rectitude perfects the other; even so the truth of natural knowledge is of one kind, and the truth of infused or acquired knowledge is of another.

SECOND ARTICLE.

WHETHER THERE IS LOVE OF CHOICE IN THE ANGELS?

We proceed thus to the Second Article:—
Objection 1. It would seem that there is no love of choice in the angels. For love of choice appears to be rational love; since choice follows counsel, which lies in inquiry, as stated in *Ethic.* iii., 3. Now rational love is contrasted with intellectual, which is proper to angels; as is said (*Div. Nom.* iv.). Therefore there is no love of choice in the angels.

Obj. 2. Further, the angels have only natural knowledge besides such as is infused: since they do not proceed from principles to acquire the knowledge of conclusions. Hence they are disposed to everything they can know, as our intellect is disposed towards first principles, which it can know naturally. Now love follows knowledge, as has been already stated (A. 1; Q. XVI., A. 1). Consequently, besides their infused love, there is only natural love in the angels. Therefore there is no love of choice in them.

On the contrary, We neither merit nor demerit by our natural acts. But by their love the angels merit or demerit. Therefore there is love of choice in them.

I answer that, There exists in the angels a natural love, and a love of choice. Their natural love is the principle of their love of choice; because, what belongs to that which precedes, has always the nature of a principle. Wherefore, since nature is first in everything, what belongs to nature must be a principle in everything.

This is clearly evident in man, with respect to both his intellect and his will. For the intellect knows principles naturally; and from such knowledge in man comes the knowledge of conclusions, which are known by him not naturally, but by discovery, or by teaching. In like manner, the end acts in the will in the same way as the principle does in the intellect, as is laid down in *Phys.* ii., text. 89. Consequently the will tends naturally to its last end; for every man naturally wills happiness: and all other desires are caused by this natural desire; since whatever a man wills he wills on account of the end. Therefore the love of that good, which a man naturally wills as an end, is his natural love; but the love which comes of this, which is of something loved for the end's sake, is the love of choice.

There is however a difference on the part of the intellect and on the part of the will. Because, as was stated already (Q. LIX., A. 2), the mind's knowledge is brought about by the inward presence of the known within the knower. It comes of the imperfection of man's intellectual nature that his mind does not simultaneously possess all things capable of being understood, but only a few things from which he is moved in a measure to grasp other things. The act of the appetitive faculty, on the contrary, follows the inclination of man towards things; some of which are good in themselves, and consequently are appetible in themselves; others being good only in relation to something else, and being appetible on account of something else. Consequently it does not argue imperfection in the person desiring, for him to seek one thing naturally as his end, and something else from choice as ordained to such end. Therefore, since the intellectual nature of the angels is perfect, only natural and not deductive knowledge is to be found in them, but there is to be found in them both natural love and love of choice.

In saying all this, we are passing over all that regards

THE LOVE OF THE ANGELS

things which are above nature, since nature is not the sufficient principle thereof: but we shall speak of them later on (Q. LXII.).

Reply Obj. 1. Not all love of choice is rational love, according as rational is distinguished from intellectual love. For rational love is so called which follows deductive knowledge: but, as was said above (Q. LIX., A. 3, *ad* 1), when treating of free-will, every choice does not follow a discursive act of the reason; but only human choice. Consequently the conclusion does not follow.

The reply to the second objection follows from what has been said.

THIRD ARTICLE.

WHETHER THE ANGEL LOVES HIMSELF WITH BOTH NATURAL LOVE, AND LOVE OF CHOICE?

We proceed thus to the Third Article:—

Objection 1. It would seem that the angel does not love himself both with a natural love and a love of choice. For, as was said (A. 2), natural love regards the end itself; while love of choice regards the means to the end. But the same thing, with regard to the same, cannot be both the end and a means to the end. Therefore natural love and the love of choice cannot have the same object.

Obj. 2. Further, as Dionysius observes (*Div. Nom.* iv.): *Love is a uniting and a binding power.* But uniting and binding imply various things brought together. Therefore the angel cannot love himself.

Obj. 3. Further, love is a kind of movement. But every movement tends towards something else. Therefore it seems that an angel cannot love himself with either natural or elective love.

On the contrary, The Philosopher says (*Ethic.* ix., 8) : *Love for others comes of love for oneself.*

I answer that, Since the object of love is good, and good is to be found both in substance and in accident, as is clear from *Ethic.* i., 6, a thing may be loved in two ways; first of all as a subsisting good; and secondly as an accidental or inherent good. That is loved as a subsisting good, which is so loved that we wish well to it. But that which we wish unto another, is loved as an accidental or inherent good: thus knowledge is loved, not that any good may come to it but that it may be possessed. This kind of love has been called by the name of *concupiscence*, while the first is called *friendship*.

Now it is manifest that in things devoid of knowledge, everything naturally seeks to procure what is good for itself; as fire seeks to mount upwards. Consequently both angel and man naturally seek their own good and perfection. This is to love self. Hence angel and man naturally love self, in so far as by natural appetite each desires what is good for self. On the other hand, each loves self with the love of choice, in so far as from choice he wishes for something which will benefit himself.

Reply Obj. 1. It is not under the same but under quite different aspects that an angel or a man loves self with natural and with elective love, as was observed above.

Reply Obj. 2. As to be one is better than to be united, so there is more oneness in love which is directed to self than in love which unites one to others. Dionysius used the terms *uniting* and *binding* in order to show the derivation of love from self to things outside self; as uniting is derived from unity.

Reply Obj. 3. As love is an action which remains within the agent, so also is it a movement which abides within the lover, but does not of necessity tend towards something else; yet it can be reflected back upon the lover so that he loves himself; just as knowledge is reflected back upon the knower, in such a way that he knows himself.

Fourth Article.
WHETHER AN ANGEL LOVES ANOTHER WITH NATURAL LOVE AS HE LOVES HIMSELF?

We proceed thus to the Fourth Article:—

Objection 1. It would seem that an angel does not love another with natural love as he loves himself. For love follows knowledge. But an angel does not know another as he knows himself; because he knows himself by his essence, while he knows another by his similitude, as was said above (Q. LVI., AA. 1, 2). Therefore it seems that one angel does not love another with natural love as he loves himself.

Obj. 2. Further, the cause is more powerful than the effect; and the principle than what is derived from it. But love for another comes of love for self, as the Philosopher says (*Ethic.* ix., 8). Therefore one angel does not love another as himself, but loves himself more.

Obj. 3. Further, natural love is of something as an end, and is unremovable. But no angel is the end of another; and again, such love can be severed from him, as is the case with the demons, who have no love for the good angels. Therefore an angel does not love another with natural love as he loves himself.

On the contrary, That seems to be a natural property which is found in all, even in such as are devoid of reason. But, *every beast loves its like,* as is said, Ecclus. xiii. 19. Therefore an angel naturally loves another as he loves himself.

I answer that, As was observed (A. 3), both angel and man naturally loves self. Now what is one with a thing, is that thing itself: consequently every thing loves what is one with itself. So, if this be one with it by natural union, it loves it with natural love; but if it be one with it by non-natural union, then it loves it with non-natural love. Thus a man loves his fellow townsman with a social love, while he loves a blood relation with natural affection, in so far as he is one with him in the principle of natural generation.

Now it is evident that what is generically or specifically one with another, is one according to nature. And so everything loves another which is one with it in species, with a natural affection, in so far as it loves its own species. This is manifest even in things devoid of knowledge: for fire has a natural inclination to communicate its form to another thing, wherein consists this other thing's good; as it is naturally inclined to seek its own good, namely, to be borne upwards.

So then, it must be said that one angel loves another with natural affection, in so far as he is one with him in nature. But so far as an angel has something else in common with another angel, or differs from him in other respects, he does not love him with natural love.

Reply Obj. 1. The expression *as himself* can in one way qualify the knowledge and the love on the part of the one known and loved: and thus one angel knows another as himself, because he knows the other to be even as he knows himself to be. In another way the expression can qualify the knowledge and the love on the part of the knower and lover. And thus one angel does not know another as himself, because he knows himself by his essence, and the other not by the other's essence. In like manner he does not love another as he loves himself, because he loves himself by his own will; but he does not love another by the other's will.

Reply Obj. 2. The expression *as* does not denote equality, but likeness. For since natural affection rests upon natural unity, the angel naturally loves less what is less one with him. Consequently he loves more what is numerically one with himself, than what is one only generically or specifically. But it is natural for him to have a like love for another as for himself, in this respect, that as he loves self in wishing well to self, so he loves another in wishing well to him.

Reply Obj. 3. Natural love is said to be of the end, not

as of that end to which good is willed, but rather as of that good which one wills for oneself, and in consequence for another, as united to oneself. Nor can such natural love be stripped from the wicked angels, without their still retaining a natural affection towards the good angels, in so far as they share the same nature with them. But they hate them, in so far as they are unlike them according to righteousness and unrighteousness.

FIFTH ARTICLE.

WHETHER AN ANGEL BY NATURAL LOVE LOVES GOD MORE THAN HE LOVES HIMSELF?

We proceed thus to the Fifth Article :—
Objection 1. It would seem that the angel does not love God by natural love more than he loves himself. For, as was stated (A. 4), natural love rests upon natural union. Now the Divine nature is far above the angelic nature. Therefore, according to natural love, the angel loves God less than self, or even than another angel.

Obj. 2. Further, *That on account of which a thing is such, is yet more so.* But every one loves another with natural love for his own sake : because one thing loves another as good for itself. Therefore the angel does not love God more than self with natural love.

Obj. 3. Further, nature is self-centred in its operation ; for we behold every agent acting naturally for its own preservation. But nature's operation would not be self-centred were it to tend towards anything else more than to nature itself. Therefore the angel does not love God more than himself from natural love.

Obj. 4. Further, it is proper to charity to love God more than self. But to love from charity is not natural to the angels; for *it is poured out upon their hearts by the Holy Spirit Who is given to them,* as Augustine says (*De Civ. Dei* xii. 9). Therefore the angels do not love God more than themselves by natural love.

Obj. 5. Further, natural love lasts while nature endures. But the love of God more than self does not remain in the angel or man who sins; for, as Augustine says (*De Civ. Dei* xiv.), *Two loves have made two cities; namely, love of self unto the contempt of God has made the earthly city; while love of God unto the contempt of self has made the heavenly city.* Therefore it is not natural to love God more than self.

On the contrary, All the moral precepts of the law come of the law of nature. But the precept of loving God more than self is a moral precept of the law. Therefore, it is of the law of nature. Consequently from natural love the angel loves God more than himself.

I answer that, There have been some who maintained that an angel loves God more than himself with natural love, both as to the love of concupiscence, through his seeking the Divine good for himself rather than his own good; and, in a fashion, as to the love of friendship, in so far as he naturally desires a greater good to God than to himself; because he naturally wishes God to be God, while as for himself, he wills to have his own nature. But absolutely speaking, out of natural love he loves himself more than he does God, because he naturally loves himself before God, and with greater intensity.

' The falsity of such an opinion stands in evidence, if one but consider whither natural movement tends in the natural order of things; because the natural tendency of things devoid of reason shows the nature of the natural inclination residing in the will of an intellectual nature. Now, in natural things, everything which, as such, naturally belongs to another, is principally and more strongly inclined to that other to which it belongs, than towards itself. Such a natural tendency is evidenced from things which are moved according to nature: because *according as a thing is moved naturally, it has an inborn aptitude to be thus moved,* as stated in *Phys.* ii., text. 78. For we observe that the part naturally exposes itself in order to safeguard the whole; as, for instance, the hand is without deliberation exposed to the blow for the whole body's safety. And since reason copies nature, we find the same inclination among the social virtues; for it behoves the virtuous citizen to expose himself to the danger of death for the public weal of the state; and if man were a natural part of the city, then such inclination would be natural to him.

Consequently, since God is the universal good, and under this good both man and angel and all creatures are comprised, because every creature in regard to its entire being naturally belongs to God, it follows that from natural love angel and man alike love God before themselves and with a greater love. Otherwise, if either of them loved self more than God, it would follow that natural love would be perverse, and that it would not be perfected but destroyed by charity.

Reply Obj. 1. Such reasoning holds good of things adequately divided, whereof one is not the cause of the existence and goodness of the other; for in such natures each loves itself naturally more than it does the other, inasmuch as it is more one with itself than it is with the other. But where one is the whole cause of the existence and goodness of the other, that one is naturally more loved than self; because, as we said above, each part naturally loves the whole more than itself : and each individual naturally loves the good of the species more than its own individual good. Now God is not only the good of one species, but is absolutely the universal good; hence everything in its own way naturally loves God more than itself.

Reply Obj. 2. When it is said that God is loved by an angel *in so far* as He is good to the angel, if the expression *in so far* denotes an end, then it is false; for he does not naturally love God for his own good, but for God's sake. If it denotes the nature of love on the lover's part, then it is true; for it would not be in the nature of anyone to love God, except from this—that everything is dependent on that good which is God.

Reply Obj. 3. Nature's operation is self-centred not

merely as to certain particular details, but much more as to what is common; for everything is inclined to preserve not merely its individuality, but likewise its species. And much more has everything a natural inclination towards what is the absolutely universal good.

Reply Obj. 4. God, in so far as He is the universal good, from Whom every natural good depends, is loved by everything with natural love. So far as He is the good which of its very nature beatifies all with supernatural beatitude, He is loved with the love of charity.

Reply Obj. 5. Since God's substance and universal goodness are one and the same, all who behold God's essence are by the same movement of love moved towards the Divine essence as it is distinct from other things, and according as it is the universal good. And because He is naturally loved by all so far as He is the universal good, it is impossible that whoever sees Him in His essence should not love Him. But such as do not behold His essence, know Him by some particular effects, which are sometimes opposed to their will. So in this way they are said to hate God; yet nevertheless, so far as He is the universal good of all, every thing naturally loves God more than itself.

QUESTION LXI.

OF THE PRODUCTION OF THE ANGELS IN THE ORDER OF NATURAL BEING.

(*In Four Articles.*)

AFTER dealing with the nature of the angels, their knowledge and will, it now remains for us to treat of their creation, or, speaking in a general way, of their origin. Such consideration is threefold. In the first place we must see how they were brought into natural existence; secondly, how they were made perfect in grace or glory; and thirdly, how some of them became wicked.

Under the first heading there are four points of inquiry : (1) Whether the angel has a cause of his existence? (2) Whether he has existed from eternity? (3) Whether he was created before corporeal creatures? (4) Whether the angels were created in the empyrean heaven?

FIRST ARTICLE.

WHETHER THE ANGELS HAVE A CAUSE OF THEIR EXISTENCE?

We proceed thus to the First Article:—

Objection 1. It would seem that the angels have no cause of their existence. For the first chapter of Genesis treats of things created by God. But there is no mention of angels. Therefore the angels were not created by God.

Obj. 2. Further, the Philosopher says (*Metaph.* viii., text. 16) that if any substance be a form without matter, *straightway it has being and unity of itself, and has no cause of its being and unity.* But the angels are immaterial forms, as was shown above (Q. L., A. 2). Therefore they have no cause of their being.

Obj. 3. Further, whatever is produced by any agent,

from the very fact of its being produced, receives form from it. But since the angels are forms, they do not derive their form from any agent. Therefore the angels have no active cause.

On the contrary, It is said (Ps. cxlviii. 2) : *Praise ye Him all His angels;* and further on, *verse* 5 : *For He spoke and they were made.*

I answer that, It must be affirmed that angels and everything existing, except God, were made by God. God alone in His own existence; while in everything else the essence differs from the existence, as was shown above (Q. III., A. 4). From this it is clear that God alone exists of His own essence : while all other things have their existence by participation. Now whatever exists by participation is caused by what exists essentially; as everything ignited is caused by fire. Consequently the angels, of necessity, were made by God.

Reply Obj. 1. Augustine says (*De Civ. Dei* xi. 50) that the angels were not passed over in that account of the first creation of things, but are designated by the name of *heavens,* or of *light.* And they were either passed over, or else designated by the names of corporeal things, because Moses was addressing an uncultured people, as yet incapable of understanding an incorporeal nature; and if it had been divulged that there were creatures existing beyond corporeal nature, it would have proved to them an occasion of idolatry, to which they were inclined, and from which Moses especially meant to safeguard them.

Reply Obj. 2. Substances that are subsisting forms have no *formal* cause of their existence and unity, nor such active cause as produces its effect by changing the matter from a state of potentiality to actuality; but they have a cause productive of their entire substance.

From this the solution of the third difficulty is manifest.

SECOND ARTICLE.

WHETHER THE ANGEL WAS PRODUCED BY GOD FROM ETERNITY?

We proceed thus to the Second Article:—

Objection 1. It would seem that the angel was produced by God from eternity. For God is the cause of the angel by His being : for He does not act through something besides His essence. But His being is eternal. Therefore He produced the angels from eternity.

Obj. 2. Further, everything which exists at one period and not at another, is subject to time. But the angel is above time, as is laid down in the *Book De Causis*. Therefore the angel is not at one time existing and at another non-existing, but exists always.

Obj. 3. Further, Augustine (*De Trin.* xiii.) proves the soul's incorruptibility by the fact that the mind is capable of truth. But as truth is incorruptible, so is it eternal. Therefore the intellectual nature of the soul and of the angel is not only incorruptible, but likewise eternal.

On the contrary, It is said (Proverbs viii. 22), in the person of begotten Wisdom : *The Lord possessed me in the beginning of His ways, before He made anything from the beginning.* But, as was shown above (A. 1), the angels were made by God. Therefore at one time the angels were not.

I answer that, God alone, Father, Son, and Holy Ghost, is from eternity. Catholic Faith holds this without doubt; and everything to the contrary must be rejected as heretical. For God so produced creatures that He made them *from nothing;* that is, after they had not been.

Reply Obj. 1. God's being is His will. So the fact that God produced the angels and other creatures by His being does not exclude that He made them also by His will. But, as was shown above (Q. XIX., A. 3; Q. XLVI., A. 1), God's will does not act by necessity in producing creatures. Therefore He produced such as He willed, and when He willed.

Reply Obj. 2. An angel is above that time which is the measure of the movement of the heavens; because he is above every movement of a corporeal nature. Nevertheless he is not above the time which is the measure of the succession of his existence after his non-existence, and which is also the measure of the succession which is in his operations. Hence Augustine says (*Gen. ad lit.* viii. 20, 21) that *God moves the spiritual creature according to time.*

Reply Obj. 3. Angels and intelligent souls are incorruptible by the very fact of their having a nature whereby they are capable of truth. But they did not possess this nature from eternity; it was bestowed upon them when God Himself willed it. Consequently it does not follow that the angels existed from eternity.

THIRD ARTICLE.

WHETHER THE ANGELS WERE CREATED BEFORE THE CORPOREAL WORLD?

We proceed thus to the Third Article:—

Objection 1. It would seem that the angels were created before the corporeal world. For Jerome says (*In Ep. ad Tit.* i. 2): *Six thousand years of our time have not yet elapsed; yet how shall we measure the time, how shall we count the ages, in which the Angels, Thrones, Dominations, and the other orders served God?* Damascene also says (*De Fid. Orth.* ii.): *Some say that the angels were begotten before all creation; as Gregory the Theologian declares, He first of all devised the angelic and heavenly powers, and the devising was the making thereof.*

Obj. 2. Further, the angelic nature stands midway between the Divine and the corporeal natures. But the Divine nature is from eternity; while corporeal nature is from time. Therefore the angelic nature was produced ere time was made, and after eternity.

Obj. 3. Further, the angelic nature is more remote from the corporeal nature than one corporeal nature is from another. But one corporeal nature was made before another; hence the six days of the production of things are set forth in the opening of Genesis. Much more, therefore, was the angelic nature made before every corporeal nature.

On the contrary, It is said (Gen. 1. 1): *In the beginning God created heaven and earth.* Now, this would not be true if anything had been created previously. Consequently the angels were not created before corporeal nature.

I answer that, There is a twofold opinion on this point to be found in the writings of the Fathers. The more probable one holds that the angels were created at the same time as corporeal creatures. For the angels are part of the universe: they do not constitute a universe of themselves; but both they and corporeal natures unite in constituting one universe. This stands in evidence from the relationship of creature to creature; because the mutual relationship of creatures makes up the good of the universe. But no part is perfect if separate from the whole. Consequently it is improbable that God, Whose *works are perfect,* as it is said Deut. xxxii. 4, should have created the angelic creature before other creatures. At the same time the contrary is not to be deemed erroneous; especially on account of the opinion of Gregory Nazianzen, *whose authority in Christian doctrine is of such weight that no one has ever raised objection to his teaching, as is also the case with the doctrine of Athanasius,* as Jerome says.

Reply Obj. 1. Jerome is speaking according to the teaching of the Greek Fathers; all of whom hold the creation of the angels to have taken place previously to that of the corporeal world.

Reply Obj. 2. God is not a part of, but far above, the whole universe, possessing within Himself the entire perfection of the universe in a more eminent way. But an angel is a part of the universe. Hence the comparison does not hold.

Reply Obj. 3. All corporeal creatures are one in matter; while the angels do not agree with them in matter. Consequently the creation of the matter of the corporeal creature involves in a manner the creation of all things; but the creation of the angels does not involve creation of the universe.

If the contrary view be held, then in the text of Genesis i., *In the beginning God created heaven and earth*, the words, *In the beginning*, must be interpreted, " In the Son," or " In the beginning of time " : but not, " In the beginning, before which there was nothing," unless we say, " Before which there was nothing of the nature of corporeal creatures."

FOURTH ARTICLE.

WHETHER THE ANGELS WERE CREATED IN THE EMPYREAN HEAVEN?

We proceed thus to the Fourth Article:—
Objection 1. It would seem that the angels were not created in the empyrean heaven. For the angels are incorporeal substances. Now a substance which is incorporeal is not dependent upon a body for its existence; and as a consequence, neither is it for its creation. Therefore the angels were not created in any corporeal place.

Obj. 2. Further, Augustine remarks (*Gen. ad lit.* iii. 10.), that the angels were created in the upper atmosphere : therefore not in the empyrean heaven.

Obj. 3. Further, the empyrean heaven is said to be the highest heaven. If therefore the angels were created in the empyrean heaven, it would not beseem them to mount up to a still higher heaven. And this is contrary to what is said in Isaias, speaking in the person of the sinning angel : *I will ascend into heaven* (Isa. xiv. 13).

On the contrary, Strabus, commenting on the text *In the beginning God created heaven and earth,* says : *By heaven he does not mean the visible firmament, but the empyrean, that is, the fiery or intellectual firmament, which is not so styled from its heat, but from its splendour; and which was filled with angels directly it was made.*

I answer that, As was observed (A. 3), the universe is

ANGELIC NATURE Q. 61. ART. 4

made up of corporeal and spiritual creatures. Consequently spiritual creatures were so created as to bear some relationship to the corporeal creature, and to rule over every corporeal creature. Hence it was fitting for the angels to be created in the highest corporeal place, as presiding over all corporeal nature; whether it be styled the empyrean heaven, or whatever else it be called. So Isidore says that the highest heaven is the heaven of the angels, explaining the passage of Deuteronomy x. 14: *Behold heaven is the Lord's thy God, and the heaven of heaven.*

Reply Obj. 1. The angels were created in a corporeal place, not as if depending upon a body either as to their existence or as to their being made; because God could have created them before all corporeal creation, as many holy Doctors hold. They were made in a corporeal place in order to show their relationship to corporeal nature, and that they are by their power in touch with bodies.

Reply Obj. 2. By the uppermost atmosphere Augustine possibly means the highest part of heaven, to which the atmosphere has a kind of affinity owing to its subtlety and transparency. Or else he is not speaking of all the angels; but only of such as sinned, who, in the opinion of some, belonged to the inferior orders. But there is nothing to hinder us from saying that the higher angels, as having an exalted and universal power over all corporeal things, were created in the highest place of the corporeal creature; while the other angels, as having more restricted powers, were created among the inferior bodies.

Reply Obj. 3. Isaias is not speaking there of any corporeal heaven, but of the heaven of the Blessed Trinity; unto which the sinning angel wished to ascend, when he desired to be equal in some manner to God, as will appear later on (Q. LXIII., A. 3).

QUESTION LXII.

OF THE PERFECTION OF THE ANGELS IN THE ORDER OF GRACE AND OF GLORY.

(In Nine Articles.)

IN due sequence we have to inquire how the angels were made in the order of grace and of glory; under which heading there are nine points of inquiry: (1) Were the angels created in beatitude? (2) Did they need grace in order to turn to God? (3) Were they created in grace? (4) Did they merit their beatitude? (5) Did they at once enter into beatitude after merit? (6) Did they receive grace and glory according to their natural capacities? (7) After entering into glory, did their natural love and knowledge remain? (8) Could they have sinned afterwards? (9) After entering into glory, could they advance farther?

FIRST ARTICLE.

WHETHER THE ANGELS WERE CREATED IN BEATITUDE?

We proceed thus to the First Article:—

Objection 1. It would seem that the angels were created in beatitude. For it is stated (*De Eccl. Dogm.* xxix.) that *the angels who continue in the beatitude wherein they were created, do not of their nature possess the excellence they have.* Therefore the angels were created in beatitude.

Obj. 2. Further, the angelic nature is nobler than the corporeal creature. But the corporeal creature straightway from its creation was made perfect and complete; nor did its lack of form take precedence in time, but only in nature, as Augustine says (*Gen. ad lit.* i. 15). Therefore neither did God create the angelic nature imperfect and incomplete.

But its formation and perfection are derived from its beatitude, whereby it enjoys God. Therefore it was created in beatitude.

Obj. 3. Further, according to Augustine (*Gen. ad lit.* iv. 34; v. 5), the things which we read of as being made in the works of the six days, were all made together at one time; and so all the six days must have existed instantly from the beginning of creation. But, according to his exposition, in those six days, *the morning* was the angelic knowledge, according to which they knew the Word and things in the Word. Therefore straightway from their creation they knew the Word, and things in the Word. But the bliss of the angels comes of seeing the Word. Consequently the angels were in beatitude straightway from the very beginning of their creation.

On the contrary, To be established or confirmed in good is of the nature of beatitude. But the angels were not confirmed in good as soon as they were created; the fall of some of them shows this. Therefore the angels were not in beatitude from their creation.

I answer that, By the name of beatitude is understood the ultimate perfection of rational or of intellectual nature; and hence it is that it is naturally desired, since everything naturally desires its ultimate perfection. Now there is a twofold ultimate perfection of rational or of intellectual nature. The first is one which it can procure of its own natural power; and this is in a measure called beatitude or happiness. Hence Aristotle (*Ethic.* x.) says that man's ultimate happiness consists in his most perfect contemplation, whereby in this life he can behold the best intelligible object; and that is God. Above this happiness there is still another, which we look forward to in the future, whereby *we shall see God as He is.* This is beyond the nature of every created intellect, as was shown above (Q. XII., A. 4).

So, then, it remains to be said, that, as regards this first beatitude, which the angel could procure by his natural power, he was created already blessed. Because the angel does not acquire such beatitude by any progressive action, as man does, but, as was observed above (Q. LVIII., AA. 3, 4), is straightway in possession thereof, owing to his natural dignity. But the angels did not have from the beginning of their creation that ultimate beatitude which is beyond the power of nature; because such beatitude is no part of their nature, but its end; and consequently they ought not to have it immediately from the beginning.

Reply Obj. 1. Beatitude is there taken for that natural perfection which the angel had in the state of innocence.

Reply Obj. 2. The corporeal creature instantly in the beginning of its creation could not have the perfection to which it is brought by its operation; consequently, according to Augustine (*Gen. ad lit.* v. 4, 23; viii. 3), the growing of plants from the earth did not take place at once among the first works, in which only the germinating power of the plants was bestowed upon the earth. In the same way, the angelic creature in the beginning of its existence had the perfection of its nature; but it did not have the perfection to which it had to come by its operation.

Reply Obj. 3. The angel has a twofold knowledge of the Word; the one which is natural, and the other according to glory. He has a natural knowledge whereby he knows the Word through a similitude thereof shining in his nature; and he has a knowledge of glory whereby he knows the Word through His essence. By both kinds of knowledge the angel knows things in the Word; imperfectly by his natural knowledge, and perfectly by his knowledge of glory. Therefore the first knowledge of things in the Word was present to the angel from the outset of his creation; while the second was not, but only when the angels became blessed by turning to the good. And this is properly termed their morning knowledge.

ANGELS' GRACE AND GLORY Q. 62. ART. 2

SECOND ARTICLE.

WHETHER AN ANGEL NEEDS GRACE IN ORDER TO TURN TO GOD?

We proceed thus to the Second Article:—
Objection 1. It would seem that the angel had no need of grace in order to turn to God. For, we have no need of grace for what we can accomplish naturally. But the angel naturally turns to God: because he loves God naturally, as is clear from what has been said (Q. LX., A. 5). Therefore an angel did not need grace in order to turn to God.

Obj. 2. Further, seemingly we need help only for difficult tasks. Now it was not a difficult task for the angel to turn to God; because there was no obstacle in him to such turning. Therefore the angel had no need of grace in order to turn to God.

Obj. 3. Further, to turn oneself to God is to dispose oneself for grace; hence it is said (Zach. i. 3): *Turn ye to Me, and I will turn to you.* But we do not stand in need of grace in order to prepare ourselves for grace: for thus we should go on to infinity. Therefore the angel did not need grace to turn to God.

On the contrary, It was by turning to God that the angel reached to beatitude. If, then, he had needed no grace in order to turn to God, it would follow that he did not require grace in order to possess everlasting life. But this is contrary to the saying of the Apostle (Rom. vi. 23): *The grace of God is life everlasting.*

I answer that, The angels stood in need of grace in order to turn to God, as the object of beatitude. For, as was observed above (Q. LX., A. 2), the natural movement of the will is the principle of all things that we will. But the will's natural inclination is directed towards what is in keeping with its nature. Therefore, if there is anything which is above nature, the will cannot be inclined towards it, unless helped by some other supernatural principle. Thus it is clear that fire has a natural tendency to give forth heat, and to generate fire; whereas to generate flesh is beyond the natural power of fire : consequently, fire has no tendency thereto, except in so far as it is moved instrumentally by the nutritive soul.

Now it was shown above (Q. XII., AA. 4, 5), when we were treating of God's knowledge, that to see God in His essence, wherein the ultimate beatitude of the rational creature consists, is beyond the nature of every created intellect. Consequently no rational creature can have the movement of the will directed towards such beatitude, except it be moved thereto by a supernatural agent. This is what we call the help of grace. Therefore it must be said that an angel could not of his own will be turned to such beatitude, except by the help of grace.

Reply Obj. 1. The angel loves God naturally, so far as God is the author of his natural being. But here we are speaking of turning to God, so far as God bestows beatitude by the vision of His essence.

Reply Obj. 2. A thing is *difficult* which is beyond a power; and this happens in two ways. First of all, because it is beyond the natural capacity of the power. Thus, if it can be attained by some help, it is said to be *difficult;* but if it can in no way be attained, then it is *impossible;* thus it is impossible for a man to fly. In another way a thing may be beyond the power, not according to the natural order of such power, but owing to some intervening hindrance; as to mount upwards is not contrary to the natural order of the motive power of the soul; because the soul, considered in itself, can be moved in any direction; but is hindered from so doing by the weight of the body; consequently it is difficult for a man to mount upwards. To be turned to his ultimate beatitude is difficult for man, both because it is beyond his nature, and because he has a hindrance from the corruption of the body and the infection of sin. But it is difficult for an angel, only because it is supernatural.

Reply Obj. 3. Every movement of the will towards God can be termed a conversion to God. And so there is a threefold turning to God. The first is by the perfect love of God; this belongs to the creature enjoying the possession of God; and for such conversion, consummate grace is required. The next turning to God is that which merits beatitude; and for this there is required habitual grace, which is the principle of merit. The third conversion is that whereby a man disposes himself so that he may have grace; for this no habitual grace is required; but the operation of God, Who draws the soul towards Himself, according to Lament. v. 21 : *Convert us, O Lord, to Thee, and we shall be converted.* Hence it is clear that there is no need to go on to infinity.

Third Article.
WHETHER THE ANGELS WERE CREATED IN GRACE?

We proceed thus to the Third Article:—

Objection 1. It would seem that the angels were not created in grace. For Augustine says (*Gen. ad lit.* ii. 8) that the angelic nature was first made without form, and was called *heaven*: but afterwards it received its form, and was then called *light*. But such formation comes from grace. Therefore they were not created in grace.

Obj. 2. Further, grace turns the rational creature towards God. If, therefore, the angel had been created in grace, no angel would ever have turned away from God.

Obj. 3. Further, grace comes midway between nature and glory. But the angels were not beatified in their creation. Therefore it seems that they were not created in grace; but that they were first created in nature only, and then received grace, and that last of all they were beatified.

On the contrary, Augustine says (*De Civ. Dei* xii. 9), *Who wrought the good will of the angels? Who, save Him Who created them with His will, that is, with the pure love wherewith they cling to Him; at the same time building up their nature and bestowing grace on them?*

I answer that, Although there are conflicting opinions on this point, some holding that the angels were created only in a natural state, while others maintain that they were created in grace; yet it seems more probable, and more in keeping with the sayings of holy men, that they were created in sanctifying grace. For we see that all things which, in the process of time, being created by the work of Divine Providence, were produced by the operation of God, were created in the first fashioning of things according to seedlike forms, as Augustine says (*Gen. ad lit.* viii. 3), such as trees, animals, and the rest. Now it is evident that sanctifying grace bears the same relation to beatitude as the seedlike form in nature does to the natural effect; hence (1 Jo. iii. 9) grace is called the *seed* of God. As, then, in Augustine's opinion it is contended that the seedlike forms of all natural effects were implanted in the creature when corporeally created, so, straightway from the beginning the angels were created in grace.

Reply Obj. 1. Such absence of form in the angels can be understood either by comparison with their formation in glory; and so the absence of formation preceded formation by priority of time. Or else it can be understood of the formation according to grace: and so it did not precede in the order of time, but in the order of nature; as Augustine holds with regard to the formation of corporeal things (*Gen. ad lit.* 1. 15).

Reply Obj. 2. Every form inclines the subject after the mode of the subject's nature. Now it is the mode of an intellectual nature to be inclined freely towards the objects it desires. Consequently the movement of grace does not impose necessity; but he who has grace can fail to make use of it, and can sin.

Reply Obj. 3. Although in the order of nature grace comes midway between nature and glory, nevertheless, in the order of time, in created nature, glory is not simultaneous with nature; because glory is the end of the operation of nature helped by grace. But grace stands not as the end of operation, because it is not of works, but as the principle of right operation. Therefore it was fitting for grace to be given straightway with nature.

Fourth Article.

WHETHER AN ANGEL MERITS HIS BEATITUDE?

We proceed thus to the Fourth Article:—

Objection 1. It would seem that the angel did not merit his beatitude. For merit arises from the difficulty of the meritorious act. But the angel experienced no difficulty in acting rightly. Therefore righteous action was not meritorious for him.

Obj. 2. Further, we do not merit by merely natural operations. But it was quite natural for the angel to turn to God. Therefore he did not thereby merit beatitude.

Obj. 3. Further, if a beatified angel merited his beatitude, he did so either before he had it, or else afterwards. But it was not before; because, in the opinion of many, he had no grace before whereby to merit it. Nor did he merit it afterwards, because thus he would be meriting it now; which is clearly false, because in that case a lower angel could by meriting rise up to the rank of a higher, and the distinct degrees of grace would not be permanent; which is not admissible. Consequently the angel did not merit his beatitude.

On the contrary, It is stated (Apoc. xxi. 17) that the *measure of the angel* in that heavenly Jerusalem is *the measure of a man*. But man can only reach beatitude by merit. Therefore the same is the case with the angel.

I answer that, Perfect beatitude is natural only to God, because existence and beatitude are one and the same thing in Him. Beatitude, however, is not of the nature of the creature, but is its end. Now everything attains its last end by its operation. Such operation leading to the end is either productive of the end, when such end is not beyond the power of the agent working for the end, as the healing art is productive of health; or else it is deserving of the end, when such end is beyond the capacity of the agent striving to attain it; wherefore it is looked for from another's bestowing. Now it is evident from what has gone before (AA. 1, 2; Q. XII., AA. 4, 5), ultimate beatitude exceeds both the angelic and the human nature. It remains, then, that both man and angel merited their beatitude.

And if the angel was created in grace, without which there is no merit, there would be no difficulty in saying that he merited beatitude: as also, if one were to say that he had grace in any way before he had glory.

But if he had no grace before entering upon beatitude, it would then have to be said that he had beatitude without merit, even as we have grace. This, however, is quite foreign to the idea of beatitude; which conveys the notion of an end, and is the reward of virtue, as even the Philosopher says (*Ethic.* i. 9). Or else it will have to be said, as some others have maintained, that the angels merit beatitude by their present ministrations, while in beatitude. This is quite contrary, again, to the notion of merit: since merit conveys the idea of a means to an end; while what is already in its end cannot, properly speaking, be moved towards such end; and so no one merits to procure what he already enjoys. Or else it will have to be said that one and the same act of turning to God, so far as it comes of freewill, is meritorious; and so far as it attains the end, is the fruition of beatitude. Even this view will not stand, because free-will is not the sufficient cause of merit; and, consequently, an act cannot be meritorious as coming from freewill, except in so far as it is informed by grace; but it cannot at the same time be informed by imperfect grace, which is the principle of meriting, and by perfect grace, which is the principle of enjoying. Hence it does not appear to be possible for anyone to enjoy beatitude, and at the same time to merit it.

Consequently it is better to say that the angel had grace ere he was admitted to beatitude, and that by such grace he merited beatitude.

Reply Obj. 1. The angel's difficulty of working righteously does not come from any contrariety or hindrance of natural powers; but from the fact that the good work is beyond his natural capacity.

Reply Obj. 2. An angel did not merit beatitude by natural movement towards God; but by the movement of charity, which comes of grace.

The answer to the third objection is evident from what we have said.

FIFTH ARTICLE.

WHETHER THE ANGEL OBTAINED BEATITUDE IMMEDIATELY AFTER ONE ACT OF MERIT?

We proceed thus to the Fifth Article:—

Objection 1. It would seem that the angel did not possess beatitude instantly after one act of merit. For it is more difficult for a man to do well than for an angel. But man is not rewarded at once after one act of merit. Therefore neither was the angel.

Obj. 2. Further, an angel could act at once, and in an instant, from the very outset of his creation, for even natural bodies begin to be moved in the very instant of their creation; and if the movement of a body could be instantaneous, like operations of mind and will, it would have movement in the first instant of its generation. Consequently, if the angel merited beatitude by one act of his will, he merited it in the first instant of his creation; and so, if their beatitude was not retarded, then the angels were in beatitude in the first instant.

Obj. 3. Further, there must be many intervals between things which are far apart. But the beatific state of the angels is very far remote from their natural condition, while merit comes midway between. Therefore the angel would have to pass through many stages of merit in order to reach beatitude.

On the contrary, Man's soul and an angel are ordained alike for beatitude: consequently equality with angels is promised to the saints. Now the soul separated from the body, if it has merit deserving beatitude, enters at once into beatitude, unless there be some obstacle. Therefore so does an angel. Now an angel instantly, in his first act of charity, had the merit of beatitude. Therefore, since there was no obstacle within him, he passed at once into beatitude by only one meritorious act.

I answer that, The angel was beatified instantly after the first act of charity, whereby he merited beatitude. The reason whereof is because grace perfects nature according to the manner of the nature; as every perfection is received in the subject capable of perfection, according to its mode. Now it is proper to the angelic nature to receive its natural perfection not by passing from one stage to another; but to have it at once naturally, as was shown above (A. 1; Q. LVIII., AA. 3, 4). But as the angel is of his nature inclined to natural perfection, so is he by merit inclined to glory. Hence instantly after merit the angel secured beatitude. Now the merit of beatitude in angel and man alike can be from merely one act; because man merits beatitude by every act informed by charity. Hence it remains that an angel was beatified straightway after one act of charity.

Reply Obj. 1. Man was not intended to secure his ultimate perfection at once, like the angel. Hence a longer way was assigned to man than to the angel for securing beatitude.

Reply Obj. 2. The angel is above the time of corporeal things; hence the various instants regarding the angels are not to be taken except as reckoning the succession of their acts. Now their act which merited beatitude could not be in them simultaneously with the act of beatitude, which is fruition; since the one belongs to imperfect grace and the other to consummate grace. Consequently, it remains for different instants to be conceived, in one of which the angel merited beatitude, and in another was beatified.

Reply Obj. 3. It is of the nature of an angel instantly to attain the perfection unto which he is ordained. Consequently, only one meritorious act is required; which act can so far be called an interval as through it the angel is brought to beatitude.

SIXTH ARTICLE.

WHETHER THE ANGELS RECEIVED GRACE AND GLORY ACCORDING TO THE DEGREE OF THEIR NATURAL GIFTS?

We proceed thus to the Sixth Article:—

Objection 1. It would seem that the angels did not receive grace and glory according to the degree of their natural gifts. For grace is bestowed of God's absolute will. Therefore the degree of grace depends on God's will, and not on the degree of their natural gifts.

Obj. 2. Further, a moral act seems to be more closely allied with grace than nature is; because a moral act is preparatory to grace. But grace does not come *of works,* as is said Rom. xi. 6. Therefore much less does the degree of grace depend upon the degree of their natural gifts.

Obj. 3. Further, man and angel are alike ordained for beatitude or grace. But man does not receive more grace according to the degree of his natural gifts. Therefore neither does the angel.

On the contrary, Is the saying of the Master of the Sentences (*Sent.* ii. D. 3), that *those angels who were created with more subtle natures and of keener intelligence in wisdom, were likewise endowed with greater gifts of grace.*

I answer that, It is reasonable to suppose that gifts of graces and perfection of beatitude were bestowed on the angels according to the degree of their natural gifts. The reason for this can be drawn from two sources. First of all, on the part of God, Who, in the order of His wisdom, established various degrees in the angelic nature. Now as the angelic nature was made by God for attaining grace and beatitude, so likewise the grades of the angelic nature seem to be ordained for the various degrees of grace and glory; just as when, for example, the builder chisels the stones for building a house, from the fact that he prepares some more artistically and more fittingly than others, it is clear that he is setting them apart for the more ornate part of the house.

So it seems that God destined those angels for greater gifts of grace and fuller beatitude, whom He made of a higher nature.

Secondly, the same is evident on the part of the angel. The angel is not a compound of different natures, so that the inclination of the one thwarts or retards the tendency of the other; as happens in man, in whom the movement of his intellective part is either retarded or thwarted by the inclination of his sensitive part. But when there is nothing to retard or thwart it, nature is moved with its whole energy. So it is reasonable to suppose that the angels who had a higher nature, were turned to God more mightily and efficaciously. The same thing happens in men, since greater grace and glory are bestowed according to the greater earnestness of their turning to God. Hence it appears that the angels who had the greater natural powers, had the more grace and glory.

Reply Obj. 1. As grace comes of God's will alone, so likewise does the nature of the angel: and as God's will ordained nature for grace, so did it ordain the various degrees of nature to the various degrees of grace.

Reply Obj. 2. The acts of the rational creature are from the creature itself; whereas nature is immediately from God. Accordingly it seems rather that grace is bestowed according to degree of nature than according to works.

Reply Obj. 3. Diversity of natural gifts is in one way in the angels, who are themselves different specifically; and in quite another way in men, who differ only numerically. For specific difference is on account of the end; while numerical difference is because of the matter. Furthermore, there is something in man which can thwart or impede the movement of his intellective nature; but not in the angels. Consequently the argument is not the same for both.

SEVENTH ARTICLE.

WHETHER NATURAL KNOWLEDGE AND LOVE REMAIN IN THE BEATIFIED ANGELS?

We proceed thus to the Seventh Article:—

Objection 1. It would seem that natural knowledge and love do not remain in the beatified angels. For it is said (1 Cor. xiii. 10): *When that which is perfect is come, then that which is in part shall be done away.* But natural love and knowledge are imperfect in comparison with beatified knowledge and love. Therefore, in beatitude, natural knowledge and love cease.

Obj. 2. Further, where one suffices, another is superfluous. But the knowledge and love of glory suffice for the beatified angels. Therefore it would be superfluous for their natural knowledge and love to remain.

Obj. 3. Further, the same faculty has not two simultaneous acts, as the same line cannot, at the same end, be terminated in two points. But the beatified angels are always exercising their beatified knowledge and love; for, as is said *Ethic.* i. 8, happiness consists not in habit, but in act. Therefore there can never be natural knowledge and love in the angels.

On the contrary, So long as a nature endures, its operation remains. But beatitude does not destroy nature, since it is its perfection. Therefore it does not take away natural knowledge and love.

I answer that, Natural knowledge and love remain in the angels. For as principles of operations are mutually related, so are the operations themselves. Now it is manifest that nature is to beatitude as first to second; because beatitude is superadded to nature. But the first must ever be preserved in the second. Consequently nature must be preserved in beatitude: and in like manner the act of nature must be preserved in the act of beatitude.

Reply Obj. 1. The advent of a perfection removes the opposite imperfection. Now the imperfection of nature is not opposed to the perfection of beatitude, but underlies it; as the imperfection of the power underlies the perfection of the form, and the power is not taken away by the form, but the privation which is opposed to the form. In the same way, the imperfection of natural knowledge is not opposed to the perfection of the knowledge in glory; for nothing hinders us from knowing a thing through various mediums, as a thing may be known at the one time through a probable medium and through a demonstrative one. In like manner, an angel can know God by His essence, and this appertains to his knowledge of glory; and at the same time he can know God by his own essence, which belongs to his natural knowledge.

Reply Obj. 2. All things which make up beatitude are sufficient of themselves. But in order for them to exist, they presuppose the natural gifts; because no beatitude is self-subsisting, except the uncreated beatitude.

Reply Obj. 3. There cannot be two operations of the one faculty at the one time, except the one be ordained to the other. But natural knowledge and love are ordained to the knowledge and love of glory. Accordingly there is nothing to hinder natural knowledge and love from existing in the angel conjointly with those of glory.

Eighth Article.
WHETHER A BEATIFIED ANGEL CAN SIN?

We proceed thus to the Eighth Article:—

Objection 1. It would seem that a beatified angel can sin. For, as was said above (A. 7), beatitude does not do away with nature. But it is of the very notion of created nature, that it can fail. Therefore a beatified angel can sin.

Obj. 2. Further, the rational powers are referred to opposites, as the Philosopher observes (*Metaph.* iv., text. 3). But the will of the angel in beatitude does not cease to be rational. Therefore it is inclined towards good and evil.

Obj. 3. Further, it belongs to the liberty of free-will for man to be able to choose good or evil. But the freedom of the will is not lessened in the beatified angels. Therefore they can sin.

On the contrary, Augustine says (*Gen. ad lit.* xi.) that *there is in the holy angels that nature which cannot sin.* Therefore the holy angels cannot sin.

I answer that, The beatified angels cannot sin. The reason for this is, because their beatitude consists in seeing God through His essence. Now, God's essence is the very essence of goodness. Consequently the angel beholding God is disposed towards God in the same way as anyone else not seeing God is to the common form of goodness. Now it is impossible for any man either to will or to do anything except aiming at what is good; or for him to wish to turn away from good precisely as such. Therefore the beatified angel can neither will nor act, except as aiming towards God. Now whoever wills or acts in this manner cannot sin. Consequently the beatified angel cannot sin.

Reply Obj. 1. Created good, considered in itself, can fail. But from its perfect union with the uncreated good, such as is the union of beatitude, it is rendered unable to sin, for the reason already alleged.

Reply Obj. 2. The rational powers are referred to opposites in the things to which they are not inclined naturally; but as to the things whereunto they have a natural tendency, they are not referred to opposites. For the intellect cannot but assent to naturally known principles; in the same way, the will cannot help clinging to good, formally as good; because the will is naturally ordained to good as to its proper object. Consequently the will of the angels is referred to opposites, as to doing many things, or not doing them. But they have no tendency to opposites with regard to God Himself, Whom they see to be the very nature of goodness; but in all things their aim is towards God, whichever alternative they choose, that is not sinful.

Reply Obj. 3. Free-will in its choice of means to an end is disposed just as the intellect is to conclusions. Now it is evident that it belongs to the power of the intellect to be able to proceed to different conclusions, according to given principles; but for it to proceed to some conclusion by passing out of the order of the principles, comes of its own defect. Hence it belongs to the perfection of its liberty for the free-will to be able to choose between opposite things, keeping the order of the end in view; but it comes of the defect of liberty for it to choose anything by turning away from the order of the end; and this is to sin. Hence there is greater liberty of will in the angels, who cannot sin, than there is in ourselves, who can sin.

NINTH ARTICLE.

WHETHER THE BEATIFIED ANGELS ADVANCE IN BEATITUDE?

We proceed thus to the Ninth Article:—

Objection 1. It would seem that the beatified angels can advance in beatitude. For charity is the principle of merit. But there is perfect charity in the angels. Therefore the beatified angels can merit. Now, as merit increases, the reward of beatitude increases. Therefore the beatified angels can progress in beatitude.

Obj. 2. Further, Augustine says (*De Doct. Christ.* i.) that *God makes use of us for our own gain, and for His own goodness. The same thing happens to the angels, whom He uses for spiritual ministrations;* since *they are all* ministering spirits, sent to minister for them who shall receive the inheritance of salvation* (Heb. i. 14). This would not be for their profit were they not to merit thereby, nor to advance in beatitude. It remains, then, that the beatified angels can merit, and can advance in beatitude.

Obj. 3. Further, it argues imperfection for anyone not occupying the foremost place not to be able to advance. But the angels are not in the highest degree of beatitude. Therefore, if unable to ascend higher, it would appear that there is imperfection and defect in them; which is not admissible.

On the contrary, Merit and progress belong to this

* Vulg., *Are they not all . . . ?*

present condition of life. But angels are not wayfarers travelling towards beatitude, they are already in possession of beatitude. Consequently the beatified angels can neither merit nor advance in beatitude.

I answer that, In every movement the mover's intention is centred upon one determined end, to which he intends to lead the movable subject; because intention looks to the end, to which infinite progress is repugnant. Now it is evident, since the rational creature cannot of its own power attain to its beatitude, which consists in the vision of God, as is clear from what has gone before (Q. XII., A. 4), that it needs to be moved by God towards its beatitude. Therefore there must be some one determined thing to which every rational creature is directed as to its last end.

Now this one determinate object cannot, in the vision of God, consist precisely in that which is seen; for the Supreme Truth is seen by all the blessed in various degrees: but it is on the part of the mode of vision, that diverse terms are fixed beforehand by the intention of Him Who directs towards the end. For it is impossible that as the rational creature is led on to the vision of the Supreme Essence, it should be led on in the same way to the supreme mode of vision, which is comprehension, for this belongs to God only; as is evident from what was said above (Q. XII., A. 7; Q. XIV., A. 3). But since infinite efficacy is required for comprehending God, while the creature's efficacy in beholding is only finite; and since every finite thing is in infinite degrees removed from the infinite; it comes to pass that the rational creature understands God more or less clearly according to infinite degrees. And as beatitude consists in vision, so the degree of vision lies in a determinate mode of the vision.

Therefore every rational creature is so led by God to the end of its beatitude, that from God's predestination it is brought even to a determinate degree of beatitude. Consequently, when that degree is once secured, it cannot pass to a higher degree.

Reply Obj. 1. Merit belongs to a subject which is

moving towards its end. Now the rational creature is moved towards its end, not merely passively, but also by working actively. If the end is within the power of the rational creature, then its action is said to procure the end; as man acquires knowledge by reflection: but if the end be beyond its power, and is looked for from another, then the action will be meritorious of such end. But what is already in the ultimate term is not said to be moved, but to have been moved. Consequently, to merit belongs to the imperfect charity of this life; whereas perfect charity does not merit but rather enjoys the reward. Even as in acquired habits, the operation preceding the habit is productive of the habit; but the operation from an acquired habit is both perfect and enjoyable. In the same way the act of perfect charity has no quality of merit, but belongs rather to the perfection of the reward.

Reply Obj. 2. A thing can be termed useful in two ways. First of all, as being on the way to an end; and so the merit of beatitude is useful. Secondly, as the part is useful for the whole; as the wall for a house. In this way the angelic ministerings are useful for the beatified angels, inasmuch as they are a part of their beatitude; for to pour out acquired perfection upon others is of the nature of what is perfect, considered as perfect.

Reply Obj. 3. Although a beatified angel is not absolutely in the highest degree of beatitude, yet, in his own regard he is in the highest degree, according to Divine predestination. Nevertheless the joy of the angels can be increased with regard to the salvation of such as are saved by their ministrations, according to Luke xv. 10: *There is* (Vulg., *shall be*) *joy before the angels of God upon one sinner doing penance.* Such joy belongs to their accidental reward, which can be increased unto the judgment day. Hence some writers say that they can merit as to their accidental reward. But it is better to say that the Blessed can in no wise merit, without being at the same time a wayfarer and a comprehensor; like Christ, Who alone was such. For the Blessed acquire such joy from the virtue of their beatitude, rather than merit it.

QUESTION LXIII.

THE MALICE OF THE ANGELS WITH REGARD TO SIN.
(In Nine Articles.)

IN the next place we must consider how angels became evil: first of all with regard to the evil of fault; and secondly, as to the evil of punishment. Under the first heading there are nine points for consideration: (1) Can there be evil of fault in the angels? (2) What kind of sins can be in them? (3) What did the angel seek in sinning? (4) Supposing that some became evil by a sin of their own choosing, are any of them naturally evil? (5) Supposing that it is not so, could any one of them become evil in the first instant of his creation by an act of his own will? (6) Supposing that he did not, was there any interval between his creation and fall? (7) Was the highest of them who fell, absolutely the highest among the angels? (8) Was the sin of the foremost angel the cause of the others sinning? (9) Did as many sin as remained steadfast?

FIRST ARTICLE.

WHETHER THE EVIL OF FAULT CAN BE IN THE ANGELS?

We proceed thus to the First Article:—

Objection 1. It would seem that there can be no evil of fault in the angels. For there can be no evil except in things which are in potentiality, as is said by the Philosopher (*Metaph.* ix., text. 19), because the subject of privation is a being in potentiality. But the angels have not being in potentiality, since they are subsisting forms. Therefore there can be no evil in them.

Obj. 2. Further, the angels are higher than the heavenly bodies. But philosophers say that there cannot be evil in the heavenly bodies. Therefore neither can there be in the angels.

Obj. 3. Further, what is natural to a thing is always in it. But it is natural for the angels to be moved by the movement of love towards God. Therefore such love cannot be withdrawn from them. But in loving God they do not sin. Consequently the angels cannot sin.

Obj. 4. Further, desire is only of what is good or apparently good. Now for the angels there can be no apparent good which is not a true good; because in them either there can be no error at all, or at least not before guilt. Therefore the angels can desire only what is truly good. But no one sins by desiring what is truly good. Consequently the angel does not sin by desire.

On the contrary, It is said (Job. iv. 18): *In His angels He found wickedness.*

I answer that, An angel or any other rational creature considered in his own nature, can sin; and to whatever creature it belongs not to sin, such creature has it as a gift of grace, and not from the condition of nature. The reason of this is, because sinning is nothing else than a deviation from that rectitude which an act ought to have; whether we speak of sin in nature, art, or morals. That act alone, the rule of which is the very virtue of the agent, can never fall short of rectitude. Were the craftsman's hand the rule itself engraving, he could not engrave the wood otherwise than rightly; but if the rightness of engraving be judged by another rule, then the engraving may be right or faulty. Now the Divine will is the sole rule of God's act, because it is not referred to any higher end. But every created will has rectitude of act so far only as it is regulated according to the Divine will, to which the last end is to be referred: as every desire of a subordinate ought to be regulated by the will of his superior; for instance, the soldier's will, according to the will of his commanding officer. Thus only in the Divine will can there be no sin;

whereas there can be sin in the will of every creature; considering the condition of its nature.

Reply Obj. 1. In the angels there is no potentiality to natural existence. Yet there is potentiality in their intellective part, as regards their being inclined to this or the other object. In this respect there can be evil in them.

Reply Obj. 2. The heavenly bodies have none but a natural operation. Therefore as there can be no evil of corruption in their nature; so neither can there be evil of disorder in their natural action. But besides their natural action there is the action of free-will in the angels, by reason of which evil may be in them.

Reply Obj. 3. It is natural for the angel to turn to God by the movement of love, according as God is the principle of his natural being. But for him to turn to God as the object of supernatural beatitude, comes of infused love, from which he could be turned away by sinning.

Reply Obj. 4. Mortal sin occurs in two ways in the act of free-will. First, when something evil is chosen; as man sins by choosing adultery, which is evil of itself. Such sin always comes of ignorance or error; otherwise what is evil would never be chosen as good. The adulterer errs in the particular, choosing this delight of an inordinate act as something good to be performed now, from the inclination of passion or of habit; even though he does not err in his universal judgment, but retains a right opinion in this respect. In this way there can be no sin in the angel; because there are no passions in the angels to fetter reason or intellect, as is manifest from what has been said above (Q. LIX., A. 4); nor, again, could any habit inclining to sin precede their first sin. In another way sin comes of free-will by choosing something good in itself, but not according to proper measure or rule; so that the defect which induces sin is only on the part of the choice which is not properly regulated, but not on the part of the thing chosen; as if one were to pray, without heeding the order established by the Church. Such a sin does not presuppose ignorance, but merely absence of consideration of the things which ought to be considered. In this way the angel sinned, by seeking his own good, from his own free-will, insubordinately to the rule of the Divine will.

SECOND ARTICLE.

WHETHER ONLY THE SIN OF PRIDE AND ENVY CAN EXIST IN AN ANGEL?

We proceed thus to the Second Article:—
Objection 1. It would seem that there can be other sins in the angels besides those of pride and envy. Because whosoever can delight in any kind of sin, can fall into the sin itself. But the demons delight even in the obscenities of carnal sins; as Augustine says (*De Civ. Dei* xiv. 3). Therefore there can also be carnal sins in the demons.

Obj. 2. Further, as pride and envy are spiritual sins, so are sloth, avarice, and anger. But spiritual sins are concerned with the spirit, just as carnal sins are with the flesh. Therefore not only can there be pride and envy in the angels; but likewise sloth and avarice.

Obj. 3. Further, according to Gregory (*Moral.* xxxi.), many vices spring from pride; and in like manner from envy. But, if the cause is granted, the effect follows. If, therefore, there can be pride and envy in the angels, for the same reason there can likewise be other vices in them.

On the contrary, Augustine says (*De Civ. Dei* xiv. 3) that the devil *is not a fornicator nor a drunkard, nor anything of the like sort; yet he is proud and envious.*

I answer that, Sin can exist in a subject in two ways: first of all by actual guilt, and secondly by affection. As to guilt, all sins are in the demons; since by leading men to sin they incur the guilt of all sins. But as to affection, only those sins can be in the demons which can belong to a spiritual nature. Now a spiritual nature cannot be affected by such pleasures as appertain to bodies, but only by such as are in keeping with spiritual things; because nothing is affected except with regard to something which is in some way suited to its nature. But there can be no sin when anyone is incited to good of the spiritual order; unless in such affection the rule of the superior be not kept. Such is precisely the sin of pride,—not to be subject to a superior where subjection is due. Consequently the first sin of the angel can be none other than pride.

Yet, as a consequence, it was possible for envy also to be in them, since for the appetite to tend to the desire of something involves on its part resistance to anything contrary. Now the envious man repines over the good possessed by another, inasmuch as he deems his neighbour's good to be a hindrance to his own. But another's good could not be deemed a hindrance to the good coveted by the wicked angel, except inasmuch as he coveted a singular excellence, which would cease to be singular because of the excellence of some other. So, after the sin of pride, there followed the evil of envy in the sinning angel, whereby he grieved over man's good, and also over the Divine excellence, according as against the devil's will God makes use of man for the Divine glory.

Reply Obj. 1. The demons do not delight in the obscenities of the sins of the flesh, as if they themselves were disposed to carnal pleasures: it is wholly through envy that they take pleasure in all sorts of human sins, so far as these are hindrances to a man's good.

Reply Obj. 2. Avarice, considered as a special kind of sin, is the immoderate greed of temporal possessions which serve the use of human life, and which can be estimated in value by money; to these demons are not at all inclined, any more than they are to carnal pleasures. Consequently avarice properly so called cannot be in them. But if every immoderate greed of possessing any created good be termed avarice, in this way avarice is contained under the pride which is in the demons. Anger implies passion, and so does concupiscence; consequently they can only exist metaphorically in the demons. Sloth is a kind of sadness, whereby a man becomes sluggish in spiritual exercises because they weary the body; which does not apply to the demons. So it is evident that pride and envy are the only spiritual sins which can be found in demons; yet so that envy is not to be taken for a passion, but for a will resisting the good of another.

Reply Obj. 3. Under envy and pride, as found in the demons, are comprised all other sins derived from them.

THIRD ARTICLE.

WHETHER THE DEVIL DESIRED TO BE AS GOD?

We proceed thus to the Third Article:—

Objection 1. It would seem that the devil did not desire to be as God. For what does not fall under apprehension, does not fall under desire; because the good which is apprehended moves the appetite, whether sensible, rational, or intellectual; and sin consists only in such desire. But for any creature to be God's equal does not fall under apprehension, because it implies a contradiction; for if the finite equals the infinite, then it would itself be infinite. Therefore an angel could not desire to be as God.

Obj. 2. Further, the natural end can always be desired without sin. But to be likened unto God is the end to which every creature naturally tends. If, therefore, the angel desired to be as God, not by equality, but by likeness, it would seem that he did not thereby sin.

Obj. 3. Further, the angel was created with greater fulness of wisdom than man. But no man, save a fool, ever makes choice of being the equal of an angel, still less of God; because choice regards only things which are possible, regarding which one takes deliberation. Therefore much less did the angel sin by desiring to be as God.

On the contrary, It is said, in the person of the devil (Isa. xiv. 13, 14), *I will ascend into heaven. . . . I will be like the Most High.* And Augustine (*De Qu. Vet. Test.,* cxiii.) says that being *inflated with pride, he wished to be called God.*

I answer that, Without doubt the angel sinned by seeking to be as God. But this can be understood in two ways: first, by equality; secondly, by likeness. He could not seek to be as God in the first way; because by natural knowledge he knew that this was impossible: and there was no habit preceding his first sinful act, nor any passion fettering his mind, so as to lead him to choose what was impossible by failing in some particular; as sometimes happens in ourselves. And even supposing it were possible, it would be against the natural desire; because there exists in everything the natural desire of preserving its own nature; which would not be preserved were it to be changed into another nature. Consequently, no creature of a lower order can ever covet the grade of a higher nature; just as an ass does not desire to be a horse: for were it to be so upraised, it would cease to be itself. But herein the imagination plays us false; for one is liable to think that, because a man seeks to occupy a higher grade as to accidentals, which can increase without the destruction of the subject, he can also seek a higher grade of nature, to which he could not attain without ceasing to exist. Now it is quite evident that God surpasses the angels, not merely in accidentals, but also in degree of nature; and one angel, another. Consequently it is impossible for one angel of lower degree to desire equality with a higher; and still more to covet equality with God.

To desire to be as God according to likeness can happen in two ways. In one way, as to that likeness whereby everything is made to be likened unto God. And so, if anyone desire in this way to be Godlike, he commits no sin; provided that he desires such likeness in proper order, that is to say, that he may obtain it of God. But he would sin were he to desire to be like unto God even in the right way, as of his own, and not of God's power. In another way one may desire to be like unto God in some respect which is not natural to one; as if one were to desire to create heaven and earth, which is proper to God; in which desire there would be sin. It was in this way that the devil desired to be as God. Not that he desired to resemble God by being subject to no one else absolutely; for so he would be desiring his own *not-being;* since no creature can exist except by holding its existence under God. But he desired resemblance with God in this respect,—by desiring, as his last end of beatitude, something which he could attain by the virtue of his own nature, turning his appetite away from supernatural beatitude, which is attained by God's grace. Or, if he desired as his last end that likeness of God which is bestowed by grace, he sought to have it by the power of his own nature; and not from Divine assistance according to God's ordering. This harmonizes with Anselm's opinion, who says* that *he sought that to which he would have come had he stood fast.* These two views in a manner coincide; because according to both, he sought to have final beatitude of his own power, whereas this is proper to God alone.

Since, then, what exists of itself is the cause of what exists of another, it follows from this furthermore that he sought to have dominion over others; wherein he also perversely wished to be like unto God.

From this we have the answer to all the objections.

Fourth Article.

WHETHER ANY OF THE DEMONS ARE NATURALLY WICKED?

We proceed thus to the Fourth Article:—

Objection 1. It would seem that some demons are naturally wicked. For Porphyry says, as quoted by Augustine (*De Civ. Dei* x. 11): *There is a class of demons of crafty nature, pretending that they are gods and the souls of the dead.* But to be deceitful is to be evil. Therefore some demons are naturally wicked.

Obj. 2. Further, as the angels are created by God, so are men. But some men are naturally wicked, of whom it is said (Wisd. xii. 10): *Their malice* was *natural.* Therefore some angels may be naturally wicked.

Obj. 3. Further, some irrational animals have wicked

* *De casu diaboli,* iv.

MALICE OF ANGELS AS TO SIN Q. 63. ART. 4

dispositions by nature : thus the fox is naturally sly, and the wolf naturally rapacious; yet they are God's creatures. Therefore, although the demons are God's creatures, they may be naturally wicked.

On the contrary, Dionysius says (*Div. Nom.* iv.) that *the demons are not naturally wicked.*

I answer that, Everything which exists, so far as it exists and has a particular nature, tends naturally towards some good; since it comes from a good principle; because the effect always reverts to its principle. Now a particular good may happen to have some evil connected with it; thus fire has this evil connected with it that it consumes other things : but with the universal good no evil can be connected. If, then, there be anything whose nature is inclined towards some particular good, it can tend naturally to some evil; not as evil, but accidentally, as connected with some good. But if anything of its nature be inclined to good in general, then of its own nature it cannot be inclined to evil. Now it is manifest that every intellectual nature is inclined towards good in general, which it can apprehend and which is the object of the will. Hence, since the demons are intellectual substances, they can in no wise have a natural inclination towards any evil whatsoever; consequently they cannot be naturally evil.

Reply Obj. 1. Augustine rebukes Porphyry for saying that the demons are naturally deceitful; himself maintaining that they are not naturally so, but of their own will. Now the reason why Porphyry held that they are naturally deceitful was that, as he contended, demons are animals with a sensitive nature. Now the sensitive nature is inclined towards some particular good, with which evil may be connected. In this way, then, it can have a natural inclination to evil; yet only accidentally, inasmuch as evil is connected with good.

Reply Obj. 2. The malice of some men can be called natural, either because of custom which is a second nature; or on account of the natural proclivity on the part of the sensitive nature to some inordinate passion, as some people are said to be naturally wrathful or lustful; but not on the part of the intellectual nature.

Reply Obj. 3. Brute beasts have a natural inclination in their sensitive nature towards certain particular goods, with which certain evils are connected; thus the fox in seeking its food has a natural inclination to do so with a certain skill coupled with deceit. Wherefore it is not evil in the fox to be sly, since it is natural to him; as it is not evil in the dog to be fierce, as Dionysius observes (*De Div. Nom.* iv.).

FIFTH ARTICLE.

WHETHER THE DEVIL WAS WICKED BY THE FAULT OF HIS OWN WILL IN THE FIRST INSTANT OF HIS CREATION?

We proceed thus to the Fifth Article:—

Objection 1. It would seem that the devil was wicked by the fault of his own will in the first instant of his creation. For it is said of the devil (Jo. viii. 44): *He was a murderer from the beginning.*

Obj. 2. Further, according to Augustine (*Gen. ad lit.* i. 15), the lack of form in the creature did not precede its formation in order of time, but merely in order of nature. Now according to him (*ibid.* ii. 8), the *heaven*, which is said to have been created in the beginning, signifies the angelic nature while as yet not fully formed: and when it is said that God said: *Be light made: and light was made*, we are to understand the full formation of the angel by turning to the Word. Consequently, the nature of the angel was created, and light was made, in the one instant. But at the same moment that light was made, it was made distinct from *darkness*, whereby the angels who sinned are denoted. Therefore in the first instant of their creation some of the angels were made blessed, and some sinned.

Obj. 3. Further, sin is opposed to merit. But some intellectual nature can merit in the first instant of its creation; as the soul of Christ, or also the good angels. Therefore the demons likewise could sin in the first instant of their creation.

MALICE OF ANGELS AS TO SIN

Obj. 4. Further, the angelic nature is more powerful than the corporeal nature. But a corporeal thing begins to have its operation in the first instant of its creation; as fire begins to move upwards in the first instant it is produced. Therefore the angel could also have his operation in the first instant of his creation. Now this operation was either ordinate or inordinate. If ordinate, then, since he had grace, he thereby merited beatitude. But with the angels the reward follows immediately upon merit; as was said above (Q. LXII., A. 5). Consequently they would have become blessed at once; and so would never have sinned, which is false. It remains, then, that they sinned by inordinate action in their first instant.

On the contrary, It is written (Gen. i. 31): *God saw all the things that He had made, and they were very good.* But among them were also the demons. Therefore the demons were at some time good.

I answer that, Some have maintained that the demons were wicked straightway in the first instant of their creation; not by their nature, but by the sin of their own will; because, as soon as he was made, the devil refused righteousness. To this opinion, as Augustine says (*De Civ. Dei* xi. 13), if anyone subscribes, he does not agree with those Manichean heretics who say that the devil's nature is evil of itself. Since this opinion, however, is in contradiction with the authority of Scripture,—for it is said of the devil under the figure of the prince of Babylon (Isa. xiv. 12): *How art thou fallen . . . O Lucifer, who didst rise in the morning!* and it is said to the devil in the person of the King of Tyre (Ezech. xxviii. 13): *Thou wast in the pleasures of the paradise of God,*—consequently, this opinion was reasonably rejected by the masters as erroneous.

Hence others have said that the angels, in the first instant of their creation, could have sinned, but did not. Yet this view also is repudiated by some, because, when two operations follow one upon the other, it seems impossible for each operation to terminate in the one instant. Now it is clear that the angel's sin was an act subsequent to his creation. But the term of the creative act is the angel's very being, while the term of the sinful act is the being wicked. It seems, then, an impossibility for the angel to have been wicked in the first instant of his existence.

This argument, however, does not satisfy. For it holds good only in such movements as are measured by time, and take place successively; thus, if local movement follows a change, then the change and the local movement cannot be terminated in the same instant. But if the changes are instantaneous, then all at once and in the same instant there can be a term to the first and the second change; thus in the same instant in which the moon is lit up by the sun, the atmosphere is lit up by the moon. Now, it is manifest that creation is instantaneous; so also is the movement of free-will in the angels; for, as has been already stated, they have no occasion for comparison or discursive reasoning (Q. LVIII., A. 3). Consequently, there is nothing to hinder the term of creation and of free-will from existing in the same instant.

We must therefore reply that, on the contrary, it was impossible for the angel to sin in the first instant by an inordinate act of free-will. For although a thing can begin to act in the first instant of its existence, nevertheless, that operation which begins with the existence comes of the agent from which it drew its nature; just as upward movement in fire comes of its productive cause. Therefore, if there be anything which derives its nature from a defective cause, which can be the cause of a defective action, it can in the first instant of its existence have a defective operation; just as the leg, which is defective from birth, through a defect in the principle of generation, begins at once to limp. But the agent which brought the angels into existence, namely, God, cannot be the cause of sin. Consequently it cannot be said that the devil was wicked in the first instant of his creation.

Reply Obj. 1. As Augustine says (*De Civ. Dei* xi. 15), when it is stated that " the devil sins from the beginning," he is not to be thought of as sinning from the beginning wherein he was created, but from the beginning of sin: that is to say, because he never went back from his sin.

Reply Obj. 2. That distinction of light and darkness, whereby the sins of the demons are understood by the term darkness, must be taken as according to God's foreknowledge. Hence Augustine says (*ibid.*), that *He alone could discern light and darkness, Who also could foreknow, before they fell, those who would fall.*

Reply Obj. 3. All that is in merit is from God; and consequently an angel could merit in the first instant of his creation. The same reason does not hold good of sin, as has been said.

Reply Obj. 4. God did not distinguish between the angels before the turning away of some of them, and the turning of others to Himself, as Augustine says (*ibid.*). Therefore, as all were created in grace, all merited in their first instant. But some of them at once placed an impediment to their beatitude, thereby destroying their preceding merit; and consequently they were deprived of the beatitude which they had merited.

Sixth Article.

WHETHER THERE WAS ANY INTERVAL BETWEEN THE CREATION AND THE FALL OF THE ANGEL?

We proceed thus to the Sixth Article:—

Objection 1. It would seem that there was some interval between the angel's creation and his fall. For, it is said (Ezech. xxviii. 15): *Thou didst walk perfect* in thy ways from the day of thy creation, until iniquity was found in thee.* But since walking is continuous movement, it requires an interval. Therefore there was some interval between the devil's creation and his fall.

Obj. 2. Further, Origen says (*Hom.* i. *in Ezech.*) that *the serpent of old did not from the first walk upon his breast*

* Vulg., *Thou hast walked in the midst of the stones of fire, thou wast perfect.* . . .

and belly; which refers to his sin. Therefore the devil did not sin at once after the first instant of his creation.

Obj. 3. Further, capability of sinning is common alike to man and angel. But there was some delay between man's formation and his sin. Therefore, for the like reason there was some interval between the devil's formation and his sin.

Obj. 4. Further, the instant wherein the devil sinned was distinct from the instant wherein he was created. But there is a middle time between every two instants. Therefore there was an interval between his creation and his fall.

On the contrary, It is said of the devil (Jo. viii. 44): *He stood not in the truth:* and, as Augustine says (*De Civ. Dei* xi. 15), *we must understand this in the sense, that he was in the truth, but did not remain in it.*

I answer that, There is a twofold opinion on this point. But the more probable one, which is also more in harmony with the teachings of the Saints, is that the devil sinned at once after the first instant of his creation. This must be maintained if it be held that he elicited an act of free-will in the first instant of his creation, and that he was created in grace; as we have said (Q. LXII., A. 3). For since the angels attain beatitude by one meritorious act, as was said above (Q. LXII., A. 5), if the devil, created in grace, merited in the first instant, he would at once have received beatitude after that first instant, if he had not placed an impediment by sinning.

If, however, it be contended that the angel was not created in grace, or that he could not elicit an act of free-will in the first instant, then there is nothing to prevent some interval being interposed between his creation and fall.

Reply Obj. 1. Sometimes in Holy Scripture spiritual instantaneous movements are represented by corporeal movements which are measured by time. In this way by *walking* we are to understand the movement of free-will tending towards good.

Reply Obj. 2. Origen says, *The serpent of old did not*

from the first walk upon his breast and belly, because of the first instant in which he was not wicked.

Reply Obj. 3. An angel has an inflexible free-will after once choosing; consequently, if after the first instant, in which he had a natural movement to good, he had not at once placed a barrier to beatitude, he would have been confirmed in good. It is not so with man; and therefore the argument does not hold good.

Reply Obj. 4. It is true to say that there is a middle time between every two instants, so far as time is continuous, as it is proved *Phys.* vi., text. 2. But in the angels, who are not subject to the heavenly movement, which is primarily measured by continuous time, time is taken to mean the succession of their mental acts, or of their affections. So the first instant in the angels is understood to respond to the operation of the angelic mind, whereby it introspects itself by its evening knowledge; because on the first day evening is mentioned, but not morning. This operation was good in them all. From such operation some of them were converted to the praise of the Word by their morning knowledge : while others, absorbed in themselves, became night, *swelling up with pride,* as Augustine says (*Gen. ad lit.* iv. 24). Hence the first act was common to them all; but in their second they were separated. Consequently they were all of them good in the first instant; but in the second the good were set apart from the wicked.

SEVENTH ARTICLE.

WHETHER THE HIGHEST ANGEL AMONG THOSE WHO SINNED WAS THE HIGHEST OF ALL?

We proceed thus to the Seventh Article :—

Objection 1. It would seem that the highest among the angels who sinned was not the highest of all. For it is stated (Ezech. xxviii. 14) : *Thou wast a cherub stretched out, and protecting, and I set thee in the holy mountain of God.* Now the order of the Cherubim is under the order of the Seraphim, as Dionysius says (*Cœl. Hier.* vi., vii.). Therefore, the highest angel among those who sinned was not the highest of all.

Obj. 2. Further, God made intellectual nature in order that it might attain to beatitude. If therefore the highest of the angels sinned, it follows that the Divine ordinance was frustrated in the noblest creature; which is unfitting.

Obj. 3. Further, the more a subject is inclined towards anything, so much the less can it fall away from it. But the higher an angel is, so much the more is he inclined towards God. Therefore so much the less can he turn away from God by sinning. And so it seems that the angel who sinned was not the highest of all, but one of the lower angels.

On the contrary, Gregory (*Hom.* xxxiv. *in Ev.*) says that the chief angel who sinned, *being set over all the hosts of angels, surpassed them in brightness, and was by comparison the most illustrious among them.*

I answer that, Two things have to be considered in sin, namely, the proneness to sin; and the motive for sinning. If, then, in the angels we consider the proneness to sin, it seems that the higher angels were less likely to sin than the lower. On this account Damascene says (*De Fid. Orth.* ii.), that the highest of those who sinned was set over the terrestrial order. This opinion seems to agree with the view of the Platonists, which Augustine quotes (*De Civ. Dei* vii. 6, 7; x. 9, 10, 11). For they said that all the gods were good; whereas some of the demons were good, and some bad; naming as *gods* the intellectual substances which are above the lunar sphere, and calling by the name of *demons* the intellectual substances which are beneath it, yet higher than men in the order of nature. Nor is this opinion to be rejected as contrary to faith; because the whole corporeal creation is governed by God through the angels, as Augustine says (*De Trin.* iii. 4, 5). Consequently there is nothing to prevent us from saying that the lower angels were divinely set aside for presiding over the lower bodies, the higher over the higher bodies; and the highest to stand

MALICE OF ANGELS AS TO SIN Q. 63 ART. 7

before God. And in this sense Damascene says (*De Fid. Orth.* ii.) that they who fell were of the lower grade of angels; yet in that order some of them remained good.

But if the motive for sinning be considered, we find that it existed in the higher angels more than in the lower. For, as has been said (A. 2), the demons' sin was pride; and the motive of pride is excellence, which was greater in the higher spirits. Hence Gregory says that he who sinned was the very highest of all. This seems to be the more probable view : because the angels' sin did not come of any proneness, but of free choice alone. Consequently that argument seems to have the more weight which is drawn from the motive in sinning. Yet this must not be prejudicial to the other view; because there might be some motive for sinning in him also who was the chief of the lower angels.

Reply Obj. 1. *Cherubim* is interpreted *fulness of knowledge,* while *Seraphim* means *those who are on fire,* or *who set on fire.* Consequently Cherubim is derived from knowledge; which is compatible with mortal sin; but Seraphim is derived from the heat of charity, which is incompatible with mortal sin. Therefore the first angel who sinned is called, not a Seraph, but a Cherub.

Reply Obj. 2. The Divine intention is not frustrated either in those who sin, or in those who are saved; for God knows beforehand the end of both; and He procures glory from both, saving these of His goodness, and punishing those of His justice. But the intellectual creature, when it sins, falls away from its due end. Nor is this unfitting in any exalted creature; because the intellectual creature was so made by God, that it lies within its own will to act for its end.

Reply Obj. 3. However great was the inclination towards good in the highest angel, there was no necessity imposed upon him : consequently it was in his power not to follow it.

Eighth Article.

WHETHER THE SIN OF THE HIGHEST ANGEL WAS THE CAUSE OF THE OTHERS SINNING?

We proceed thus to the Eighth Article:—

Objection 1. It would seem that the sin of the highest angel was not the cause of the others sinning. For the cause precedes the effect. But, as Damascene observes (*De Fid. Orth.* ii.), they all sinned at the one time. Therefore the sin of one was not the cause of the others sinning.

Obj. 2. Further, an angel's first sin can only be pride, as was shown above (A. 2). But pride seeks excellence. Now it is more contrary to excellence for anyone to be subject to an inferior than to a superior; and so it does not appear that the angels sinned by desiring to be subject to a higher angel rather than to God. Yet the sin of one angel would have been the cause of the others sinning, if he had induced them to be his subjects. Therefore it does not appear that the sin of the highest angel was the cause of the others sinning.

Obj. 3. Further, it is a greater sin to wish to be subject to another against God, than to wish to be over another against God; because there is less motive for sinning. If, therefore, the sin of the foremost angel was the cause of the others sinning, in that he induced them to subject themselves to him, then the lower angels would have sinned more deeply than the highest one; which is contrary to a gloss on Ps. ciii. 26: *This dragon which Thou hast formed:—He who was the more excellent than the rest in nature, became the greater in malice.* Therefore the sin of the highest angel was not the cause of the others sinning.

On the contrary, It is said (Apoc. xii. 4) that the dragon drew with him *the third part of the stars of heaven.*

I answer that, The sin of the highest angel was the cause of the others sinning; not as compelling them, but as inducing them by a kind of exhortation. A token thereof appears in this, that all the demons are subjects of that

MALICE OF ANGELS AS TO SIN Q 63. ART. 8

highest one; as is evident from our Lord's words: *Go* (Vulg., *Depart from Me*), *you cursed, into everlasting fire, which was prepared for the devil and his angels* (Matth. xxv. 41). For the order of Divine justice exacts that whosoever consents to another's evil suggestion, shall be subjected to him in his punishment; according to (2 Pet. ii. 19): *By whom a man is overcome, of the same also he is the slave.*

Reply Obj. 1. Although the demons all sinned in the one instant, yet the sin of one could be the cause of the rest sinning. For the angel needs no delay of time for choice, exhortation, or consent, as man, who requires deliberation in order to choose and consent, and vocal speech in order to exhort; both of which are the work of time. And it is evident that even man begins to speak in the very instant when he takes thought; and in the last instant of speech, another who catches his meaning can assent to what is said; as is especially evident with regard to primary concepts, *which everyone accepts directly they are heard.*[*] Taking away, then, the time for speech and deliberation which is required in us; in the same instant in which the highest angel expressed his affection by intelligible speech, it was possible for the others to consent thereto.

Reply Obj. 2. Other things being equal, the proud would rather be subject to a superior than to an inferior. Yet he chooses rather to be subject to an inferior than to a superior, if he can procure an advantage under an inferior which he cannot under a superior. Consequently it was not against the demons' pride for them to wish to serve an inferior by yielding to his rule; for they wanted to have him as their prince and leader, so that they might attain their ultimate beatitude of their own natural powers; especially because in the order of nature they were even then subject to the highest angel.

Reply Obj. 3. As was observed above (Q. LXII., A. 6), an angel has nothing in him to retard his action, and with

[*] Boethius, *De hebdom.*

his whole might he is moved to whatsoever he is moved, be it good or bad. Consequently since the highest angel had greater natural energy than the lower angels, he fell into sin with intenser energy, and therefore he became the greater in malice.

NINTH ARTICLE.

WHETHER THOSE WHO SINNED WERE AS MANY AS THOSE WHO REMAINED FIRM?

We proceed thus to the Ninth Article:—

Objection 1. It would seem that more angels sinned than stood firm. For, as the Philosopher says (*Ethic.* ii. 6): *Evil is in many, but good is in few.*

Obj. 2. Further, justice and sin are to be found in the same way in men and in angels. But there are more wicked men to be found than good; according to Eccles. i. 15: *The number of fools is infinite.* Therefore for the same reason it is so with the angels.

Obj. 3. Further, the angels are distinguished according to persons and orders. Therefore if more angelic persons stood firm, it would appear that those who sinned were not from all the orders.

On the contrary, It is said (4 Kings vi. 16): *There are more with us than with them:* which is expounded of the good angels who are with us to aid us, and the wicked spirits who are our foes.

I answer that, More angels stood firm than sinned. Because sin is contrary to the natural inclination; while that which is against the natural order happens with less frequency; for nature procures its effect either always, or more often than not.

Reply Obj. 1. The Philosopher is speaking with regard to men, in whom evil comes to pass from seeking after sensible pleasures, which are known to most men, and from forsaking the good dictated by reason, which good is known to the few. In the angels there is only an intellectual nature; hence the argument does not hold.

And from this we have the answer to the second difficulty.

Reply Obj. 3. According to those who hold that the chief devil belonged to the lower order of the angels, who are set over earthly affairs, it is evident that some of every order did not fall, but only those of the lowest order. According to those who maintain that the chief devil was of the highest order, it is probable that some fell of every order; just as men are taken up into every order to supply for the angelic ruin. In this view the liberty of free-will is more established; which in every degree of creature can be turned to evil. In the Sacred Scripture, however, the names of some orders, as of Seraphim and Thrones, are not attributed to demons; since they are derived from the ardour of love and from God's indwelling, which are not consistent with mortal sin. Yet the names of Cherubim, Powers, and Principalities are attributed to them; because these names are derived from knowledge and from power, which can be common to both good and bad.

QUESTION LXIV.

THE PUNISHMENT OF THE DEMONS.

(In Four Articles.)

IT now remains as a sequel to deal with the punishment of the demons; under which heading there are four points of inquiry: (1) Of their darkness of intellect. (2) Of their obstinacy of will. (3) Of their grief. (4) Of their place of punishment.

FIRST ARTICLE.

WHETHER THE DEMONS' INTELLECT IS DARKENED BY PRIVATION OF THE KNOWLEDGE OF ALL TRUTH?

We proceed thus to the First Article:—

Objection 1. It would seem that the demons' intellect is darkened by being deprived of the knowledge of all truth. For if they knew any truth at all, they would most of all know themselves; which is to know separated substances. But this is not in keeping with their unhappiness: for this seems to belong to great happiness, insomuch that some writers have assigned as man's last happiness the knowledge of the separated substances. Therefore the demons are deprived of all knowledge of truth.

Obj. 2. Further, what is most manifest in its nature, seems to be specially manifest to the angels, whether good or bad. That the same is not most manifest with regard to ourselves, comes from the weakness of our intellect which draws its knowledge from phantasms; as it comes from the weakness of its eye that the owl cannot behold the light of the sun. But the demons cannot know God, Who is most manifest of Himself, because He is the sovereign truth; and this is because they are not clean of heart, whereby alone can God be seen. Therefore neither can they know other things.

Obj. 3. Further, according to Augustine (*Gen. ad lit.* iv. 22), the proper knowledge of the angels is twofold; namely, morning and evening. But the demons have no morning knowledge, because they do not see things in the Word; nor have they the evening knowledge, because this evening knowledge refers the things known to the Creator's praise (hence, after *evening* comes *morning*, [Gen. i.]). Therefore the demons can have no knowledge of things.

Obj. 4. Further, the angels at their creation knew the mystery of the kingdom of God, as Augustine says (*Gen. ad lit.* v. 19; *De Civ. Dei* xi.). But the demons are deprived of such knowledge : *for if they had known it, they would never have crucified the Lord of glory*, as is said 1 Cor. ii. 8. Therefore, for the same reason, they are deprived of all other knowledge of truth.

Obj. 5. Further, whatever truth anyone knows is known either naturally, as we know first principles; or by deriving it from someone else, as we know by learning; or by long experience, as the things we learn by discovery. Now, the demons cannot know the truth by their own nature, because, as Augustine says (*De Civ. Dei* xi. 19, 33), the good angels are separated from them as light is from darkness; and every manifestation is made through light, as is said Eph. v. 13. In like manner they cannot learn by revelation, nor by learning from the good angels : because *there is no fellowship of light with darkness** (2 Cor. vi. 14). Nor can they learn by long experience : because experience comes of the senses. Consequently there is no knowledge of truth in them.

On the contrary, Dionysius says (*Div. Nom.* iv.) that, *certain gifts were bestowed upon the demons which, we say, have not been changed at all, but remain entire and most brilliant.* Now, the knowledge of truth stands among those natural gifts. Consequently there is some knowledge of truth in them.

* Vulg., *What fellowship hath* . . ?

I answer that, The knowledge of truth is twofold: one which comes of nature, and one which comes of grace. The knowledge which comes of grace is likewise twofold: the first is purely speculative, as when Divine secrets are imparted to an individual; the other is effective, and produces love for God; which knowledge properly belongs to the gift of wisdom.

Of these three kinds of knowledge the first was neither taken away nor lessened in the demons. For it follows from the very nature of the angel, who, according to his nature, is an intellect or mind: since on account of the simplicity of his substance, nothing can be withdrawn from his nature, so as to punish him by subtracting from his natural powers, as a man is punished by being deprived of a hand or foot or of something else. Therefore Dionysius says (*loc. cit.*) that the natural gifts remain entire in them. Consequently their natural knowledge was not diminished. The second kind of knowledge, however, which comes of grace, and consists in speculation, has not been utterly taken away from them, but lessened; because, of these Divine secrets only so much is revealed to them as is necessary; and that is done either by means of the angels, or *through some temporal workings of Divine power,* as Augustine says (*De Civ. Dei* ix. 21); but not in the same degree as to the holy angels, to whom many more things are revealed, and more fully, in the Word Himself. But of the third knowledge, as likewise of charity, they are utterly deprived.

Reply Obj. 1. Happiness consists in self-application to something higher. The separated substances are above us in the order of nature; hence man can have happiness of a kind by knowing the separated substances, although his perfect happiness consists in knowing the first substance, namely, God. But it is quite natural for one separate substance to know another; as it is natural for us to know sensible natures. Hence, as man's happiness does not consist in knowing sensible natures; so neither does the angel's happiness consist in knowing separated substances.

Reply Obj. 2. What is most manifest in its nature is hidden from us by its surpassing the bounds of our intellect; and not merely because our intellect draws knowledge from phantasms. Now the Divine substance surpasses the proportion not only of the human intellect, but even of the angelic. Consequently, not even an angel can of his own nature know God's substance. Yet on account of the perfection of his intellect he can of his nature have a higher knowledge of God than man can have. Such knowledge of God remains also in the demons. Although they do not possess the purity which comes with grace, nevertheless they have purity of nature, and this suffices for the knowledge of God which belongs to them from their nature.

Reply Obj. 3. The creature is darkness in comparison with the excellence of the Divine light; and therefore the creature's knowledge in its own nature is called *evening* knowledge. For the evening is akin to darkness, yet it possesses some light : but when the light fails utterly, then it is night. So then the knowledge of things in their own nature, when referred to the praise of the Creator, as it is in the good angels, has something of the Divine light, and can be called evening knowledge; but if it be not referred to God, as is the case with the demons, it is not called evening, but *nocturnal* knowledge. Accordingly we read in Genesis (i. 5) that the darkness, which God separated from the light, *He called night*.

Reply Obj. 4. All the angels had some knowledge from the very beginning respecting the mystery of God's kingdom, which found its completion in Christ; and most of all from the moment when they were beatified by the vision of the Word, which vision the demons never had. Yet all the angels did not fully nor equally apprehend it; hence the demons much less fully understood the mystery of the Incarnation, when Christ was in the world. For, as Augustine observes (*De Civ. Dei* ix. 21), *It was not manifested to them as it was to the holy angels, who enjoy a participated eternity of the Word; but it was made known by some temporal effects, so as to strike terror into them.*

For had they fully and certainly known that he was the Son of God and the effect of His passion, they would never have procured the crucifixion of the Lord of glory.

Reply Obj. 5. The demons know a truth in three ways: first of all by the subtlety of their nature; for although they are darkened by privation of the light of grace, yet they are enlightened by the light of their intellectual nature: secondly, by revelation from the holy angels; for while not agreeing with them in conformity of will, they do agree, nevertheless, by their likeness of intellectual nature, according to which they can accept what is manifested by others: thirdly, they know by long experience; not as deriving it from the senses; but when the similitude of their innate intelligible species is completed in individual things, they know some things as present, which they previously did not know would come to pass, as we said when dealing with the knowledge of the angels (Q. LVII., A. 3 *ad* 3).

Second Article.

WHETHER THE WILL OF THE DEMONS IS OBSTINATE IN EVIL?

We proceed thus to the Second Article:—

Objection 1. It would seem that the will of the demons is not obstinate in evil. For liberty of will belongs to the nature of an intellectual being, which nature remains in the demons, as we said above (A. 1). But liberty of will is directly and firstly ordained to good rather than to evil. Therefore the demons' will is not so obstinate in evil as not to be able to return to what is good.

Obj. 2. Further, since God's mercy is infinite, it is greater than the demons' malice, which is finite. But no one returns from the malice of sin to the goodness of justice save through God's mercy. Therefore the demons can likewise return from their state of malice to the state of justice.

Obj. 3. Further, if the demons have a will obstinate in evil, then their will would be especially obstinate in

PUNISHMENT OF THE DEMONS Q. 64. ART. 2

the sin whereby they fell. But that sin, namely, pride, is in them no longer; because the motive for the sin no longer endures, namely, excellence. Therefore the demon is not obstinate in malice.

Obj. 4. Further, Gregory says (*Moral.* iv.) that man can be reinstated by another, since he fell through another. But, as was observed already (Q. LXIII., A. 8), the lower demons fell through the highest one. Therefore their fall can be repaired by another. Consequently they are not obstinate in malice.

Obj. 5. Further, whoever is obstinate in malice, never performs any good work. But the demon performs some good works: for he confesses the truth, saying to Christ: *I know Who Thou art, the holy one of God* (Mark i. 24). *The demons also believe and tremble* (Jas ii. 19). And Dionysius observes (*Div. Nom.* iv.), that *they desire what is good and best, which is, to be, to live, to understand.* Therefore they are not obstinate in malice.

On the contrary, It is said (Ps. lxxiii. 23): *The pride of them that hate Thee, ascendeth continually;* and this is understood of the demons. Therefore they remain ever obstinate in their malice.

I answer that, It was Origen's opinion* that every will of the creature can by reason of free-will be inclined to good and evil; with the exception of the soul of Christ on account of the union of the Word. Such a statement deprives angels and saints of true beatitude, because everlasting stability is of the very nature of true beatitude; hence it is termed *life everlasting.* It is also contrary to the authority of Sacred Scripture, which declares that demons and wicked men shall be sent *into everlasting punishment,* and the good brought *into everlasting life.* Consequently such an opinion must be considered erroneous, while according to Catholic Faith, it must be held firmly both that the will of the good angels is confirmed in good, and that the will of the demons is obstinate in evil.

We must seek for the cause of this obstinacy, not in

* *Peri Archon* i. 6.

the gravity of the sin, but in the condition of their nature or state. For as Damascene says (*De Fid. Orth.* ii.), *death is to men, what the fall is to the angels.* Now it is clear that all the mortal sins of men, grave or less grave, are pardonable before death; whereas after death they are without remission, and endure for ever.

To find the cause, then, of this obstinacy, it must be borne in mind that the appetitive power is in all things proportioned to the apprehensive, whereby it is moved, as the movable by its mover. For the sensitive appetite seeks a particular good; while the will seeks the universal good, as was said above (Q. LIX., A. 1); as also the sense apprehends particular objects, while the intellect considers universals. Now the angel's apprehension differs from man's in this respect, that the angel by his intellect apprehends immovably, as we apprehend immovably first principles which are the object of the habit of *intelligence;* whereas man by his reason apprehends movably, passing from one consideration to another; and having the way open by which he may proceed to either of two opposites. Consequently man's will adheres to a thing movably, and with the power of forsaking it and of clinging to the opposite; whereas the angel's will adheres fixedly and immovably. Therefore, if his will be considered before its adhesion, it can freely adhere either to this or to its opposite (namely, in such things as he does not will naturally); but after he has once adhered, he clings immovably. So it is customary to say that man's free-will is flexible to the opposite both before and after choice; but the angel's free-will is flexible to either opposite before the choice, but not after. Therefore the good angels who adhered to justice, were confirmed therein; whereas the wicked ones, sinning, are obstinate in sin. Later on we shall treat of the obstinacy of men who are damned. (*Suppl.,* Q. XCVIII., AA. 1, 2.)

Reply Obj. 1. The good and wicked angels have free-will, but according to the manner and condition of their state, as has been said.

Reply Obj. 2. God's mercy delivers from sin those who repent. But such as are not capable of repenting, cling immovably to sin, and are not delivered by the Divine mercy.

Reply Obj. 3. The devil's first sin still remains in him according to desire; although not as to his believing that he can obtain what he desired. Even so, if a man were to believe that he can commit murder, and wills to commit it, and afterwards the power is taken from him; nevertheless, the will to murder can stay with him, so that he would he had done it, or still would do it if he could.

Reply Obj. 4. The fact that man sinned from another's suggestion, is not the whole cause for man's sin being pardonable. Consequently the argument does not hold good.

Reply Obj. 5. A demon's act is twofold. One comes of deliberate will; and this is properly called his own act. Such an act on the demon's part is always wicked; because, although at times he does something good, yet he does not do it well; as when he tells the truth in order to deceive; and when he believes and confesses, yet not willingly, but compelled by the evidence of things. Another kind of act is natural to the demon; this can be good, and bears witness to the goodness of nature. Yet he abuses even such good acts to evil purpose.

THIRD ARTICLE.

WHETHER THERE IS SORROW IN THE DEMONS?

We proceed thus to the Third Article:—

Objection 1. It would seem that there is no sorrow in the demons. For since sorrow and joy are opposites, they cannot be together in the same subject. But there is joy in the demons: for Augustine writing against the Manichees (*De Gen. contra Manich.* ii. 17) says: *The devil has power over them who despise God's commandments, and he rejoices over this sinister power.* Therefore there is no sorrow in the demons.

Obj. 2. Further, sorrow is the cause of fear; for those things cause fear while they are future, which cause sorrow when they are present. But there is no fear in the demons, according to Job. xli. 24, *Who was made to fear no one.* Therefore there is no grief in the demons.

Obj. 3. Further, it is a good thing to be sorry for evil. But the demons can do no good action. Therefore they cannot be sorry, at least for the evil of sin; which applies to the worm of conscience.

On the contrary, The demon's sin is greater than man's sin. But man is punished with sorrow on account of the pleasure taken in sin, according to Apoc. xviii. 7, *As much as she hath glorified herself, and lived in delicacies, so much torment and sorrow give ye to her.* Consequently much more is the devil punished with the grief of sorrow, because he especially glorified himself.

I answer that, Fear, sorrow, joy, and the like, so far as they are passions, cannot exist in the demons; for thus they are proper to the sensitive appetite, which is a power in a corporeal organ. According, however, as they denote simple acts of the will, they can be in the demons. And it must be said that there is sorrow in them; because sorrow, as denoting a simple act of the will, is nothing else than the resistance of the will to what is, or to what is not. Now it is evident that the demons would wish many things not to be, which are, and others to be, which are not: for, out of envy, they would wish others to be damned, who are saved. Consequently, sorrow must be said to exist in them: and especially because it is of the very notion of punishment for it to be repugnant to the will. Moreover, they are deprived of happiness, which they desire naturally; and their wicked will is curbed in many respects.

Reply Obj. 1. Joy and sorrow about the same thing are opposites, but not about different things. Hence there is nothing to hinder a man from being sorry for one thing, and joyful for another; especially so far as sorrow and joy imply simple acts of the will; because, not merely in different things, but even in one and the same thing, there can be something that we will, and something that we will not.

Reply Obj. 2. As there is sorrow in the demons over present evil, so also there is fear of future evil. Now when it is said, *He was made to fear no one,* this is to be understood of the fear of God which restrains from sin. For it is written elsewhere that *the devils believe and tremble* (Jas. ii. 19).

Reply Obj. 3. To be sorry for the evil of sin on account of the sin bears witness to the goodness of the will, to which the evil of sin is opposed. But to be sorry for the evil of punishment, or for the evil of sin on account of the punishment, bears witness to the goodness of nature, to which the evil of punishment is opposed. Hence Augustine says (*De Civ. Dei* xix. 13), that *sorrow for good lost by punishment, is the witness to a good nature.* Consequently, since the demon has a perverse and obstinate will, he is not sorry for the evil of sin.

FOURTH ARTICLE.

WHETHER OUR ATMOSPHERE IS THE DEMONS' PLACE OF PUNISHMENT?

We proceed thus to the Fourth Article:—

Objection 1. It would seem that this atmosphere is not the demons' place of punishment. For a demon is a spiritual nature. But a spiritual nature is not affected by place. Therefore there is no place of punishment for demons.

Obj. 2. Further, man's sin is not graver than the demons'. But man's place of punishment is hell. Much more, therefore, is it the demons' place of punishment; and consequently not the darksome atmosphere.

Obj. 3. Further, the demons are punished with the pain of fire. But there is no fire in the darksome atmosphere. Therefore the darksome atmosphere is not the place of punishment for the demons.

On the contrary, Augustine says (*Gen. ad lit.* iii. 10), that *the darksome atmosphere is as a prison to the demons until the judgment day.*

I answer that, The angels in their own nature stand midway between God and men. Now the order of Divine providence so disposes, that it procures the welfare of the inferior orders through the superior. But man's welfare is disposed by Divine providence in two ways: first of all, directly, when a man is brought unto good and withheld from evil; and this is fittingly done through the good angels. In another way, indirectly, as when anyone assailed is exercised by fighting against opposition. It was fitting for this procuring of man's welfare to be brought about through the wicked spirits, lest they should cease to be of service in the natural order. Consequently a twofold place of punishment is due to the demons: one, by reason of their sin, and this is hell; and another, in order that they may tempt men, and thus the darksome atmosphere is their due place of punishment.

Now the procuring of men's salvation is prolonged even to the judgment day: consequently, the ministry of the angels and wrestling with demons endure until then. Hence until then the good angels are sent to us here; and the demons are in this dark atmosphere for our trial: although some of them are even now in hell, to torment those whom they have led astray; just as some of the good angels are with the holy souls in heaven. But after the judgment day all the wicked, both men and angels, will be in hell, and the good in heaven.

Reply Obj. 1. A place is not penal to angel or soul as if affecting the nature by changing it, but as affecting the will by saddening it: because the angel or the soul apprehends that it is in a place not agreeable to its will.

Reply Obj. 2. One soul is not set over another in the order of nature, as the demons are over men in the order of nature; consequently there is no parallel.

Reply Obj. 3. Some have maintained that the pain of sense for demons and souls is postponed until the judgment day : and that the beatitude of the saints is likewise postponed until the judgment day. But this is erroneous, and contrary to the teaching of the Apostle (2 Cor. v. 1) : *If our earthly house of this habitation be dissolved, we have a house in heaven.* Others, again, while not admitting the same of souls, admit it as to demons. But it is better to say that the same judgment is passed upon wicked souls and wicked angels, even as on good souls and good angels.

Consequently, it must be said that, although a heavenly place belongs to the glory of the angels, yet their glory is not lessened by their coming to us, for they consider that place to be their own ; in the same way as we say that the bishop's honour is not lessened while he is not actually sitting on his throne In like manner it must be said, that although the demons are not actually bound within the fire of hell while they are in this dark atmosphere, nevertheless their punishment is none the less; because they know that such confinement is their due. Hence it is said in a gloss upon Jas. iii. 6 : *They carry the fire of hell with them wherever they go.* Nor is this contrary to what is said (Luke viii. 31), *They besought the Lord not to cast them into the abyss;* for they asked for this, deeming it to be a punishment for them to be cast out of a place where they could injure men. Hence it is stated, *They* (Vulg., *He*) *besought Him that He would not expel them* (Vulg., *him*) *out of the country* (Mark v. 10).

TREATISE ON THE WORK OF THE SIX DAYS

QUESTION LXV.

THE WORK OF CREATION OF CORPOREAL CREATURES.

(*In Four Articles.*)

FROM the consideration of spiritual creatures we proceed to that of corporeal creatures, in the production of which, as Holy Scripture makes mention, three works are found, namely, the work of creation, as given in the words, *In the beginning God created heaven and earth;* the work of distinction as given in the words, *He divided the light from the darkness, and the waters that are above the firmament from the waters that are under the firmament;* and the work of adornment, expressed thus, *Let there be lights in the firmament.*

First, then, we must consider the work of creation; secondly, the work of distinction; and thirdly, the work of adornment. Under the first head there are four points of inquiry : (1) Whether corporeal creatures are from God? (2) Whether they were created on account of God's goodness? (3) Whether they were created by God through the medium of the angels? (4) Whether the forms of bodies are from the angels or immediately from God.

FIRST ARTICLE.

WHETHER CORPOREAL CREATURES ARE FROM GOD?

We proceed thus to the First Article:—

Objection 1. It would seem that corporeal creatures are not from God. For it is said (Eccles. iii. 14) : *I have learned that all the works which God hath made, continue for ever.* But visible bodies do not continue for ever, for it is said

(2 Cor. iv. 18): *The things which are seen are temporal, but the things which are not seen are eternal.* Therefore God did not make visible bodies.

Obj. 2. Further, it is said (Gen. i. 31): *God saw all the things that He had made, and they were very good.* But corporeal creatures are evil, since we find them harmful in many ways; as may be seen in serpents, in the sun's heat, and other like things. Now a thing is called evil, in so far as it is harmful. Corporeal creatures, therefore, are not from God.

Obj. 3. Further, what is from God does not withdraw us from God, but leads us to Him. But corporeal creatures withdraw us from God. Hence the Apostle says (2 Cor. iv. 18): *While we look not at the things which are seen.* Corporeal creatures, therefore, are not from God.

On the contrary, It is said (Ps. cxlv. 6): *Who made heaven and earth, the sea, and all things that are in them.*

I answer that, Certain heretics maintain that visible things are not created by the good God, but by an evil principle, and allege in proof of their error the words of the Apostle (2 Cor. iv. 4), *The god of this world hath blinded the minds of unbelievers.* But this position is altogether untenable. For, if things that differ agree in some point, there must be some cause for that agreement, since things diverse in nature cannot be united of themselves. Hence whenever in different things some one thing common to all is found, it must be that these different things receive that one thing from some one cause, as different bodies that are hot receive their heat from fire But being is found to be common to all things, however otherwise different. There must, therefore, be one principle of being from which all things in whatever way existing have their being, whether they are invisible and spiritual, or visible and corporeal. But the devil is called the god of this world, not as having created it, but because worldlings serve him, of whom also the Apostle says, speaking in the same sense, *Whose god is their belly* (Phil. iii. 19).

Reply Obj. 1. All the creatures of God in some respects continue for ever, at least as to matter, since what is created will never be annihilated, even though it be corruptible. And the nearer a creature approaches God, Who is immovable, the more it also is immovable. For corruptible creatures endure for ever as regards their matter, though they change as regards their substantial form. But incorruptible creatures endure with respect to their substance, though they are mutable in other respects, such as place, for instance, the heavenly bodies; or the affections, as spiritual creatures. But the Apostle's words, *The things which are seen are temporal*, though true even as regards such things considered in themselves (in so far as every visible creature is subject to time, either as to being or as to movement), are intended to apply to visible things in so far as they are offered to man as rewards. For such rewards, as consist in these visible things, are temporal; while those that are invisible endure for ever. Hence he said before (*ibid.* 17): It *worketh for us . . . an eternal weight of glory*.

Reply Obj. 2. Corporeal creatures according to their nature are good, though this good is not universal, but partial and limited, the consequence of which is a certain opposition of contrary qualities, though each quality is good in itself. To those, however, who estimate things, not by the nature thereof, but by the good they themselves can derive therefrom, everything which is harmful to themselves seems simply evil. For they do not reflect that what is in some way injurious to one person, to another is beneficial, and that even to themselves the same thing may be evil in some respects, but good in others. And this could not be, if bodies were essentially evil and harmful.

Reply Obj. 3. Creatures of themselves do not withdraw us from God, but lead us to Him; for *the invisible things of God are clearly seen, being understood by the things that are made* (Rom. i. 20). If, then, they withdraw men from God, it is the fault of those who use them foolishly.

Thus it is said (Wis. xiv. 11): *Creatures are turned into a snare to the feet of the unwise*. And the very fact that they can thus withdraw us from God proves that they came from Him, for they cannot lead the foolish away from God except by the allurements of some good that they have from Him.

SECOND ARTICLE.

WHETHER CORPOREAL THINGS WERE MADE ON ACCOUNT OF GOD'S GOODNESS?

We proceed thus to the Second Article:—

Objection 1. It would seem that corporeal creatures were not made on account of God's goodness. For it is said (Wis. i. 14) that God *created all things that they might be*. Therefore all things were created for their own being's sake, and not on account of God's goodness.

Obj. 2. Further, good has the nature of an end; therefore the greater good in things is the end of the lesser good. But spiritual creatures are related to corporeal creatures, as the greater good to the lesser. Corporeal creatures, therefore, are created for the sake of spiritual creatures, and not on account of God's goodness.

Obj. 3. Further, justice does not give unequal things except to the unequal. Now God is just: therefore inequality not created by God must precede all inequality created by Him. But an inequality not created by God can only arise from free-will, and consequently all inequality results from the different movements of free-will. Now, corporeal creatures are unequal to spiritual creatures. Therefore the former were made on account of movements of free-will, and not on account of God's goodness.

On the contrary, It is said (Prov. xvi. 4): *The Lord hath made all things for Himself*.

I answer that, Origen laid down* that corporeal creatures were not made according to God's original purpose, but in punishment of the sin of spiritual creatures. For he main-

* *Peri Archon* ii.

tained that God in the beginning made spiritual creatures only, and all of equal nature; but that of these by the use of free-will some turned to God, and, according to the measure of their conversion, were given a higher or a lower rank, retaining their simplicity; while others turned from God, and became bound to different kinds of bodies according to the degree of their turning away. But this position is erroneous. In the first place, because it is contrary to Scripture, which, after narrating the production of each kind of corporeal creatures, subjoins, *God saw that it was good* (Gen. i.), as if to say that everything was brought into being for the reason that it was good for it to be. But according to Origen's opinion, the corporeal creature was made, not because it was good that it should be, but that the evil in another might be punished. Secondly, because it would follow that the arrangement, which now exists, of the corporeal world would arise from mere chance. For if the sun's body was made what it is, that it might serve for a punishment suitable to some sin of a spiritual creature, it would follow, if other spiritual creatures had sinned in the same way as the one to punish whom the sun had been created, that many suns would exist in the world; and so of other things. But such a consequence is altogether inadmissible. Hence we must set aside this theory as false, and consider that the entire universe is constituted by all creatures, as a whole consists of its parts.

Now if we wish to assign an end to any whole, and to the parts of that whole, we shall find, first, that each and every part exists for the sake of its proper act, as the eye for the act of seeing; secondly, that less honourable parts exist for the more honourable, as the senses for the intellect, the lungs for the heart; and, thirdly, that all parts are for the perfection of the whole, as the matter for the form, since the parts are, as it were, the matter of the whole. Furthermore, the whole man is on account of an extrinsic end, that end being the fruition of God. So, therefore, in the parts of the universe also every creature exists for its own proper act and perfection, and the less noble for the nobler, as those creatures that are less noble than man exist for the sake of man, whilst each and every creature exists for the perfection of the entire universe. Furthermore, the entire universe, with all its parts, is ordained towards God as its end, inasmuch as it imitates, as it were, and shows forth the Divine goodness, to the glory of God. Reasonable creatures, however, have in some special and higher manner God as their end, since they can attain to Him by their own operations, by knowing and loving Him. Thus it is plain that the Divine goodness is the end of all corporeal things.

Reply Obj. 1. In the very fact of any creature possessing being, it represents the Divine Being and Its goodness. And, therefore, that God created all things, that they might have being, does not exclude that He created them for His own goodness.

Reply Obj. 2. The proximate end does not exclude the ultimate end. Therefore that corporeal creatures were, in a manner, made for the sake of the spiritual, does not prevent their being made on account of God's goodness.

Reply Obj. 3. Equality of justice has its place in retribution, since equal rewards or punishments are due to equal merit or demerit. But this does not apply to things as at first instituted. For just as an architect, without injustice, places stones of the same kind in different parts of a building, not on account of any antecedent difference in the stones, but with a view to securing that perfection of the entire building, which could not be obtained except by the different positions of the stones; even so, God from the beginning, to secure perfection in the universe, has set therein creatures of various and unequal natures, according to His wisdom, and without injustice, since no diversity of merit is presupposed.

Third Article.

WHETHER CORPOREAL CREATURES WERE PRODUCED BY GOD THROUGH THE MEDIUM OF THE ANGELS?

We proceed thus to the Third Article:—

Objection 1. It would seem that corporeal creatures were produced by God through the medium of the angels. For, as all things are governed by the Divine wisdom, so by it were all things made, according to Ps. ciii. 24 : *Thou hast made all things in wisdom.* But it belongs to wisdom to *ordain*, as stated in the beginning of the *Metaphysics* (i. 2). Hence in the government of things the lower is ruled by the higher in a certain fitting order, as Augustine says (*De Trin.* iii. 4). Therefore in the production of things it was ordained that the corporeal should be produced by the spiritual, as the lower by the higher.

Obj. 2. Further, diversity of effects shows diversity of causes, since like always produces like. If then all creatures, both spiritual and corporeal, were produced immediately by God, there would be no diversity in creatures, for one would not be further removed from God than another. But this is clearly false; for the Philosopher says that some things are corruptible because they are far removed from God (*De Gen. et Corrup.* ii., text. 59).

Obj. 3. Further, infinite power is not required to produce a finite effect. But every corporeal thing is finite. Therefore, it could be, and was, produced by the finite power of spiritual creatures : for in suchlike beings there is no distinction between what is and what is possible : especially as no dignity befitting a nature is denied to that nature, unless it be in punishment of a fault.

On the contrary, It is said (Gen. i. 1) :*In the beginning God created heaven and earth;* by which are understood corporeal creatures. These, therefore, were produced immediately by God.

I answer that, Some have maintained that creatures proceeded from God by degrees, in such a way that the first creature proceeded from Him immediately, and in its turn produced another, and so on until the production of corporeal creatures. But this position is untenable, since the first production of corporeal creatures is by creation, by which matter itself is produced: for in the act of coming into being the imperfect must be made before the perfect: and it is impossible that anything should be created, save by God alone.

In proof whereof it must be borne in mind that the higher the cause, the more numerous the objects to which its causation extends. Now the underlying principle in things is always more universal than that which informs and restricts it; thus, being is more universal than living, living than understanding, matter than form. The more widely, then, one thing underlies others, the more directly does that thing proceed from a higher cause. Thus the thing that underlies primarily all things, belongs properly to the causality of the supreme cause. Therefore no secondary cause can produce anything, unless there is presupposed in the thing produced something that is caused by a higher cause. But creation is the production of a thing in its entire substance, nothing being presupposed either uncreated or created. Hence it remains that nothing can create except God alone, Who is the first cause. Therefore, in order to show that all bodies were created immediately by God, Moses said: *In the beginning God created heaven and earth.*

Reply Obj. 1. In the production of things an order exists, but not such that one creature is created by another, for that is impossible; but rather such that by the Divine wisdom diverse grades are constituted in creatures.

Reply Obj. 2. God Himself, though one, has knowledge of many and different things without detriment to the simplicity of His nature, as has been shown above (Q. XV., A. 2); so that by His wisdom He is the cause of diverse things, produced according to the diversity of things as known by Him, even as an artificer, by apprehending diverse forms, produces diverse works of art.

Reply Obj. 3. The amount of the power of an agent is measured not only by the thing made, but also by the manner of making it; for one and the same thing is made in one way by a higher power, in another by a lower. But the production of finite things, where nothing is presupposed as existing, is the work of infinite power, and, as such, can belong to no creature.

FOURTH ARTICLE.

WHETHER THE FORMS OF BODIES ARE FROM THE ANGELS?

We proceed thus to the Fourth Article:—

Objection 1. It would seem that the forms of bodies are from the angels. For Boethius says (*De Trin.* i.) : *From forms that are without matter come the forms that are in matter.* But forms that are without matter are spiritual substances, and forms that are in matter are the forms of bodies. Therefore, the forms of bodies are from spiritual substances.

Obj. 2. Further, all that is such by participation is reduced to that which is such by its essence. But spiritual substances are forms essentially, whereas corporeal creatures have forms by participation. Therefore the forms of corporeal things are derived from spiritual substances.

Obj. 3. Further, spiritual substances have more power of causation than the heavenly bodies. But the heavenly bodies give form to things here below, for which reason they are said to cause generation and corruption. Much more, therefore, are material forms derived from spiritual substances.

On the contrary, Augustine says (*De Trin.* iii. 8) : *We must not suppose that this corporeal matter serves the angels at their nod, but rather that it obeys God thus.* But corporeal matter may be said thus to serve that from which it receives its form. Corporeal forms, then, are not from the angels, but from God.

I answer that, It was the opinion of some that all corporeal forms are derived from spiritual substances, which we call the angels. And there are two ways in which this has been stated. For Plato held that the forms of corporeal matter are derived from, and formed by, forms immaterially subsisting, by a kind of participation. Thus he held that there exists an immaterial man, and an immaterial horse, and so forth, and that from such the individual sensible things that we see are constituted, in so far as in corporeal matter there abides the impression received from these separate forms, by a kind of assimilation, or as he calls it, *participation* (*Phædo* xlix.). And, according to the Platonists, the order of forms corresponds to the order of those separate substances; for example, that there is a single separate substance, which is a horse and the cause of all horses, whilst above this is separate life, or *per se* life, as they term it, which is the cause of all life, and that above this again is that which they call being itself, which is the cause of all being. Avicenna, however, and certain others, have maintained that the forms of corporeal things do not subsist *per se* in matter, but in the intellect only. Thus they say that from forms existing in the intellect of spiritual creatures (called *intelligences* by them, but *angels* by us) proceed all the forms of corporeal matter, as the form of his handiwork proceeds from the forms in the mind of the craftsman. This theory seems to be the same as that of certain heretics of modern times, who say that God indeed created all things, but that the devil formed corporeal matter, and differentiated it into species.

But all these opinions seem to have a common origin; they all, in fact, sought for a cause of forms as though the form were of itself brought into being. Whereas, as Aristotle (*Metaph.* vii., text. 26, 27, 28), proves, what is, properly speaking, made, is the *composite*. Now, such are the forms of corruptible things that at one time they exist and at another exist not, without being themselves generated or corrupted, but by reason of the generation or corruption of the *composite;* since even forms have not being, but composites have being through forms: for, according to a thing's mode of being, is the mode in which it is brought into being. Since, then, like is produced from like, we must not look for the cause of corporeal forms in any immaterial form, but in something that is composite, as this fire is generated by that fire. Corporeal forms, therefore, are caused, not as emanations from some immaterial form, but by matter being brought from potentiality into act by some composite agent. But since the composite agent, which is a body, is moved by a created spiritual substance, as Augustine says (*De Trin.* iii. 4, 5), it follows further that even corporeal forms are derived from spiritual substances, not as emanating from them, but as the term of their movement. And, further still, the species of the angelic intellect, which are, as it were, the seminal types of corporeal forms, must be referred to God as the first cause. But in the first production of corporeal creatures no transmutation from potentiality to act can have taken place, and accordingly, the corporeal forms that bodies had when first produced came immediately from God, whose bidding alone matter obeys, as its own proper cause. To signify this, Moses prefaces each work with the words, *God said, Let this thing be,* or *that,* to denote the formation of all things by the Word of God, from Whom, according to Augustine,* is *all form and fitness and concord of parts.*

Reply Obj. 1. By immaterial forms Boëthius understands the types of things in the mind of God. Thus the Apostle says (Heb. xi. 3) : *By faith we understand that the world was framed by the Word of God; that from invisible things visible things might be made.* But if by immaterial forms he understands the angels, we say that from them come material forms, not by emanation, but by motion.

Reply Obj. 2. Forms received into matter are to be referred, not to self-subsisting forms of the same type, as

* *Tract.* i. in *Joan.,* and *Gen. ad lit.* i. 4.

the Platonists held, but either to intelligible forms of the angelic intellect, from which they proceed by movement, or, still higher, to the types in the Divine intellect, by which the seeds of forms are implanted in created things, that they may be able to be brought by movement into act.

Reply Obj. 3. The heavenly bodies inform earthly ones by movement, not by emanation.

QUESTION LXVI.

ON THE ORDER OF CREATION TOWARDS DISTINCTION.

(*In Four Articles.*)

WE must next consider the work of distinction; first, the ordering of creation towards distinction; secondly, the distinction itself. Under the first head there are four points of inquiry: (1) Whether formlessness of created matter preceded in time its formation? (2) Whether the matter of all corporeal things is the same? (3) Whether the empyrean heaven was created contemporaneously with formless matter? (4) Whether time was created simultaneously with it?

First Article.

WHETHER FORMLESSNESS OF CREATED MATTER PRECEDED IN TIME ITS FORMATION?

We proceed thus to the First Article:—

Objection 1. It would seem that formlessness of matter preceded in time its formation. For it is said (Gen. i. 2): *The earth was void and empty,* or *invisible and shapeless,* according to another version;* by which is understood the formlessness of matter, as Augustine says (*Conf.* xii. 12). Therefore matter was formless until it received its form.

Obj. 2. Further, nature in its working imitates the working of God, as a secondary cause imitates a first cause. But in the working of nature formlessness precedes form in time. It does so, therefore, in the Divine working.

Obj. 3. Further, matter is higher than accident, for matter is part of substance. But God can effect that accident exist without substance, as in the Sacrament of the

---

* The Septuagint.

Altar. He could, therefore, cause matter to exist without form.

On the contrary, An imperfect effect proves imperfection in the agent. But God is an agent absolutely perfect; wherefore it is said of Him (Deut. xxxii. 4) : *The works of God are perfect.* Therefore the work of His creation was at no time formless. Further, the formation of corporeal creatures was effected by the work of distinction. But confusion is opposed to distinction, as formlessness to form. If, therefore, formlessness preceded in time the formation of matter, it follows that at the beginning confusion, called by the ancients chaos, existed in the corporeal creation.

I answer that, On this point holy men differ in opinion. Augustine, for instance (*Gen ad lit.* i. 15), believes that the formlessness of matter was not prior in time to its formation, but only in origin or the order of nature, whereas others, as Basil (*Hom.* ii. *In Hexæm.*), Ambrose (*In Hexæm.* i.), and Chrysostom (*Hom.* ii. *In Gen.*), hold that formlessness of matter preceded in time its formation. And although these opinions seem mutually contradictory, in reality they differ but little; for Augustine takes the formlessness of matter in a different sense from the others. In his sense it means the absence of all form, and if we thus understand it we cannot say that the formlessness of matter was prior in time either to its formation or to its distinction. As to formation, the argument is clear. For if formless matter preceded in duration, it already existed; for this is implied by duration, since the end of creation is being in act : and act itself is a form. To say, then, that matter preceded, but without form, is to say that being existed actually, yet without act, which is a contradiction in terms. Nor can it be said that it possessed some common form, on which afterwards supervened the different forms, that distinguish it. For this would be to hold the opinion of the ancient natural philosophers, who maintained that primary matter was some corporeal thing in act, as fire, air, water, or some intermediate substance. Hence, it followed that to be made means merely to be changed; for since that preceding form bestowed actual substantial being, and made some particular thing to be, it would result that the supervening form would not simply make an actual being, but *this* actual being; which is the proper effect of an accidental form. Thus the consequent forms would be merely accidents, implying not generation, but alteration. Hence we must assert that primary matter was not created altogether formless, nor under any one common form, but under distinct forms. And so, if the formlessness of matter be taken as referring to the condition of primary matter, which in itself is formless, this formlessness did not precede in time its formation or distinction, but only in origin and nature, as Augustine says; in the same way as potentiality is prior to act, and the part to the whole. But the other holy writers understand by formlessness, not the exclusion of all form, but the absence of that beauty and comeliness which are now apparent in the corporeal creation. Accordingly they say that the formlessness of corporeal matter preceded its form in duration. And so, when this is considered, it appears that Augustine agrees with them in some respects, and in others disagrees, as will be shown later (Q. LXIX., A. 1; and Q. LXXIV., A. 2).

As far as may be gathered from the text of Genesis a threefold beauty was wanting to corporeal creatures, for which reason they are said to be without form. For the beauty of light was wanting to all that transparent body, which we call the heavens, whence it is said that *darkness was upon the face of the deep*. And the earth lacked beauty in two ways: first, that beauty which it acquired when its watery veil was withdrawn, and so we read that *the earth was void*, or *invisible*, inasmuch as the waters covered and concealed it from view; secondly, that which it derives from being adorned by herbs and plants, for which reason it is called *empty*, or, according to another reading,* *shapeless*—that is, unadorned Thus after

---
* The Septuagint

mention of two created natures, the heaven and the earth, the formlessness of the heaven is indicated by the words, *darkness was upon the face of the deep*, since the air is included under heaven; and the formlessness of the earth, by the words, *the earth was void and empty*.

Reply Obj. 1. The word earth is taken differently in this passage by Augustine, and by other writers. Augustine holds that by the words *earth* and *water*, in this passage, primary matter itself is signified, on account of its being impossible for Moses to make the idea of such matter intelligible to an ignorant people, except under the similitude of well-known objects. Hence he uses a variety of figures in speaking of it, calling it not water only, nor earth only, lest they should think it to be in very truth water or earth. At the same time it has so far a likeness to earth, in that it is susceptible of form, and to water in its adaptability to a variety of forms. In this respect, then, the earth is said to be *void and empty*, or *invisible and shapeless*, that matter is known by means of form. Hence, considered in itself, it is called *invisible* or *void*, and its potentiality is completed by form; thus Plato says that matter is *place*.* But other holy writers understand by earth the element of earth, and we have said (A. 1) how, in this sense, the earth was, according to them, without form.

Reply Obj. 2. Nature produces effect in act from being in potentiality; and consequently in the operations of nature potentiality must precede act in time, and formlessness precede form. But God produces being in act out of nothing, and can, therefore, produce a perfect thing in an instant, according to the greatness of His power.

Reply Obj. 3. Accident, inasmuch as it is a form, is a kind of act; whereas matter, as such, is essentially being in potentiality. Hence it is more repugnant that matter should be in act without form, than for accident to be without subject.

In reply to the first argument in the contrary sense, we

* *Timæus*, quoted by Aristotle, *Phys.* iv., text 15

say that if, according to some holy writers, formlessness was prior in time to the informing of matter, this arose, not from want of power on God's part, but from His wisdom, and from the design of preserving due order in the disposition of creatures by developing perfection from imperfection.

In reply to the second argument, we say that certain of the ancient natural philosophers maintained confusion devoid of all distinction; except Anaxagoras, who taught that the intellect alone was distinct and without admixture. But previous to the work of distinction Holy Scripture enumerates several kinds of differentiation, the first being that of the heaven from the earth, in which even a material distinction is expressed, as will be shown later (A. 3; Q. LXVIII., A. 1). This is signified by the words, *In the beginning God created heaven and earth.* The second distinction mentioned is that of the elements according to their forms, since both earth and water are named. That air and fire are not mentioned by name is due to the fact that the corporeal nature of these would not be so evident as that of earth and water, to the ignorant people to whom Moses spoke. Plato,* nevertheless, understood air to be signified by the words, *Spirit of God,* since spirit is another name for air, and considered that by the word heaven is meant fire, for he held heaven to be composed of fire, as Augustine relates (*De Civ. Dei* viii. 11). But Rabbi Moses,† though otherwise agreeing with Plato, says that fire is signified by the word darkness, since, said he, fire does not shine in its own sphere. However, it seems more reasonable to hold to what we stated above; because by the words *Spirit of God* Scripture usually means the Holy Ghost, Who is said to " move over the waters," not, indeed, in bodily shape, but as the craftsman's will may be said to move over the material to which he intends to give a form. The third distinction is that of place; since the earth is said to be under the waters that rendered it invisible, whilst the air, the subject of darkness, is described

* *Timæus* xxvi.   † *Perplex.* ii.

as being above the waters, in the words: *Darkness was upon the face of the deep*. The remaining distinctions will appear from what follows (Q. LXXI.).

SECOND ARTICLE.

WHETHER THE FORMLESS MATTER OF ALL CORPOREAL THINGS IS THE SAME?

We proceed thus to the Second Article:—

Objection 1. It would seem that the formless matter of all corporeal things is the same. For Augustine says (*Conf.* xii. 12): *I find two things Thou hast made, one formed, the other formless,* and he says that the latter was the earth invisible and shapeless, whereby, he says, the matter of all corporeal things is designated. Therefore the matter of all corporeal things is the same.

Obj. 2. Further, the Philosopher says (*Metaph.* v., text. 10): *Things that are one in genus are one in matter.* But all corporeal things are in the same genus of body. Therefore the matter of all bodies is the same.

Obj. 3. Further, different acts befit different potentialities, and the same act befits the same potentiality. But all bodies have the same form, corporeity. Therefore all bodies have the same matter.

Obj. 4. Further, matter, considered in itself, is only in potentiality. But distinction is due to form. Therefore matter considered in itself is the same in all corporeal things.

On the contrary, Things of which the matter is the same are mutually interchangeable, and mutually active or passive, as is said (*De Gener.* i., text. 50). But heavenly and earthly bodies do not act upon each other mutually. Therefore their matter is not the same.

I answer that, On this question the opinions of philosophers have differed. Plato and all who preceded Aristotle held that all bodies are of the nature of the four elements. Hence, because the four elements have one common matter, as their mutual generation and corruption prove, it followed that the matter of all bodies is the same. But the fact of the incorruptibility of some bodies was ascribed by Plato, not to the condition of matter, but to the will of the artificer, God, Whom he represents as saying to the heavenly bodies : *By your own nature you are subject to dissolution, but by My will you are indissoluble, for My will is more powerful than the link that binds you together.* But this theory Aristotle* disproves by the natural movements of bodies. For since, he says, the heavenly bodies have a natural movement, different from that of the elements, it follows that they have a different nature from them. For movement in a circle, which is proper to the heavenly bodies, is not by contraries, whereas the movements of the elements are mutually opposite, one tending upwards, another downwards : so, therefore, the heavenly body is without contrariety, whereas the elemental bodies have contrariety in their nature. And as generation and corruption are from contraries, it follows that, whereas the elements are corruptible, the heavenly bodies are incorruptible. But in spite of this difference of natural corruption and incorruption, Avicebron taught unity of matter in all bodies, arguing from their unity of form. And, indeed, if corporeity were one form in itself, on which the other forms that distinguish bodies from each other supervene, this argument would necessarily be true, for this form of corporeity would inhere in matter immutably, and so far all bodies would be incorruptible. But corruption would then be merely accidental through the disappearance of successive forms—that is to say, it would be corruption, not pure and simple, but partial, since a being in act would subsist under the transient form. Thus the ancient natural philosophers taught that the substratum of bodies was some actual being, such as air or fire. But supposing that no form exists in corruptible bodies which remains subsisting beneath generation and corruption, it follows necessarily that the matter of cor-

* *De cœlo* 1., text. 5.

ruptible and incorruptible bodies is not the same. For matter, as it is in itself, is in potentiality to form.

Considered in itself, then, it is in potentiality in respect to all those forms to which it is common, and in receiving any one form it is in act only as regards that form. Hence it remains in potentiality to all other forms. And this is the case even where some forms are more perfect than others, and contain these others virtually in themselves. For potentiality in itself is indifferent with respect to perfection and imperfection, so that under an imperfect form it is in potentiality to a perfect form, and *vice versa*. Matter, therefore, whilst existing under the form of an incorruptible body, would be in potentiality to the form of a corruptible body; and as it does not actually possess the latter, it has both form and the privation of form; for want of a form in that which is in potentiality thereto is privation. But this condition implies corruptibility. It is therefore impossible that bodies by nature corruptible, and those by nature incorruptible, should possess the same matter.

Neither can we say, as Averroes* imagines, that a heavenly body itself is the matter of the heaven—beings in potentiality with regard to place, though not to being, and that its form is a separate substance united to it as its motive force. For it is impossible to suppose any being in act, unless in its totality it be act and form, or be something which has act or form. Setting aside, then, in thought, the separate substance stated to be endowed with motive power, if the heavenly body is not something having form—that is, something composed of a form and the subject of that form—it follows that in its totality it is form and act. But every such thing is something actually understood, which the heavenly bodies are not, being sensible. It follows, then, that the matter of the heavenly bodies, considered in itself, is in potentiality to that form alone which it actually possesses. Nor does it concern the point at issue to inquire whether this is a

* *De substantia orbis* ii.

soul or any other thing. Hence this form perfects this matter in such a way that there remains in it no potentiality with respect to being, but only to place, as Aristotle* says. So, then, the matter of the heavenly bodies and of the elements is not the same, except by analogy, in so far as they agree in the character of potentiality.

Reply Obj. 1. Augustine follows in this the opinion of Plato, who does not admit a fifth essence. Or we may say that formless matter is one with the unity of order, as all bodies are one in the order of corporeal creatures.

Reply Obj. 2. If genus is taken in a physical sense, corruptible and incorruptible things are not in the same genus, on account of their different modes of potentiality, as is said *Metaph.* x., text. 26. Logically considered, however, there is but one genus of all bodies, since they are all included in the one notion of corporeity.

Reply Obj. 3. The form of corporeity is not one and the same in all bodies, being no other than the various forms by which bodies are distinguished, as stated above.

Reply Obj. 4. As potentiality is directed towards act, potential beings are differentiated by their different acts, as sight is by colour, hearing by sound. Therefore for this reason the matter of the celestial bodies is different from that of the elemental, that the matter of the celestial is not in potentiality to an elemental form.

THIRD ARTICLE.

WHETHER THE EMPYREAN HEAVEN WAS CREATED AT THE SAME TIME AS FORMLESS MATTER?

We proceed thus to the Third Article:—

Objection 1. It would seem that the empyrean heaven was not created at the same time as formless matter. For the empyrean, if it is anything at all, must be a sensible body. But all sensible bodies are movable, and the empyrean heaven is not movable. For if it were so, its movement would be ascertained by the movement of some visible body, which is not the case. The empyrean

* *De cœlo* i., text. 20.

heaven, then, was not created contemporaneously with formless matter.

Obj. 2. Further, Augustine says (*De Trin.* iii. 4) that *the lower bodies are governed by the higher in a certain order.* If, therefore, the empyrean heaven is the highest of bodies, it must necessarily exercise some influence on bodies below it. But this does not seem to be the case, especially as it is presumed to be without movement; for one body cannot move another unless itself also be moved. Therefore the empyrean heaven was not created together with formless matter.

Obj. 3. Further, if it is held that the empyrean heaven is the place of contemplation, and not ordained to natural effects; on the contrary, Augustine says (*De Trin.* iv. 20): *In so far as we mentally apprehend eternal things, so far are we not of this world;* from which it is clear that contemplation lifts the mind above the things of this world. Corporeal place, therefore, cannot be the seat of contemplation.

Obj. 4. Further, among the heavenly bodies exists a body, partly transparent and partly luminous, which we call the sidereal heaven. There exists also a heaven wholly transparent, called by some the aqueous or crystalline heaven. If, then, there exists a still higher heaven, it must be wholly luminous. But this cannot be, for then the air would be constantly illuminated, and there would be no night. Therefore the empyrean heaven was not created together with formless matter.

On the contrary, Strabus says that in the passage, *In the beginning God created heaven and earth,* heaven denotes not the visible firmament, but the empyrean or fiery heaven.

I answer that, The empyrean heaven rests only on the authority of Strabus and Bede, and also of Basil; all of whom agree in one respect, namely, in holding it to be the place of the blessed. Strabus and Bede say that as soon as created it was filled with the angels; and Basil* says: *Just*

* *Hom.* ii. *in Hexæm.*

as the lost are driven into the lowest darkness, so the reward for worthy deeds is laid up in the light beyond this world, where the just shall obtain the abode of rest. But they differ in the reasons on which they base their statement. Strabus and Bede teach that there is an empyrean heaven, because the firmament, which they take to mean the empyrean heaven, is said to have been made, not in the beginning, but on the second day: whereas the reason given by Basil is that otherwise God would seem to have made darkness His first work, as the Manicheans falsely assert, when they call the God of the Old Testament the God of darkness. These reasons, however, are not very cogent. For the question of the firmament, said to have been made on the second day, is solved in one way by Augustine, and in another by other holy writers. But the question of the darkness is explained, according to Augustine,* by supposing that formlessness, signified by darkness, preceded form not by duration, but by origin. According to others, however, since darkness is no creature, but a privation of light, it is a proof of Divine wisdom, that the things it created from nothing it produced first of all in an imperfect state, and afterwards brought them to perfection. But a better reason can be drawn from the state of glory itself. For in the reward to come a twofold glory is looked for, spiritual and corporeal, not only in the human body to be glorified, but in the whole world which is to be made new. Now the spiritual glory began with the beginning of the world, in the blessedness of the angels, equality with whom is promised to the saints. - It was fitting, then, that even from the beginning there should be made some beginning of bodily glory in something corporeal, free at the very outset from the servitude of corruption and change, and wholly luminous, even as the whole bodily creation, after the Resurrection, is expected to be. So, then, that heaven is called the empyrean, *i.e.*, fiery, not from its heat, but from its brightness. It is to be noticed, however, that Augustine (*De Civ. Dei* x. 9, 27)

* *Gen. ad lit.* i.; vii.

says that Porphyry sets the demons apart from the angels by supposing that the former inhabit the air, the latter the ether, or empyrean. But Porphyry, as a Platonist, held the heaven, known as sidereal, to be fiery, and therefore called it empyrean or ethereal, taking ethereal to denote the burning of flame, and not as Aristotle understands it, swiftness of movement (*De Cœl.* i., text. 22). This much has been said to prevent anyone from supposing that Augustine maintained an empyrean heaven in the sense understood by modern writers.

Reply Obj. 1. Sensible corporeal things are movable in the present state of the world, for by the movement of corporeal creatures is secured the multiplication of the elements. But when glory is finally consummated, the movement of bodies will cease. And such must have been from the beginning the condition of the empyrean.

Reply Obj. 2. It is sufficiently probable, as some assert, that the empyrean heaven, having the state of glory for its ordained end, does not influence inferior bodies of another order—those, namely, that are directed only to natural ends. Yet it seems still more probable that it does influence bodies that are moved, though itself motionless, just as angels of the highest rank, who assist,* influence those of lower degree who act as messengers, though they themselves are not sent, as Dionysius teaches (*Cœl. Hier.* xiii.). For this reason it may be said that the influence of the empyrean upon that which is called the first heaven, and is moved, produces therein not something that comes and goes as a result of movement, but something of a fixed and stable nature, as the power of conservation or causation, or something of the kind pertaining to dignity.

Reply Obj. 3. Corporeal place is assigned to contemplation, not as necessary, but as congruous, that the splendour without may correspond to that which is within. Hence Basil (*Hom.* ii. *in Hexæm.*) says: *The ministering spirit could not live in darkness, but made his habitual dwelling in light and joy.*

* *Infra,* Q. CXII., A. 3

Reply Obj. 4. As Basil says (*ibid.*): *It is certain that the heaven was created spherical in shape, of dense body, and sufficiently strong to separate what is outside it from what it encloses.* On this account it darkens the region external to it, the light by which itself is lit up being shut out from that region. But since the body of the firmament, though solid, is transparent, for that it does not exclude light (as is clear from the fact that we can see the stars through the intervening heavens), we may also say that the empyrean has light, not condensed so as to emit rays, as the sun does, but of a more subtle nature. Or it may have the brightness of glory which differs from mere natural brightness.

FOURTH ARTICLE.

WHETHER TIME WAS CREATED SIMULTANEOUSLY WITH FORMLESS MATTER?

We proceed thus to the Fourth Article:—

Objection 1. It would seem that time was not created simultaneously with formless matter. For Augustine says (*Conf.* xii. 12): *I find two things that Thou didst create before time was, the primary corporeal matter, and the angelic nature.* Therefore time was not created with formless matter.

Obj. 2. Further, time is divided by day and night. But in the beginning there was neither day nor night, for these began when *God divided the light from the darkness.* Therefore in the beginning time was not.

Obj. 3. Further, time is the measure of the firmament's movement; and the firmament is said to have been made on the second day. Therefore in the beginning time was not.

Obj. 4. Further, movement precedes time, and therefore should be reckoned among the first things created, rather than time.

Obj. 5. Further, as time is the extrinsic measure of created things, so is place. Place, then, as truly as time, must be reckoned among the things first created.

On the contrary, Augustine says (*Gen. ad lit.* i. 3) : *Both spiritual and corporeal creatures were created at the beginning of time.*

I answer that, It is commonly said that the first things created were these four—the angelic nature, the empyrean heaven, formless corporeal matter, and time. It must be observed, however, that this is not the opinion of Augustine. For he (*Conf.* xii. 12) specifies only two things as first created—the angelic nature and corporeal matter—making no mention of the empyrean heaven. But these two, namely, the angelic nature and formless matter, precede the formation, by nature only, and not by duration ; and therefore, as they precede formation, so do they precede movement and time. Time, therefore, cannot be included among them. But the enumeration above given is that of other holy writers, who hold that the formlessness of matter preceded by duration its form, and this view postulates the existence of time as the measure of duration : for otherwise there would be no such measure.

Reply Obj. 1. The teaching of Augustine rests on the opinion that the angelic nature and formless matter precede time by origin or nature.

Reply Obj. 2. As in the opinion of some holy writers matter was in some measure formless before it received its full form, so time was in a manner formless before it was fully formed and distinguished into day and night.

Reply Obj. 3. If the movement of the firmament did not begin immediately from the beginning, then the time that preceded was the measure, not of the firmament's movement, but of the first movement of whatsoever kind. For it is accidental to time to be the measure of the firmament's movement, in so far as this is the first movement. But if the first movement was another than this, time would have been its measure, for everything is measured by the first of its kind. And it must be granted that forthwith from the beginning, there was movement of some kind, at least in the succession of concepts and affections in the angelic mind : while movement without time cannot be conceived, since time is nothing else than *the measure of priority and succession in movement.*

Reply Obj. 4. Among the first created things are to be reckoned those which have a general relationship to things. And, therefore, among these time must be included, as having the nature of a common measure; but not movement, which is related only to the movable subject.

Reply Obj. 5. Place is implied as existing in the empyrean heaven, this being the boundary of the universe. And since place has reference to things permanent, it was created at once in its totality. But time, as not being permanent, was created in its beginning: even as actually we cannot lay hold of any part of time save the *now.*

QUESTION LXVII

ON THE WORK OF DISTINCTION IN ITSELF.
(In Four Articles.)

WE must consider next the work of distinction in itself. First, the work of the first day; secondly, the work of the second day; thirdly, the work of the third day.

Under the first head there are four points of inquiry: (1) Whether the word light is used in its proper sense in speaking of spiritual things? (2) Whether light, in corporeal things, is itself corporeal? (3) Whether light is a quality? (4) Whether light was fittingly made on the first day?

FIRST ARTICLE.

WHETHER THE WORD LIGHT IS USED IN ITS PROPER SENSE IN SPEAKING OF SPIRITUAL THINGS?

We proceed thus to the First Article:—

Objection 1. It would seem that light is used in its proper sense in spiritual things. For Augustine says (*Gen. ad lit.* iv. 28) that *in spiritual things light is better and surer; and that Christ is not called Light in the same sense as He is called the Stone; the former is to be taken literally, and the latter metaphorically.*

Obj. 2. Further, Dionysius (*Div. Nom.* iv.) includes Light among the intellectual names of God. But such names are used in their proper sense in spiritual things. Therefore light is used in its proper sense in spiritual matters.

Obj. 3. Further, the Apostle says (Eph. v. 13): *All that is made manifest is light.* But to be made manifest belongs more properly to spiritual things than to corporeal. Therefore also does light.

On the contrary, Ambrose says (*De Fid.* ii.) that *Splendour* is among those things which are said of God metaphorically.

I answer that, Any word may be used in two ways—that is to say, either in its original application or in its more extended meaning. This is clearly shown in the word *sight,* originally applied to the act of the sense, and then, as sight is the noblest and most trustworthy of the senses, extended in common speech to all knowledge obtained through the other senses. Thus we say, " *Seeing how it tastes,*" or *smells,* or *burns.* Further, sight is applied to knowledge obtained through the intellect, as in those words : *Blessed are the clean of heart, for they shall see God* (Matt. v. 8). And thus it is with the word light. In its primary meaning it signifies that which makes manifest to the senses of sight; afterwards it was extended to that which makes manifest to cognition of any kind. If, then, the word is taken in its strict and primary meaning, it is to be understood metaphorically when applied to spiritual things, as Ambrose says (*loc. cit.*) But if taken in its common and extended use, as applied to manifestation of every kind, it may properly be applied to spiritual things.

The answer to the objections will sufficiently appear from what has been said.

SECOND ARTICLE.

WHETHER LIGHT IS A BODY?

We proceed thus to the Second Article:—

Objection 1. It would seem that light is a body. For Augustine says (*De Lib. Arb.* iii. 5) that *light takes the first place among bodies.* Therefore light is a body.

Obj. 2. Further, the Philosopher says (*Topic.* v. 2) that *light is a species of fire.* But fire is a body, and therefore so is light.

Obj. 3. Further, the powers of movement, intersection,

reflection, belong properly to bodies; and all these are attributes of light and its rays. Moreover, different rays of light, as Dionysius says (*Div. Nom.* ii.), are united and separated, which seems impossible unless they are bodies. Therefore light is a body.

On the contrary, Two bodies cannot occupy the same place simultaneously. But this is the case with light and air. Therefore light is not a body.

I answer that, Light cannot be a body, for three evident reasons. First, on the part of place. For the place of any one body is different from that of any other, nor is it possible, naturally speaking, for any two bodies, of whatever nature, to exist simultaneously in the same place; since contiguity requires distinction of place.

The second reason is from movement. For if light were a body, its diffusion would be the local movement of a body. Now no local movement of a body can be instantaneous, as everything that moves from one place to another must pass through the intervening space before reaching the end: whereas the diffusion of light is instantaneous. Nor can it be argued that the time required is too short to be perceived; for though this may be the case in short distances, it cannot be so in distances so great as that which separates the East from the West. Yet as soon as the sun is at the horizon, the whole hemisphere is illuminated from end to end. It must also be borne in mind on the part of movement that whereas all bodies have their natural determinate movement, that of light is indifferent as regards direction, working equally in a circle as in a straight line. Hence it appears that the diffusion of light is not the local movement of a body.

The third reason is from generation and corruption. For if light were a body, it would follow that whenever the air is darkened by the absence of the luminary, the body of light would be corrupted, and its matter would receive a new form. But unless we are to say that darkness is a body, this does not appear to be the case. Neither does it appear from what matter a body can be daily generated large enough to fill the intervening hemisphere. Also it would be absurd to say that a body of so great bulk is corrupted by the mere absence of the luminary. And should anyone reply that it is not corrupted, but approaches and moves round with the sun, we may ask why it is that when a lighted candle is obscured by the intervening object the whole room is darkened? It is not that the light is condensed round the candle when this is done, since it burns no more brightly then than it burned before.

Since, therefore, these things are repugnant, not only to reason, but to common sense, we must conclude that light cannot be a body.

Reply Obj. 1. Augustine takes light to be a luminous body in act—in other words, to be fire, the noblest of the four elements.

Reply Obj. 2. Aristotle pronounces light to be fire existing in its own proper matter : just as fire in aerial matter is *flame,* or in earthly matter is *burning coal.* Nor must too much attention be paid to the instances adduced by Aristotle in his works on logic, as he merely mentions them as the more or less probable opinions of various writers.

Reply Obj. 3. All these properties are assigned to light metaphorically, and might in the same way be attributed to heat. For because movement from place to place is naturally first in the order of movement, as is proved *Phys.* viii., text. 55, we use terms belonging to local movement in speaking of alteration and movement of all kinds. For even the word distance is derived from the idea of remoteness of place, to that of all contraries, as is said *Metaph* x., text. 13.

THIRD ARTICLE.

WHETHER LIGHT IS A QUALITY?

We proceed thus to the Third Article.—

Objection 1. It would seem that light is not a quality. For every quality remains in its subject, though the active cause of the quality be removed, as heat remains in water removed from the fire. But light does not remain in the air when the source of light is withdrawn. Therefore light is not a quality.

Obj. 2. Further, every sensible quality has its opposite, as cold is opposed to heat, blackness to whiteness. But this is not the case with light since darkness is merely a privation of light. Light therefore is not a sensible quality.

Obj. 3. Further, a cause is more potent than its effect. But the light of the heavenly bodies is a cause of substantial forms of earthly bodies, and also gives to colours their immaterial being, by making them actually visible. Light, then, is not a sensible quality, but rather a substantial or spiritual form.

On the contrary, Damascene (*De Fid. Orth.* i.) says that light is a species of quality.

I answer that, Some writers have said that the light in the air has not a natural being such as the colour on a wall has, but only an intentional being, as a similitude of colour in the air. But this cannot be the case for two reasons. First, because light gives a name to the air, since by it the air becomes actually luminous. But colour does not do this, for we do not speak of the air as coloured. Secondly, because light produces natural effects, for by the rays of the sun bodies are warmed, and natural changes cannot be brought about by mere intentions. Others have said that light is the sun's substantial form, but this also seems impossible for two reasons. First, because substantial forms are not of themselves objects of the senses; for the object of the intellect is what a thing is, as is said *De Anima* iii., text. 26: whereas light is visible of itself. In the second place, because it is impossible that what is the substantial form of one thing should be the accidental form of another; since substantial forms of their very nature constitute species: wherefore the substantial form always and everywhere accompanies the species. But light is not the substantial form of air, for if it were, the air would be destroyed when light is withdrawn. Hence it cannot be the substantial form of the sun.

We must say, then, that as heat is an active quality consequent on the substantial form of fire, so light is an active quality consequent on the substantial form of the sun, or of another body that is of itself luminous, if there is any such body. A proof of this is that the rays of different stars produce different effects according to the diverse natures of bodies.

Reply Obj. 1. Since quality is consequent upon substantial form, the mode in which the subject receives a quality differs as the mode differs in which a subject receives a substantial form. For when matter receives its form perfectly, the qualities consequent upon the form are firm and enduring; as when, for instance, water is converted into fire. When, however, substantial form is received imperfectly, so as to be, as it were, in process of being received, rather than fully impressed, the consequent quality lasts for a time but is not permanent; as may be seen when water which has been heated returns in time to its natural state. But light is not produced by the transmutation of matter, as though matter were in receipt of a substantial form, and light were a certain inception of substantial form. For this reason light disappears on the disappearance of its active cause.

Reply Obj. 2. It is accidental to light not to have a contrary, forasmuch as it is the natural quality of the first corporeal cause of change, which is itself removed from contrariety.

Reply Obj. 3. As heat acts towards perfecting the form of fire, as an instrumental cause, by virtue of the substantial form, so does light act instrumentally, by virtue of the heavenly bodies, towards producing substantial forms; and towards rendering colours actually visible, inasmuch as it is a quality of the first sensible body.

Fourth Article

WHETHER THE PRODUCTION OF LIGHT IS FITTINGLY ASSIGNED TO THE FIRST DAY?

We proceed thus to the Fourth Article:—

Objection 1. It would seem that the production of light is not fittingly assigned to the first day. For light, as stated above (A. 3), is a quality. But qualities are accidents, and as such should have, not the first, but a subordinate place. The production of light, then, ought not to be assigned to the first day.

Obj. 2. Further, it is light that distinguishes night from day, and this is effected by the sun, which is recorded as having been made on the fourth day. Therefore the production of light could not have been on the first day.

Obj. 3. Further, night and day are brought about by the circular movement of a luminous body. But movement of this kind is an attribute of the firmament, and we read that the firmament was made on the second day. Therefore the production of light, dividing night from day, ought not to be assigned to the first day.

Obj. 4. Further, if it be said that spiritual light is here spoken of, it may be replied that the light made on the first day dispels the darkness. But in the beginning spiritual darkness was not, for even the demons were in the beginning good, as has been shown (Q. LXIII., A. 5). Therefore the production of light ought not to be assigned to the first day.

On the contrary, That without which there could not be day, must have been made on the first day. But there can be no day without light. Therefore light must have been made on the first day.

I answer that, There are two opinions as to the production of light. Augustine seems to say (*De Civ. Dei.* xi. 9, 33) that Moses could not have fittingly passed over the production of the spiritual creature, and therefore when we read, *In the beginning God created heaven and earth*, a spiritual nature as yet formless is to be understood by the word *heaven*, and formless matter of the corporeal creature by the word *earth*. And spiritual nature was formed first, as being of higher dignity than corporeal. The forming, therefore, of this spiritual nature is signified by the production of light, that is to say, of spiritual light. For a spiritual nature receives its form by the enlightenment whereby it is led to adhere to the Word of God.

Other writers think that the production of spiritual creatures was purposely omitted by Moses, and give various reasons. Basil* says that Moses begins his narrative from the beginning of time which belongs to sensible things; but that the spiritual or angelic creation is passed over, as created beforehand.

Chrysostom† gives as a reason for the omission that Moses was addressing an ignorant people, to whom material things alone appealed, and whom he was endeavouring to withdraw from the service of idols. It would have been to them a pretext for idolatry if he had spoken to them of natures spiritual in substance and nobler than all corporeal creatures; for they would have paid them Divine worship, since they were prone to worship as gods even the sun, moon, and stars, which was forbidden them (Deut. iv.).

But mention is made of several kinds of formlessness, in regard to the corporeal creature. One is where we read that *the earth was void and empty,* and another where it is said that *darkness was upon the face of the deep*. Now it seems to be required, for two reasons, that the formlessness of darkness should be removed first of all by the production of light. In the first place because light is a quality of the first body, as was stated (A. 3), and thus by means of light it was fitting that the world should first receive its form. The second reason is because light is a common quality. For light is common to terrestrial and celestial bodies. But as in knowledge we proceed from general principles, so do

* *Hom.* i. *in Hexæm.* † *Hom.* ii. *in Genes.*

we in work of every kind. For the living thing is generated before the animal, and the animal before man, as is shown in *De Gener. Anim.* ii. 3. It was fitting, then, as an evidence of the Divine wisdom, that among the works of distinction the production of light should take first place, since light is a form of the primary body, and because it is more common quality.

Basil,* indeed, adds a third reason : that all other things are made manifest by light. And there is yet a fourth, already touched upon in the objections; that day cannot be unless light exists, which was made therefore on the first day.

Reply Obj. 1. According to the opinion of those who hold that the formlessness of matter preceded its form in duration, matter must be held to have been created at the beginning with substantial forms, afterwards receiving those that are accidental, among which light holds the first place.

Reply Obj. 2. In the opinion of some the light here spoken of was a kind of luminous nebula, and that on the making of the sun this returned to the matter of which it had been formed. But this cannot well be maintained, as in the beginning of Genesis Holy Scripture records the institution of that order of nature which henceforth is to endure. We cannot, then, say that what was made at that time afterwards ceased to exist.

Others, therefore, held that this luminous nebula continues in existence, but so closely attached to the sun as to be indistinguishable. But this is as much as to say that it is superfluous, whereas none of God's works have been made in vain. On this account it is held by some that the sun's body was made out of this nebula. This, too, is impossible to those at least who believe that the sun is different in its nature from the four elements, and naturally incorruptible. For in that case its matter cannot take on another form.

I answer, then, with Dionysius (*Div. Nom.* iv.), that the light was the sun's light, formless as yet, being already the

* *Hom.* ii. *in Hexæm.*

THE WORK OF DISTINCTION Q. 67. Art. 4

solar substance, and possessing illuminative power in a general way, to which was afterwards added the special and determinative power required to produce determinate effects. Thus, then, in the production of this light a triple distinction was made between light and darkness. First, as to the cause, forasmuch as in the substance of the sun we have the cause of light, and in the opaque nature of the earth the cause of darkness. Secondly, as to place, for in one hemisphere there was light, in the other darkness. Thirdly, as to time; because there was light for one and darkness for another in the same hemisphere; and this is signified by the words *He called the light day, and the darkness night*.

Reply Obj. 3. Basil says (*Homil.* ii. *in Hexæm.*) that day and night were then caused by expansion and contraction of light, rather than by movement. But Augustine objects to this (*Gen. ad lit.* i.), that there was no reason for this vicissitude of expansion and contraction since there were neither men nor animals on the earth at that time, for whose service this was required. Nor does the nature of a luminous body seem to admit of the withdrawal of light, so long as the body is actually present; though this might be effected by miracle. As to this, however, Augustine remarks (*ibid.*) that in the first founding of the order of nature we must not look for miracles, but for what is in accordance with nature. We hold, then, that the movement of the heavens is twofold. Of these movements, one is common to the entire heaven, and is the cause of day and night. This, as it seems, had its beginning on the first day. The other varies in proportion as it affects various bodies, and by its variations is the cause of the succession of days, months, and years. Thus it is, that in the account of the first day the distinction between day and night alone is mentioned; this distinction being brought about by the common movement of the heavens. The further distinction into successive days, seasons, and years recorded as begun on the fourth day, in the words, *let them be for seasons, and for days, and years* is due to proper movements.

Reply Obj. 4. As Augustine teaches (*Conf.* xii.; *Gen. ad lit.* i. 15), formlessness did not precede forms in duration; and so we must understand the production of light to signify the formation of spiritual creatures, not, indeed, with the perfection of glory, in which they were not created, but with the perfection of grace, which they possessed from their creation as said above (Q. LXII., A. 3). Thus the division of light from darkness will denote the distinction of the spiritual creature from other created things as yet without form. But if all created things received their form at the same time, the darkness must be held to mean the spiritual darkness of the wicked, not as existing from the beginning, but such as God foresaw would exist.

QUESTION LXVIII.

ON THE WORK OF THE SECOND DAY.
(In Four Articles.)

WE must next consider the work of the second day. Under this head there are four points of inquiry : (1) Whether the firmament was made on the second day ? (2) Whether there are waters above the firmament ? (3) Whether the firmament divides waters from waters? (4) Whether there is more than one heaven ?

FIRST ARTICLE.

WHETHER THE FIRMAMENT WAS MADE ON THE SECOND DAY?

We proceed thus to the First Article:—

Objection 1. It would seem that the firmament was not made on the second day. For it is said (Gen. i. 8) : *God called the firmament heaven.* But the heaven existed before days, as is clear from the words, *In the beginning God created heaven and earth.* Therefore the firmament was not made on the second day.

Obj. 2. Further, the work of the six days is ordered conformably to the order of Divine wisdom. Now it would ill become the Divine wisdom to make afterwards that which is naturally first. But though the firmament naturally precedes the earth and the waters, these are mentioned before the formation of light, which was on the first day. Therefore the firmament was not made on the second day.

Obj. 3. Further, all that was made in the six days was formed out of matter created before days began. But the firmament cannot have been formed out of pre-existing matter, for if so it would be liable to generation and corruption. Therefore the firmament was not made on the second day.

On the contrary, It is written (Gen. i. 6): *God said: let there be a firmament,* and further on *(verse* 8): *And the evening and morning were the second day.*

I answer that, In discussing questions of this kind two rules are to be observed, as Augustine teaches *(Gen. ad lit.* i. 18). The first is, to hold the truth of Scripture without wavering. The second is that since Holy Scripture can be explained in a multiplicity of senses, one should adhere to a particular explanation, only in such measure as to be ready to abandon it, if it be proved with certainty to be false; lest Holy Scripture be exposed to the ridicule of unbelievers, and obstacles be placed to their believing.

We say, therefore, that the words which speak of the firmament as made on the second day can be understood in two senses. They may be understood, first, of the starry firmament, on which point it is necessary to set forth the different opinions of philosophers. Some of these believed it to be composed of the elements; and this was the opinion of Empedocles, who, however, held further that the body of the firmament was not susceptible of dissolution, because its parts are, so to say, not in disunion, but in harmony. Others held the firmament to be of the nature of the four elements, not, indeed, compounded of them, but being as it were a simple element. Such was the opinion of Plato, who held that element to be fire. Others, again; have held that the heaven is not of the nature of the four elements, but is itself a fifth body, existing over and above these This is the opinion of Aristotle *(De cœlo* i. text. 6, 32).

According to the first opinion, it may, strictly speaking, be granted that the firmament was made, even as to substance, on the second day. For it is part of the work of creation to produce the substance of the elements, while it belongs to the work of distinction and adornment to give forms to the elements that pre-exist.

But the belief that the firmament was made, as to its substance, on the second day is incompatible with the opinion of Plato, according to whom the making of the firmament implies the production of the element of fire. This production, however, belongs to the work of creation, at least, according to those who hold that formlessness of matter preceded in time its formation, since the first form received by matter is the elemental.

Still less compatible with the belief that the substance of the firmament was produced on the second day is the opinion of Aristotle, seeing that the mention of days denotes succession of time, whereas the firmament, being naturally incorruptible, is of a matter not susceptible of change of form; wherefore it could not be made out of matter existing antecedently in time.

Hence to produce the substance of the firmament belongs to the work of creation. But its formation, in some degree, belongs to the second day, according to both opinions: for as Dionysius says (*Div. Nom.* iv.), the light of the sun was without form during the first three days, and afterwards, on the fourth day, received its form.

If, however, we take these days to denote merely sequence in the natural order, as Augustine holds (*Gen. ad lit.* iv. 22, 24), and not succession in time, there is then nothing to prevent our saying, whilst holding any one of the opinions given above, that the substantial formation of the firmament belongs to the second day.

Another possible explanation is to understand by the firmament that was made on the second day, not that in which the stars are set, but the part of the atmosphere where the clouds are collected, and which has received the name of firmament from the firmness and density of the air. *For a body is called firm*, that is dense and solid, *thereby differing from a mathematical body* as is remarked by Basil (*Hom.* iii. *in Hexæm.*). If, then, this explanation is adopted none of these opinions will be found repugnant to reason. Augustine, in fact (*Gen. ad lit.* ii. 4), recommends it thus: *I consider this view of the question worthy* of all commendation, as neither contrary to faith nor difficult to be proved and believed.

Reply Obj. 1. According to Chrysostom (*Hom.* iii. *in Genes.*), Moses prefaces his record by speaking of the works of God collectively, in the words, *In the beginning God created heaven and earth,* and then proceeds to explain them part by part; in somewhat the same way as one might say : *This house was constructed by that builder,* and then add : *First he laid the foundations, then built the walls, and thirdly, put on the roof.* In accepting this explanation we are, therefore, not bound to hold that a different heaven is spoken of in the words : *In the beginning God created heaven and earth,* and when we read that the firmament was made on the second day.

We may also say that the heaven recorded as created in the beginning is not the same as that made on the second day; and there are several senses in which this may be understood. Augustine says (*Gen. ad lit.* i. 9) that the heaven recorded as made on the first day is the formless spiritual nature, and that the heaven of the second day is the corporeal heaven. According to Bede (*Hexæm.* i.) and Strabus, the heaven made on the first day is the empyrean, and the firmament made on the second day, the starry heaven. According to Damascene (*De Fid. Orth.* ii.), that of the first day was spherical in form and without stars, the same, in fact, that the philosophers speak of, calling it the ninth sphere, and the primary movable body that moves with a diurnal movement : while by the firmament made on the second day he understands the starry heaven. According to another theory, touched upon by Augustine,* the heaven made on the first day was the starry heaven, and the firmament made on the second day was that region of the air where the clouds are collected, which is also called heaven, but equivocally. And to show that the word is here used in an equivocal sense, it is expressly said that *God called the firmament heaven:* just as in a preceding verse it is said that *God called the light day* (since the word *day* is also

* *Gen. ad lit.* ii. 1.

WORK OF THE SECOND DAY Q 68. ART. 2

used to denote a space of twenty-four hours). Other instances of a similar use occur, as pointed out by Rabbi Moses.

The second and third objections are sufficiently answered by what has been already said.

SECOND ARTICLE.

WHETHER THERE ARE WATERS ABOVE THE FIRMAMENT?

We proceed thus to the Second Article:—

Objection 1. It would seem that there are not waters above the firmament. For water is heavy by nature, and heavy things tend naturally downwards, not upwards. Therefore there are not waters above the firmament.

Obj. 2. Further, water is fluid by nature, and fluids cannot rest on a sphere, as experience shows. Therefore, since the firmament is a sphere, there cannot be water above it.

Obj. 3. Further, water is an element, and appointed to the generation of composite bodies, according to the relation in which imperfect things stand towards perfect. But bodies of composite nature have their place upon the earth, and not above the firmament, so that water would be useless there. But none of God's works are useless. Therefore there are not waters above the firmament.

On the contrary, It is written (Gen. i. 7): *(God) divided the waters that were under the firmament, from those that were above the firmament.*

I answer with Augustine *(Gen. ad lit.* ii. 5) that, *These words of Scripture have more authority than the most exalted human intellect. Hence, whatever these waters are, and whatever their mode of existence, we cannot for a moment doubt that they are there.* As to the nature of these waters, all are not agreed. Origen says *(Hom.* i. *in Gen.)* that the waters that are above the firmament are *spiritual substances.* Wherefore it is written (Ps. cxlviii. 4): *Let the waters that are above the heavens praise the name of the Lord,* and (Dan. iii. 60): *Ye waters that are above the heavens, bless the Lord.* To this Basil answers (*Hom.* iii. *in Hexæm.*) that these words do not mean that these waters are rational creatures, but that *the thoughtful contemplation of them by those who understand fulfils the glory of the Creator.* Hence in the same context, fire, hail, and other like creatures, are invoked in the same way, though no one would attribute reason to these.

We must hold, then, these waters to be material, but their exact nature will be differently defined according as opinions on the firmament differ. For if by the firmament we understand the starry heaven, and as being of the nature of the four elements, for the same reason it may be believed that the waters above the heaven are of the same nature as the elemental waters. But if by firmament we understand the starry heaven, not, however, as being of the nature of the four elements, then the waters above the firmament will not be of the same nature as the elemental waters, but just as, according to Strabus, one heaven is called empyrean, that is, fiery, solely on account of its splendour: so this other heaven will be called aqueous solely on account of its transparence; and this heaven is above the starry heaven. Again, if the firmament is held to be of other nature than the elements, it may still be said to divide the waters, if we understand by water not the element but formless matter. Augustine, in fact, says (*Super Gen. cont. Manich.* i. 5, 7) that whatever divides bodies from bodies can be said to divide waters from waters.

If, however, we understand by the firmament that part of the air in which the clouds are collected, then the waters above the firmament must rather be the vapours resolved from the waters which are raised above a part of the atmosphere, and from which the rain falls. But to say, as some writers alluded to by Augustine (*Gen. ad lit.* ii. 4), that waters resolved into vapour may be lifted above the starry heaven, is a mere absurdity. The solid nature of the firmament, the intervening region of fire, wherein all vapour must be consumed, the tendency in light and rarefied bodies to drift to one spot beneath the vault of the moon, as well as the fact that vapours are perceived not to rise even to the tops of the higher mountains, all go to show the impossibility of this. Nor is it less absurd to say, in support of this opinion, that bodies may be rarefied infinitely, since natural bodies cannot be infinitely rarefied or divided, but up to a certain point only.

Reply Obj. 1. Some have attempted to solve this difficulty by supposing that in spite of the natural gravity of water, it is kept in its place above the firmament by the Divine power. Augustine (*Gen. ad lit.* ii. 1), however, will not admit this solution, but says, *It is our business here to inquire how God has constituted the natures of His creatures, not how far it may have pleased Him to work on them by way of miracle.* We leave this view, then, and answer that according to the last two opinions on the firmament and the waters the solution appears from what has been said. According to the first opinion, an order of the elements must be supposed different from that given by Aristotle, that is to say, that the waters surrounding the earth are of a dense consistency, and those around the firmament of a rarer consistency, in proportion to the respective density of the earth and of the heaven.

Or by the water, as stated, we may understand the matter of bodies to be signified.

Reply Obj. 2. The solution is clear from what has been said, according to the last two opinions. But according to the first opinion, Basil gives two replies (*Hom.* iii. *in Hexæm.*). He answers first, that a body seen as concave from beneath need not necessarily be rounded, or convex, above. Secondly, that the waters above the firmament are not fluid, but exist outside it in a solid state, as a mass of ice, and that this is the crystalline heaven of some writers.

Reply Obj. 3. According to the third opinion given, the waters above the firmament have been raised in the form of vapours, and serve to give rain to the earth. But according to the second opinion, they are above the heaven that is wholly transparent and starless. This, according to some, is the primary mobile, the cause of the daily revolution of the entire heaven, whereby the continuance of generation is secured. In the same way the starry heaven, by the zodiacal movement, is the cause whereby different bodies are generated or corrupted, through the rising and setting of the stars, and their various influences. But according to the first opinion these waters are set there to temper the heat of the celestial bodies, as Basil supposes (*loc. cit.*). And Augustine says (*Gen. ad lit.* ii. 5) that some have considered this to be proved by the extreme cold of Saturn owing to its nearness to the waters that are above the firmament.

THIRD ARTICLE.

WHETHER THE FIRMAMENT DIVIDES WATERS FROM WATERS?

We proceed thus to the Third Article:—

Objection 1. It would seem that the firmament does not divide waters from waters. For bodies that are of one and the same species have naturally one and the same place. But the Philosopher says (*Topic.* i. 6): *All water is the same in species.* Water therefore cannot be distinct from water by place.

Obj. 2. Further, should it be said that the waters above the firmament differ in species from those under the firmament, it may be argued, on the contrary, that things distinct in species need nothing else to distinguish them. If, then, these waters differ in species, it is not the firmament that distinguishes them.

Obj. 3. Further, it would appear that what distinguishes waters from waters must be something which is in contact with them on either side, as a wall standing in the midst of a river. But it is evident that the waters below do not reach up to the firmament. Therefore the firmament does not divide the waters from the waters.

WORK OF THE SECOND DAY   Q. 68. Art. 3

On the contrary, It is written (Gen. i. 6) : *Let there be a firmament made amidst the waters; and let it divide the waters from the waters.*

I answer that, The text of Genesis, considered superficially, might lead to the adoption of a theory similar to that held by certain philosophers of antiquity, who taught that water was a body infinite in dimension, and the primary element of all bodies. Thus in the words, *Darkness was upon the face of the deep,* the word *deep* might be taken to mean the infinite mass of water, understood as the principle of all other bodies. These philosophers also taught that not all corporeal things are confined beneath the heaven perceived by our senses, but that a body of water, infinite in extent, exists above that heaven. On this view the firmament of heaven might be said to divide the waters without from those within—that is to say, from all bodies under the heaven, since they took water to be the principle of them all.

As, however, this theory can be shown to be false by solid reasons, it cannot be held to be the sense of Holy Scripture. It should rather be considered that Moses was speaking to ignorant people, and that out of condescension to their weakness he put before them only such things as are apparent to sense. Now even the most uneducated can perceive by their senses that earth and water are corporeal, whereas it is not evident to all that air also is corporeal, for there have even been philosophers who said that air is nothing, and called a space filled with air a vacuum.

Moses, then, while. he expressly mentions water and earth, makes no express mention of air by name, to avoid setting before ignorant persons something beyond their knowledge. In order, however, to express the truth to those capable of understanding it, he implies in the words, *Darkness was upon the face of the deep,* the existence of air as attendant, so to say, upon the water. For it may be understood from these words that over the face of the water a transparent body was extended, the subject of light and darkness, which, in fact, is the air.

Whether, then, we understand by the firmament the starry heaven, or the cloudy region of the air, it is true to say that it divides the waters from the waters, according as we take water to denote formless matter, or any kind of transparent body as fittingly designated under the name of waters. For the starry heaven divides the lower transparent bodies from the higher, and the cloudy region divides that higher part of the air, where the rain and similar things are generated, from the lower part, which is connected with the water and included under that name.

Reply Obj. 1. If by the firmament is understood the starry heaven, the waters above are not of the same species as those beneath. But if by the firmament is understood the cloudy region of the air, both these waters are of the same species, and two places are assigned to them, though not for the same purpose, the higher being the place of their begetting, the lower, the place of their repose.

Reply Obj. 2. If the waters are held to differ in species, the firmament cannot be said to divide the waters, as the cause of their distinction, but only as the boundary of each.

Reply Obj. 3. On account of the air and other similar bodies being invisible, Moses includes all such bodies under the name of water, and thus it is evident that waters are found on each side of the firmament, whatever be the sense in which the word is used.

FOURTH ARTICLE.

WHETHER THERE IS ONLY ONE HEAVEN?

We proceed thus to the Fourth Article:—

Objection 1. It would seem that there is only one heaven. For the heaven is contrasted with the earth, in the words, *In the beginning God created heaven and earth.* But there is only one earth. Therefore there is only one heaven.

Obj. 2. Further, that which consists of the entire sum of its own matter, must be one; and such is the heaven, as the

Philosopher proves (*De Cœl.* i., text. 95). Therefore there is but one heaven.

Obj. 3. Further, whatever is predicated of many things univocally is predicated of them according to some common notion. But if there are more heavens than one, they are so called univocally, for if equivocally only, they could not properly be called many. If, then, they are many, there must be some common notion by reason of which each is called heaven, but this common notion cannot be assigned. Therefore there cannot be more than one heaven.

On the contrary, It is said (Ps. cxlviii. 4): *Praise Him, ye heavens of heavens.*

I answer that, On this point there seems to be a diversity of opinion between Basil and Chrysostom. The latter says that there is only one heaven (*Hom.* iv. *in Gen.*), and that the words *heavens of heavens* are merely the translation of the Hebrew idiom according to which the word is always used in the plural, just as in Latin there are many nouns that are wanting in the singular. On the other hand, Basil (*Hom.* iii. *in Hexæm.*), whom Damascene follows (*De Fid. Orth.* ii.), says that there are many heavens. The difference, however, is more nominal than real. For Chrysostom means by the one heaven the whole body that is above the earth and the water, for which reason the birds that fly in the air are called birds of heaven.* But since in this body there are many distinct parts, Basil said that there are more heavens than one.

In order, then, to understand the distinction of heavens, it must be borne in mind that Scripture speaks of heaven in a threefold sense. Sometimes it uses the word in its proper and natural meaning, when it denotes that body on high which is luminous actually or potentially, and incorruptible by nature. In this body there are three heavens; the first is the empyrean, which is wholly luminous; the second is the aqueous or crystalline, wholly transparent; and the third is called the starry heaven, in part transparent, and in part actually luminous, and divided into eight spheres. One of

* Ps. viii. 9.

these is the sphere of the fixed stars; the other seven, which may be called the seven heavens, are the spheres of the planets.

In the second place, the name heaven is applied to a body that participates in any property of the heavenly body, as sublimity and luminosity, actual or potential. Thus Damascene (*ibid.*) holds as one heaven all the space between the waters and the moon's orb, calling it the aerial. According to him, then, there are three heavens, the aerial, the starry, and one higher than both these, of which the Apostle is understood to speak when he says of himself that he was *rapt to the third heaven*.

But since this space contains two elements, namely, fire and air, and in each of these there is what is called a higher and a lower region, Rabanus subdivides this space into four distinct heavens. The higher region of fire he calls the fiery heaven; the lower, the Olympian heaven from a lofty mountain of that name: the higher region of air he calls, from its brightness, the ethereal heaven; the lower, the aerial. When, therefore, these four heavens are added to the three enumerated above, there are seven corporeal heavens in all, in the opinion of Rabanus.

Thirdly, there are metaphorical uses of the word heaven, as when this name is applied to the Blessed Trinity, Who is the Light and the Most High Spirit. It is explained by some, as thus applied, in the words, *I will ascend into heaven;* whereby the evil spirit is represented as seeking to make himself equal with God. Sometimes also spiritual blessings, the recompense of the Saints, from being the highest of all good gifts, are signified by the word heaven, and, in fact, are so signified, according to Augustine (*De Serm. Dom. in Monte*), in the words, *Your reward is very great in heaven* (Matt. v. 12).

Again, three kinds of supernatural visions, bodily, imaginative, and intellectual, are called sometimes so many heavens, in reference to which Augustine (*De Gen. ad lit.* xii.) expounds Paul's rapture *to the third heaven*.

Reply Obj. 1. The earth stands in relation to the heaven

as the centre of a circle to its circumference. But as one centre may have many circumferences, so, though there is but one earth, there may be many heavens.

Reply Obj. 2. The argument holds good as to the heaven, in so far as it denotes the entire sum of corporeal creation, for in that sense it is one.

Reply Obj. 3. All the heavens have in common sublimity and some degree of luminosity, as appears from what has been said.

QUESTION LXIX.

ON THE WORK OF THE THIRD DAY.
(*In Two Articles.*)

WE next consider the work of the third day. Under this head there are two points of inquiry : (1) About the gathering together of the waters. (2) About the production of plants.

FIRST ARTICLE.

WHETHER IT WAS FITTING THAT THE GATHERING TOGETHER OF THE WATERS SHOULD TAKE PLACE, AS RECORDED, ON THE THIRD DAY?

We proceed thus to the First Article:—

Objection 1. It would seem that it was not fitting that the gathering together of the waters should take place on the third day. For what was made on the first and second days is expressly said to have been *made* in the words, *God said: Be light made,* and *Let there be a firmament made.* But the third day is contradistinguished from the first and second days. Therefore the work of the third day should have been described as a making, not as a gathering together.

Obj. 2. Further, the earth hitherto had been completely covered by the waters, wherefore it was described as *invisible.** There was then no place on the earth to which the waters could be gathered together.

Obj. 3. Further, things which are not in continuous contact cannot occupy one place. But not all the waters are in continuous contact, and therefore all were not gathered together into one place.

Obj. 4. Further, a gathering together is a mode of local

* See Q. LXVI., A. 1., Obj. 1.

movement. But the waters flow naturally, and take their course towards the sea. In their case, therefore, a Divine precept of this kind was unnecessary.

Obj. 5. Further, the earth is given its name at its first creation by the words, *In the beginning God created heaven and earth.* Therefore the imposition of its name on the third day seems to be recorded without necessity.

On the contrary, The authority of Scripture suffices.

I answer that, It is necessary to reply differently to this question according to the different interpretations given by Augustine and other holy writers. In all these works, according to Augustine (*Gen. ad lit.* i. 15; iv. 22, 34; *De Gen. contr. Manich.* i. 5, 7), there is no order of duration, but only of origin and nature. He says that the formless spiritual and formless corporeal natures were created first of all, and that the latter are at first indicated by the words *earth* and *water.* Not that this formlessness preceded formation, in time, but only in origin; nor yet that one formation preceded another in duration, but merely in the order of nature. Agreeably, then, to this order, the formation of the highest or spiritual nature is recorded in the first place, where it is said that light was made on the first day. For as the spiritual nature is higher than the corporeal, so the higher bodies are nobler than the lower. Hence the formation of the higher bodies is indicated in the second place, by the words, *Let there be made a firmament,* by which is to be understood the impression of celestial forms on formless matter, that preceded with priority not of time, but of origin only. But in the third place the impression of elemental forms on formless matter is recorded, also with a priority of origin only. Therefore the words, *Let the waters be gathered together, and the dry land appear,* mean that corporeal matter was impressed with the substantial form of water, so as to have such movement, and with the substantial form of earth, so as to have such an appearance.

According, however, to other holy writers* an order of

* See Q. LXVI., A. 1.

duration in the works is to be understood, by which is meant that the formlessness of matter precedes its formation, and one form another, in order of time. Nevertheless, they do not hold that the formlessness of matter implies the total absence of form, since heaven, earth, and water already existed, since these three are named as already clearly perceptible to the senses; rather they understand by formlessness the want of due distinction and of perfect beauty, and in respect of these three Scripture mentions three kinds of formlessness. Heaven, the highest of them, was without form so long as *darkness* filled it, because it was the source of light. The formlessness of water, which holds the middle place, is called the *deep*, because, as Augustine says (*Contr. Faust.* xxii. 11), this word signifies the mass of waters without order. Thirdly, the formless state of the earth is touched upon when the earth is said to be *void* or *invisible,* because it was covered by the waters. Thus, then, the formation of the highest body took place on the first day. And since time results from the movement of the heaven, and is the numerical measure of the movement of the highest body, from this formation resulted the distinction of time, namely, that of night and day. On the second day the intermediate body, water, was formed, receiving from the firmament a sort of distinction and order (so that water be understood as including certain other things, as explained above, Q. LXVIII., A. 3). On the third day the earth, the lowest body, received its form by the withdrawal of the waters, and there resulted the distinction in the lowest body, namely, of land and sea. Hence Scripture, having clearly expressed the formless state of the earth, by saying that it was *invisible* or *void,* expresses the manner in which it received its form by the equally suitable words, *Let the dry land appear.*

Reply Obj. 1. According to Augustine,[*] Scripture does not say of the work of the third day, that it was made, as it says of those that precede, in order to show that higher and spiritual forms, such as the angels and the heavenly

[*] *Gen. ad lit.* ii. 7, 8; iii. 20.

WORK OF THE THIRD DAY Q. 69. ART. 1

bodies, are perfect and stable in being, whereas inferior forms are imperfect and mutable. Hence the impression of such forms is signified by the gathering of the waters, and the appearing of the land. For *water*, to use Augustine's words, *glides and flows away, the earth abides* (*Gen. ad lit.* ii. 11). Others, again, hold that the work of the third day was perfected on that day only as regards movement from place to place, and that for this reason Scripture had no reason to speak of it as made.

Reply Obj. 2. This argument is easily solved, according to Augustine's opinion (*De Gen. contr. Manich.* 1.), because we need not suppose that the earth was first covered by the waters, and that these were afterwards gathered together, but that they were produced in this very gathering together. But according to the other writers there are three solutions, which Augustine gives (*Gen. ad lit.* i. 12): The first supposes that the waters were heaped up to a greater height at the place where they were gathered together, for it has been proved in regard to the Red Sea that the sea is higher than the land, as Basil remarks (*Hom.* iv. *in Hexæm.*). The second explains the water that covered the earth as being rarefied or nebulous, which was afterwards condensed when the waters were gathered together. The third suggests the existence of hollows in the earth, to receive the confluence of waters. Of the above the first seems the most probable.

Reply Obj. 3. All the waters have the sea as their goal, into which they flow by channels hidden or apparent, and this may be the reason why they are said to be gathered together into one place. Or, *one place* is to be understood not simply, but as contrasted with the place of the dry land, so that the sense would be, *Let the waters be gathered together in one place*, that is, apart from the dry land. That the waters occupied more places than one seems to be implied by the words that follow, *The gathering together of the waters He called seas*.

Reply Obj. 4. The Divine command gives bodies their natural movement; and by these natural movements they are said to *fulfil His word*. Or we may say that it was according to the nature of water completely to cover the earth, just as the air completely surrounds both water and earth; but as a necessary means towards an end, namely, that plants and animals might be on the earth, it was necessary for the waters to be withdrawn from a portion of the earth. Some philosophers attribute this uncovering of the earth's surface to the action of the sun lifting up the vapours and thus drying the land. Scripture, however, attributes it to the Divine power, not only in the Book of Genesis, but also Job xxxviii. 10, where in the person of the Lord it is said, *I set My bounds around the sea,* and Jer. v. 22, where it is written : *Will you not then fear Me, saith the Lord, who have set the sand a bound for the sea?*

Reply Obj. 5. According to Augustine (*De Gen. contr. Manich.* i.), primary matter is meant by the word earth, where first mentioned, but in the present passage it is to be taken for the element itself. Again it may be said with Basil (*Hom.* iv. *in Hexæm.*), that the earth is mentioned in the first passage in respect of its nature, but here in respect of its principal property, namely, dryness. Wherefore it is written : *He called the dry land, Earth.* It may also be said with Rabbi Moses, that the expression, *He called,* denotes throughout an equivocal use of the name imposed. Thus we find it said at first that *He called the light day:* for the reason that later on a period of twenty-four hours is also called day, where it is said that *there was evening and morning, one day.* In like manner it is said that *the firmament,* that is, the air, *He called heaven;* for that which was first created was also called *heaven.* And here, again, it is said that *the dry land,* that is, the part from which the waters had withdrawn, *He called, Earth,* as distinct from the sea; although the name earth is equally applied to that which is covered with waters or not. So by the expression *He called* we are to understand throughout that the nature or property He bestowed corresponded to the name He gave.

WORK OF THE THIRD DAY

SECOND ARTICLE.

WHETHER IT WAS FITTING THAT THE PRODUCTION OF PLANTS SHOULD TAKE PLACE ON THE THIRD DAY?

We proceed thus to the Second Article:—

Objection 1. It would seem that it was not fitting that the production of plants should take place on the third day. For plants have life, as animals have. But the production of animals belongs to the work, not of distinction, but of adornment. Therefore the production of plants, as also belonging to the work of adornment, ought not to be recorded as taking place on the third day, which is devoted to the work of distinction.

Obj. 2. Further, a work by which the earth is accursed should have been recorded apart from the work by which it receives its form. But the words of Gen. iii. 17, *Cursed is the earth in thy work, thorns and thistles shall it bring forth to thee,* show that by the production of certain plants the earth was accursed. Therefore the production of plants in general should not have been recorded on the third day, which is concerned with the work of formation.

Obj. 3. Further, as plants are firmly fixed to the earth, so are stones and metals, which are, nevertheless, not mentioned in the work of formation. Plants, therefore, ought not to have been made on the third day.

On the contrary, It is said (Gen. i. 12): *The earth brought forth the green herb,* after which there follows, *The evening and the morning were the third day.*

I answer that, On the third day, as said (A. 1), the formless state of the earth comes to an end. But this state is described as twofold. On the other hand, the earth was *invisible* or *void*, being covered by the waters; on the other hand, it was *shapeless* or *empty*, that is, without that comeliness which it owes to the plants that clothe it, as it were, with a garment. Thus, therefore, in either respect this formless state ends on the third day: first, when *the waters were gathered together into one place and the dry land appeared;* secondly, when the *earth brought forth the green herb.* But concerning the production of plants, Augustine's opinion differs from that of others. For other commentators, in accordance with the surface meaning of the text, consider that the plants were produced in act in their various species, on this third day: whereas Augustine *(Gen. ad lit.* v. 5; viii. 3) says that the earth is said to have then produced plants and trees in their causes, that is, it received then the power to produce them. He supports this view by the authority of Scripture, for it is said (Gen. ii. 4, 5): *These are the generations of the heaven and the earth, when they were created, in the day that . . . God made the heaven and the earth, and every plant of the field before it sprung up in the earth, and every herb of the ground before it grew.* Therefore, the production of plants in their causes, within the earth, took place before they sprang up from the earth's surface. And this is confirmed by reason, as follows. In these first days God created all things in their origin or causes, and from this work He subsequently rested. Yet afterwards, by governing His creatures, in the work of propagation, *He worketh until now.* Now the production of plants from out the earth is a work of propagation, and therefore they were not produced in act on the third day, but in their causes only. However, in accordance with other writers, it may be said that the first constitution of species belongs to the work of the six days, but the reproduction among them of like from like, to the government of the universe. And Scripture indicates this in the words, *before it sprung up in the earth,* and *before it grew,* that is, before like was produced from like; just as now happens in the natural course by the production of seed. Wherefore Scripture says pointedly (Gen. i. 11): *Let the earth bring forth the green herb, and such as may seed,* as indicating the production of perfect species, from which the seed of others should arise. Nor does the question where the seminal power may reside, whether in root, stem, or fruit, affect the argument.

Reply Obj. 1. Life in plants is hidden, since they lack sense and local movement, by which the animate and the inanimate are chiefly discernible. And therefore, since they are firmly fixed in the earth, their production is treated as a part of the earth's formation.

Reply Obj. 2. Even before the earth was accursed, thorns and thistles had been produced, either virtually or actually. But they were not produced in punishment of man; as though the earth, which he tilled to gain his food, produced unfruitful and noxious plants. Hence it was said: " Shall it bring forth *to thee.*"

Reply Obj. 3. Moses put before the people such things only as were manifest to their senses, as we have said (QQ. LXVII., A. 4; LXVIII., A. 3). But minerals are generated in hidden ways within the bowels of the earth. Moreover, they seem hardly specifically distinct from earth, and would seem to be species thereof. For this reason, therefore, he makes no mention of them.

QUESTION LXX.

OF THE WORK OF ADORNMENT, AS REGARDS THE FOURTH DAY.

(In Three Articles.)

WE must next consider the work of adornment, first as to each day by itself, secondly as to all seven days in general.

In the first place, then, we consider the work of the fourth day, secondly that of the fifth day, thirdly that of the sixth day, and fourthly, such matters as belong to the seventh day.

Under the first head there are three points of inquiry: (1) As to the production of the lights? (2) As to the end of their production? (3) Whether they are living beings?

FIRST ARTICLE.

WHETHER THE LIGHTS OUGHT TO HAVE BEEN PRODUCED ON THE FOURTH DAY?

We proceed thus to the First Article:—

Objection 1. It would seem that the lights ought not to have been produced on the fourth day. For the heavenly luminaries are by nature incorruptible bodies: wherefore their matter cannot exist without their form. But as their matter was produced in the work of creation, before there was any day, so therefore were their forms. It follows, then, that the lights were not produced on the fourth day.

Obj. 2. Further, the luminaries are, as it were, vessels of light. But light was made on the first day. The luminaries, therefore, should have been made on the first day, not on the fourth.

Obj. 3. Further, the lights are fixed in the firmament,

as plants are fixed in the earth. For, the Scripture says: *He set them in the firmament.* But plants are described as produced when the earth, to which they are attached, received its form. The lights, therefore, should have been produced at the same time as the firmament, that is to say, on the second day.

Obj. 4. Further, plants are an effect of the sun, moon, and other heavenly bodies. Now, cause precedes effect in the order of nature. The lights, therefore, ought not to have been produced on the fourth day, but on the third or before.

Obj. 5. Further, as astronomers say, there are many stars larger than the moon. Therefore the sun and the moon alone are not correctly described as the *two great lights.*

On the contrary, Suffices the authority of Scripture.

I answer that, In recapitulating the Divine works, Scripture says (Gen. ii. 1) · *So the heavens and the earth were finished and all the furniture of them,* thereby indicating that the work was threefold. In the first work, that of *creation,* the heaven and the earth were produced, but as yet without form. In the second, or work of *distinction,* the heaven and the earth were perfected, either by adding substantial form to formless matter, as Augustine holds (*Gen. ad lit.* ii. 11), or by giving them the order and beauty due to them, as other holy writers suppose. To these two works is added the work of adornment, which is distinct from perfect For the perfection of the heaven and the earth regards, seemingly, those things that belong to them intrinsically, but the adornment, those that are extrinsic, just as the perfection of a man lies in his proper parts and forms, and his adornment, in clothing or such like. Now just as distinction of certain things is made most evident by their local movement, as separating one from another; so the work of adornment is set forth by the production of things having movement in the heavens, and upon the earth. But it has been stated above (Q. LXIX., A. 1), that three things are recorded as created, namely, the heaven, the water, and the earth; and these three received their form from the three days' work of distinction, so that heaven was formed on the first day; on the second day the waters were separated; and on the third, the earth was divided into sea and dry land. So also is it in the work of adornment; on the first day of this work, which is the fourth of creation, are produced the lights, to adorn the heaven by their movements; on the second day, which is the fifth, birds and fishes are called into being, to make beautiful the intermediate element, for they move in air and water, which are here taken as one; while on the third day, which is the sixth, animals are brought forth, to move upon the earth and adorn it. It must also here be noted that Augustine's opinion (*Gen. ad lit.* v. 5) on the production of the lights is not at variance with that of other holy writers, since he says that they were made actually, and not merely virtually, for the firmament has not the power of producing lights, as the earth has of producing plants. Wherefore Scripture does not say: *Let the firmament produce lights*, though it says: *Let the earth bring forth the green herb.*

Reply Obj. 1. In Augustine's opinion there is no difficulty here; for he does not hold a succession of time in these works, and so there was no need for the matter of the lights to exist under another form. Nor is there any difficulty in the opinion of those who hold the heavenly bodies to be of the nature of the four elements, for it may be said that they were formed out of matter already existing, as animals and plants were formed. For those, however, who hold the heavenly bodies to be of another nature from the elements, and naturally incorruptible, the answer must be that the lights were substantially created at the beginning, but that their substance, at first formless, is formed on this day, by receiving not its substantial form, but a determination of power. As to the fact that the lights are not mentioned *as* existing from the beginning, but only as made on the fourth day, Chrysostom (*Hom.* vi. *in Gen.*) explains this by the need of guarding the people from the danger of idolatry : since the lights are proved not to be gods, by the fact that they were not from the beginning.

Reply Obj. 2. No difficulty exists if we follow Augustine in holding the light made on the first day to be spiritual, and that made on this day to be corporeal. If, however, the light made on the first day is understood to be itself corporeal, then it must be held to have been produced on that day merely as light in general; and that on the fourth day the lights received a definite power to produce determinate effects. Thus we observe that the rays of the sun have one effect, those of the moon another, and so forth. Hence, speaking of such a determination of power, Dionysius (*De Div. Nom.* iv.) says that the sun's light which previously was without form, was formed on the fourth day.

Reply Obj. 3. According to Ptolemy the heavenly luminaries are not fixed in the spheres, but have their own movement distinct from the movement of the spheres. Wherefore Chrysostom says (*ibid.*) that He is said to have set them in the firmament, not because He fixed them there immovably, but because He bade them be there, even as He placed man in Paradise, to be there. In the opinion of Aristotle, however, the stars are fixed in their orbits, and in reality have no other movement but that of the spheres; and yet our senses perceive the movement of the luminaries and not that of the spheres (*De Cœl.* ii., text. 43). But Moses describes what is obvious to sense, out of condescension to popular ignorance, as we have already said (QQ. LXVII., A. 4; LXVIII., A. 3). The objection, however, falls to the ground if we regard the firmament made on the second day as having a natural distinction from that in which the stars are placed, even though the distinction is not apparent to the senses, the testimony of which Moses follows, as stated above (*ibid.*). For although to the senses there appears but one firmament; if we admit a higher and a lower firmament, the lower will be that which was made on the second day, and on the fourth the stars were fixed in the higher firmament.

Reply Obj. 4. In the words of Basil (*Hom.* v. *in*

Hexæm.), plants were recorded as produced before the sun and moon,·to prevent idolatry, since those who believe the heavenly bodies to be gods, hold that plants originate primarily from these bodies. Although as Chrysostom remarks (*Hom.* vi. *in Gen.*), the sun, moon, and stars co-operate in the work of production by their movements, as the husbandman co-operates by his labour.

Reply Obj. 5. As Chrysostom says, the two lights are called great, not so much with regard to their dimensions as to their influence and power. For though the stars be of greater bulk than the mnoo, yet the influence of the moon is more perceptible to the senses in this lower world. Moreover, as far as the senses are concerned, its apparent size is greater.

Second Article.

WHETHER THE CAUSE ASSIGNED FOR THE PRODUCTION OF THE LIGHTS IS REASONABLE?

We proceed thus to the Second Article:—

Objection 1. It would seem that the cause assigned for the production of the lights is not reasonable. For it is said (Jer. x. 2): *Be not afraid of the signs of heaven, which the heathens fear.* Therefore the heavenly lights were not made to be signs.

Obj. 2. Further, sign is contradistinguished from cause. But the lights are the cause of what takes place upon the earth. Therefore they are not signs.

Obj. 3. Further, the distinction of seasons and days began from the first day. Therefore the lights were not made *for seasons, and days, and years,* that is, in order to distinguish them.

Obj. 4. Further, nothing is made for the sake of that which is inferior to itself, *since the end is better than the means* (*Topic.* iii.). But the lights are nobler than the earth. Therefore they were not made *to enlighten it.*

Obj. 5. Further, the new moon cannot be said *to rule the night.* But such it probably did when first made; for men begin to count from the new moon. The moon, therefore, was not made to *rule the night.*

On the contrary, Suffices the authority of Scripture.

I answer that, As we have said above (Q. LXV., A. 2), a corporeal creature can be considered as made either for the sake of its proper act, or for other creatures, or for the whole universe, or for the glory of God. Of these reasons only that which points out the usefulness of these things to man, is touched upon by Moses, in order to withdraw his people from idolatry. Hence it is written (Deut. iv. 19): *Lest perhaps lifting up thy eyes to heaven, thou see the sun and the moon and all the stars of heaven, and being deceived by error thou adore and serve them, which the Lord thy God created for the service of all nations.* Now, he explains this service at the beginning of Genesis as threefold. First, the lights are of service to man, in regard to sight, which directs him in his works, and is most useful for perceiving objects. In reference to this he says: *Let them shine in the firmament and give life to the earth.* Secondly, as regards the changes of the seasons, which prevent weariness, preserve health, and provide for the necessities of food; all of which things could not be secured if it were always summer or winter. In reference to this he says: *Let them be for seasons, and for days, and years.* Thirdly, as regards the convenience of business and work, in so far as the lights are set in the heavens to indicate fair or foul weather, as favourable to various occupations. And in this respect he says: *Let them be for signs.*

Reply Obj. 1. The lights in the heaven are set for signs of changes effected in corporeal creatures, but not of those changes which depend upon the free-will.

Reply Obj. 2. We are sometimes brought to the knowledge of hidden effects through their sensible causes, and conversely. Hence nothing prevents a sensible cause from being a sign. But he says *signs,* rather than *causes,* to guard against idolatry.

Reply Obj. 3. The general division of time into day and

night took place on the first day, as regards the diurnal movement, which is common to the whole heaven and may be understood to have begun on that first day. But the particular distinctions of days and seasons and years, according as one day is hotter than another, one season than another, and one year than another, are due to certain particular movements of the stars : which movements may have had their beginning on the fourth day.

Reply Obj. 4. Light was given to the earth for the service of man, who, by reason of his soul, is nobler than the heavenly bodies. Nor is it untrue to say that a higher creature may be made for the sake of a lower, considered not in itself, but as ordained to the good of the universe.

Reply Obj. 5. When the moon is at its perfection it rises in the evening and sets in the morning, and thus it rules the night, and it was probably made in its full perfection as were plants yielding seed, as also were animals and man himself. For although the perfect is developed from the imperfect by natural processes, yet the perfect must exist simply before the imperfect. Augustine, however (*Gen ad lit.* ii.), does not say this, for he says that it is not unfitting that God made things imperfect, which He afterwards perfected.

Third Article.

WHETHER THE LIGHTS OF HEAVEN ARE LIVING BEINGS?

We proceed thus to the Third Article:—

Objection 1. It would seem that the lights of heaven are living beings. For the nobler a body is, the more nobly it should be adorned. But a body less noble than the heaven, is adorned with living beings, with fish, birds, and the beasts of the field. Therefore the lights of heaven, as pertaining to its adornment, should be living beings also.

Obj. 2. Further, the nobler a body is, the nobler must be its form. But the sun, moon, and stars are nobler bodies than plants or animals, and must therefore have nobler forms. Now the noblest of all forms is the soul, as being the first principle of life. Hence Augustine (*De Vera Relig.* xxix.) says: *Every living substance stands higher in the order of nature than one that has not life.* The lights of heaven, therefore, are living beings.

Obj. 3. Further, a cause is nobler than its effect. But the sun, moon, and stars are a cause of life, as is especially evidenced in the case of animals generated from putrefaction, which receive life from the power of the sun and stars. Much more, therefore, have the heavenly bodies a living soul.

Obj. 4. Further, the movements of the heaven and the heavenly bodies are natural (*De Cœlo.* i., text. 7, 8): and natural movement is from an intrinsic principle. Now the principle of movement in the heavenly bodies is a substance capable of apprehension, and is moved as the desirer is moved by the object desired (*Metaph.* xii., text. 36). Therefore, seemingly, the apprehending principle is intrinsic to the heavenly bodies: and consequently they are living beings.

Obj. 5. Further, the first of movables is the heaven. Now, of all things that are endowed with movement the first moves itself, as is proved in *Phys.* viii., text. 34, because, what is such of itself precedes that which is by another. But only beings that are living move themselves, as is shown in the same book (text. 27). Therefore the heavenly bodies are living beings.

On the contrary, Damascene says (*De Fid. Orth.* ii.), *Let no one esteem the heavens or the heavenly bodies to be living beings, for they have neither life nor sense.*

I answer that, Philosophers have differed on this question. Anaxagoras, for instance, as Augustine mentions (*De Civ. Dei* xviii. 41), *was condemned by the Athenians for teaching that the sun was a fiery mass of stone, and neither a god nor even a living being.* On the other hand, the Platonists held that the heavenly bodies have life. Nor was there less diversity of opinion among the Doctors of the Church. It was the belief of Origen (*Peri Archon* i.) and Jerome that these bodies were alive, and the latter seems to explain in that sense the words (Eccles. i. 6), *The spirit goeth forward, surveying all places round about*. But Basil (*Hom.* iii., vi. *in Hexæm.*) and Damascene (*loc. cit.*) maintain that the heavenly bodies are inanimate. Augustine leaves the matter in doubt, without committing himself to either theory, though he goes so far as to say that if the heavenly bodies are really living beings, their souls must be akin to the angelic nature (*Gen. ad lit.* ii. 18 and *Enchiridion* lviii.).

In examining the truth of this question, where such diversity of opinion exists, we shall do well to bear in mind that the union of soul and body exists for the sake of the soul and not of the body; for the form does not exist for the matter, but the matter for the form. Now the nature and power of the soul are apprehended through its operation, which is to a certain extent its end. Yet for some of these operations, as sensation and nutrition, our body is a necessary instrument. Hence it is clear that the sensitive and nutritive souls must be united to a body in order to exercise their functions. There are, however, operations of the soul, which are not exercised through the medium of the body, though the body ministers, as it were, to their production. The intellect, for example, makes use of the phantasms derived from the bodily senses, and thus far is dependent on the body, although capable of existing apart from it. It is not, however, possible that the functions of nutrition, growth, and generation, through which the nutritive soul operates, can be exercised by the heavenly bodies, for such operations are incompatible with a body naturally incorruptible. Equally impossible is it that the functions of the sensitive soul can appertain to the heavenly body, since all the senses depend on the sense of touch, which perceives elemental qualities, and all the organs of the senses require a certain proportion in the admixture of elements, whereas the nature of the heavenly bodies is not elemental. It follows, then, that of the operations of the soul the only ones left to be attributed to the heavenly bodies are those of understanding and moving; for appetite follows both sensitive and intellectual perception, and is in proportion thereto. But the operations of the intellect, which does not act through the body, do not need a body as their instrument, except to supply phantasms through the senses. Moreover, the operations of the sensitive soul, as we have seen, cannot be attributed to the heavenly bodies. Accordingly, the union of a soul to a heavenly body cannot be for the purpose of the operations of the intellect. It remains, then, only to consider whether the movement of the heavenly bodies demands a soul as the motive power, not that the soul, in order to move the heavenly body, need be united to the latter as its form; but by contact of power, as a mover is united to that which he moves. Wherefore Aristotle (*Phys.* viii., text. 42, 43), after showing that the first mover is made up of two parts, the moving and the moved, goes on to show the nature of the union between these two parts. This, he says, is effected by contact which is mutual if both are bodies; on the part of one only, if one is a body and the other not. The Platonists explain the union of soul and body in the same way, as a contact of a moving power with the object moved, and since Plato holds the heavenly bodies to be living beings, this means nothing else but that substances of spiritual nature are united to them, and act as their moving power. A proof that the heavenly bodies are moved by the direct influence and contact of some spiritual substance, and not, like bodies of specific gravity, by nature, lies in the fact that whereas nature moves to one fixed end which having attained, it rests; this does not appear in the movement of heavenly bodies. Hence it follows that they are moved by some intellectual substances. Augustine appears to be of the same opinion when he expresses his belief that all corporeal things are ruled by God through the spirit of life (*De Trin.* iii. 4).

From what has been said, then, it is clear that the heavenly bodies are not living beings in the same sense as plants and animals, and that if they are called so, it can only be equivocally. It will also be seen that the difference of opinion between those who affirm, and those who deny, that these bodies have life, is not a difference of things but of words.

Reply Obj. 1. Certain things belong to the adornment of the universe by reason of their proper movement; and in this way the heavenly luminaries agree with others that conduce to that adornment, for they are moved by a living substance.

Reply Obj. 2. One being may be nobler than another absolutely, but not in a particular respect. While, then, it is not conceded that the souls of heavenly bodies are nobler than the souls of animals absolutely, it must be conceded that they are superior to them with regard to their respective forms, since their form perfects their matter entirely, which is not in potentiality to other forms; whereas a soul does not do this. Also as regards movement the power that moves the heavenly bodies is of a nobler kind.

Reply Obj. 3. Since the heavenly body is a mover moved, it is of the nature of an instrument, which acts in virtue of the agent: and therefore since this agent is a living substance the heavenly body can impart life in virtue of that agent.

Reply Obj. 4. The movements of the heavenly bodies are natural, not on account of their active principle, but on account of their passive principle; that is to say, from a certain natural aptitude for being moved by an intelligent power.

Reply Obj. 5. The heaven is said to move itself in as far as it is compounded of mover and moved; not by the union of the mover, as the form, with the moved, as the matter, but by contact with the motive power, as we have said. So far, then, the principle that moves it may be called intrinsic, and consequently its movement natural with respect to that active principle; just as we say that voluntary movement is natural to the animal as animal (*Phys.* viii., text. 27).

QUESTION LXXI.

ON THE WORK OF THE FIFTH DAY.

(*In One Article.*)

WE must next consider the work of the fifth day.

Objection 1. It would seem that this work is not fittingly described. For the waters produce that which the power of water suffices to produce. But the power of water does not suffice for the production of every kind of fishes and birds since we find that many of them are generated from seed. Therefore the words, *Let the waters bring forth the creeping creature having life, and the fowl that may fly over the earth,* do not fittingly describe this work.

Obj. 2. Further, fishes and birds are not produced from water only, but earth seems to predominate over water in their composition, as is shown by the fact that their bodies tend naturally to the earth and rest upon it. It is not, then, fittingly said that fishes and birds are produced from water.

Obj. 3. Further, fishes move in the waters, and birds in the air. If, then, fishes are produced from the waters, birds ought to be produced from the air, and not from the waters.

Obj. 4. Further, not all fishes creep through the waters, for some, as seals, have feet and walk on land. Therefore the production of fishes is not sufficiently described by the words, *Let the waters bring forth the creeping creature having life.*

Obj. 5. Further, land animals are more perfect than birds and fishes, which appears from the fact that they have more distinct limbs, and generation of a higher order. For they bring forth living beings, whereas birds and fishes bring forth eggs. But the more perfect has precedence in the order of nature. Therefore fishes and birds ought not to have been produced on the fifth day, before land animals.

On the contrary, Suffices the authority of Scripture.

I answer that, As said above (Q. LXX., A. 1), the order of the work of adornment corresponds to the order of the work of distinction. Hence, as among the three days assigned to the work of distinction, the middle, or second, day is devoted to the work of the distinction of water, which is the intermediate body, so in the three days of the work of adornment, the middle day, which is the fifth, is assigned to the adornment of the intermediate body, by the production of birds and fishes. As, then, Moses makes mention of the lights and the light on the fourth day, to show that the fourth day corresponds to the first day on which he had said that the light was made, so on this fifth day he mentions the waters and the firmament of heaven to show that the fifth day corresponds to the second. It must, however, be observed that Augustine differs from other writers in his opinion about the production of fishes and birds, as he differs about the production of plants. For while others say that fishes and birds were produced on the fifth day actually, he holds that the nature of the waters produced them on that day potentially.

Reply Obj. 1. It was laid down by Avicenna that animals of all kinds can be generated by various minglings of the elements, and, naturally, without any kind of seed. This, however, seems repugnant to the fact that nature produces its effects by determinate means, and, consequently, those things that are naturally generated from seed cannot be generated naturally in any other way. It ought, then, rather to be said that in the natural generation of all animals that are generated from seed, the active principle lies in the formative power of the seed, but that in the case of animals generated from putrefaction, the formative power is the influence of the heavenly bodies. The material principle, however, in the generation of either kind of animals, is either some element, or something compounded of the elements. But at the first beginning of the world the active principle was the Word of God, which produced animals from material elements either in act, as some holy writers say, or virtually, as Augustine teaches. Not as though the power possessed by water or earth of producing all animals resides in the earth and water themselves, as Avicenna held, but in the power originally given to the elements of producing them from elemental matter by the power of seed or the influence of the stars.

Reply Obj. 2. The bodies of birds and fishes may be considered from two points of view. If considered in themselves, it will be evident that the earthly element must predominate, since the element that is least active, namely, the earth, must be the most abundant in quantity in order that the mingling may be duly tempered in the body of the animal. But if considered as by nature constituted to move with certain specific motions, thus they have some special affinity with the bodies in which they move; and hence the words in which their generation is described.

Reply Obj. 3. The air, as not being so apparent to the senses, is not enumerated by itself, but with other things: partly with the water, because the lower region of the air is thickened by watery exhalations; partly with the heaven as to the higher region. But birds move in the lower part of the air, and so are said to fly *beneath the firmament,* even if the firmament be taken to mean the region of clouds. Hence the production of birds is ascribed to the water.

Reply Obj. 4. Nature passes from one extreme to another through the medium; and therefore there are creatures of intermediate type between the animals of the air and those of the water, having something in common with both; and they are reckoned as belonging to that class to which they are most allied, through the characters possessed in common with that class, rather than with the other. But in order to include among fishes all such intermediate forms as have special characters like to theirs, the words, *Let the waters bring forth the creeping creature having life,* are followed by these: *God created great whales,* etc.

Reply Obj. 5. The order in which the production of these animals is given has reference to the order of those bodies which they are set to adorn, rather than to the superiority of the animals themselves. Moreover, in generation also the more perfect is reached through the less perfect.

QUESTION LXXII.

ON THE WORK OF THE SIXTH DAY.

(In One Article.)

WE must now consider the work of the sixth day.

Objection 1. It would seem that this work is not fittingly described. For as birds and fishes have a living soul, so also have land animals. But these animals are not themselves living souls. Therefore the words, *Let the earth bring forth the living creature,* should rather have been, *Let the earth bring forth the living fourfooted creatures.*

Obj. 2. Further, a genus ought not to be opposed to its species. But beasts and cattle are quadrupeds. Therefore quadrupeds ought not to be enumerated as a class with beasts and cattle.

Obj. 3. Further, as other animals belong to a determinate genus and species, so also does man. But in the making of man nothing is said of his genus and species, and therefore nothing ought to have been said about them in the production of other animals, whereas it is said *according to its genus* and *in its species.*

Obj. 4. Further, land animals are more like man, whom God is recorded to have blessed, than are birds and fishes. But as birds and fishes are said to be blessed, this should have been said, with much more reason, of the other animals as well.

Obj. 5. Further, certain animals are generated from putrefaction, which is a kind of corruption. But corruption is repugnant to the first founding of the world. Therefore such animals should not have been produced at that time.

Obj. 6. Further, certain animals are poisonous, and injurious to man. But there ought to have been nothing injurious to man before man sinned. Therefore such animals ought not to have been made by God at all, since He is the Author of good; or at least not until man had sinned.

On the contrary, Suffices the authority of Scripture.

I answer that, As on the fifth day the intermediate body, namely the water, is adorned, and thus that day corresponds to the second day; so the sixth day, on which the lowest body, or the earth, is adorned by the production of land animals, corresponds to the third day. Hence the earth is mentioned in both places. And here again Augustine says (*Gen. ad lit.,* v.) that the production was potential, and other holy writers that it was actual.

Reply Obj. 1. The different grades of life which are found in different living creatures can be discovered from the various ways in which the Scripture speaks of them, as Basil says (*Hom.* viii. *in Hexæm.*). The life of plants, for instance, is very imperfect and difficult to discern, and hence, in speaking of their production, nothing is said of their life, but only their generation is mentioned, since only in generation is a vital act observed in them. For the powers of nutrition and growth are subordinate to the generative life, as will be shown later on (Q. LXXVIII., A. 2). But amongst animals, those that live on land are, generally speaking, more perfect than birds and fishes, not because the fish is devoid of memory, as Basil upholds (*ibid.*) and Augustine rejects (*Gen. ad lit.* iii.), but because their limbs are more distinct and their generation of a higher order, (yet some imperfect animals, such as bees and ants, are more intelligent in certain ways). Scripture, therefore, does not call fishes *living creatures,* but *creeping creatures having life;* whereas it does call land animals *living creatures* on account of their more perfect life, and seems to imply that fishes are merely bodies having in them something of a soul, whilst land animals, from the higher perfection of their life, are, as it were, living souls with bodies subject to them. But the life of man, as being the most perfect grade, is not said to be produced, like the life of other animals, by the earth or water, but immediately by God.

Reply Obj. 2. By *cattle*, domestic animals are signified, which in any way are of service to man : but by *beasts*, wild animals such as bears and lions are designated. By *creeping things* those animals are meant which either have no feet and cannot rise from the earth, as serpents, or those whose feet are too short to lift them far from the ground, as the lizard and tortoise. But since certain animals, as deer and goats, seem to fall under none of these classes, the word *quadrupeds* is added. Or perhaps the word *quadruped* is used first as being the genus, to which the others are added as species, for even some reptiles, such as lizards and tortoises, are four-footed.

Reply Obj. 3. In other animals, and in plants, mention is made of genus and species, to denote the generation of like from like. But it was unnecessary to do so in the case of man, as what had already been said of other creatures might be understood of him. Again, animals and plants may be said to be produced according to their kinds, to signify their remoteness from the Divine image and likeness, whereas man is said to be made *to the image and likeness of God*.

Reply Obj. 4. The blessing of God gives power to multiply by generation, and, having been mentioned in the preceding account of the making of birds and fishes, could be understood of the beasts of the earth, without requiring to be repeated. The blessing, however, is repeated in the case of man, since in him generation of children has a special relation to the number of the elect,* and to prevent anyone from saying that there was any sin whatever in the act of begetting children. As to plants, since they experience neither desire of propagation, nor sensation in generating, they are deemed unworthy of a formal blessing.

Reply Obj. 5. Since the generation of one thing is the corruption of another, it was not incompatible with the first formation of things, that from the corruption of the

* *Cf.* Augustine, *Gen. ad lit.* iii. 12.

less perfect the more perfect should be generated. Hence animals generated from the corruption of inanimate things, or of plants, may have been generated then. But those generated from corruption of animals could not have been produced then otherwise than potentially.

Reply Obj. 6. In the words of Augustine (*Super. Gen. contr. Manich.* i.): *If an unskilled person enters the workshop of an artificer he sees in it many appliances of which he does not understand the use, and which, if he is a foolish fellow, he considers unnecessary. Moreover, should he carelessly fall into the fire, or wound himself with a sharp-edged tool, he is under the impression that many of the things there are hurtful; whereas the craftsman, knowing their use, laughs at his folly. And thus some people presume to find fault with many things in this world, through not seeing the reasons for their existence. For though not required for the furnishing of our house, these things are necessary for the perfection of the universe.* And, since man before he sinned would have used the things of this world conformably to the order designed, poisonous animals would not have injured him.

QUESTION LXXIII.

ON THE THINGS THAT BELONG TO THE SEVENTH DAY.

(*In Three Articles.*)

WE must next consider the things that belong to the seventh day. Under this head there are three points of inquiry : (1) About the completion of the works. (2) About the resting of God. (3) About the blessing and sanctifying of this day.

FIRST ARTICLE.

WHETHER THE COMPLETION OF THE DIVINE WORKS OUGHT TO BE ASCRIBED TO THE SEVENTH DAY?

We proceed thus to the First Article:—

Objection 1. It would seem that the completion of the Divine works ought not to be ascribed to the seventh day. For all things that are done in this world belong to the Divine works. But the consummation of the world will be at the end of the world (Matth. xiii. 39, 40). Moreover, the time of Christ's Incarnation is a time of completion, wherefore it is called *the time of fulness** (Gal. iv. 4). And Christ Himself, at the moment of His death, cried out, *It is consummated* (Jo. xix. 30). Hence the completion of the Divine works does not belong to the seventh day.

, *Obj.* 2. Further, the completion of a work is an act in itself. But we do not read that God acted at all on the seventh day, but rather that He rested from all His work. Therefore the completion of the works does not belong to the seventh day.

Obj. 3. Further, nothing is said to be complete to which

* Vulg , *the fulness of time*

many things are added, unless they are merely superfluous, for a thing is called perfect to which nothing is wanting that it ought to possess. But many things were made after the seventh day, as the production of many individual beings, and even of certain new species that are frequently appearing, especially in the case of animals generated from putrefaction. Also, God creates daily new souls. Again, the work of the Incarnation was a new work, of which it is said (Jer. xxxi. 22): *The Lord hath created a new thing upon the earth.* Miracles also are new works, of which it is said (Eccles. xxxvi. 6): *Renew thy signs, and work new miracles.* Moreover, all things will be made new when the Saints are glorified, according to Apoc. xxi. 5: *And He that sat on the throne said: Behold I make all things new.* Therefore the completion of the Divine works ought not to be attributed to the seventh day.

On the contrary, It is said (Gen. ii. 2): *On the seventh day God ended His work which he had made.*

I answer that, The perfection of a thing is twofold, the first perfection and the second perfection. The *first* perfection is that according to which a thing is substantially perfect, and this perfection is the form of the whole; which form results from the whole having its parts complete. But the *second* perfection is the end, which is either an operation, as the end of the harpist is to play the harp; or something that is attained by an operation, as the end of the builder is the house that he makes by building. But the first perfection is the cause of the second, because the form is the principle of operation. Now the final perfection, which is the end of the whole universe, is the perfect beatitude of the Saints at the consummation of the world; and the first perfection is the completeness of the universe at its first founding, and this is what is ascribed to the seventh day.

Reply Obj. 1. The first perfection is the cause of the second, as above said. Now, for the attaining of beatitude two things are required, nature and grace. Therefore, as said above, the perfection of beatitude will be at the end of the world. But this consummation existed previously in its causes, as to nature, at the first founding of the world, as to grace, in the Incarnation of Christ. For, *Grace and truth came by Jesus Christ* (Jo. i. 17). So, then, on the seventh day was the consummation of nature, in Christ's Incarnation the consummation of grace, and at the end of the world will be the consummation of glory.

Reply Obj. 2. God did act on the seventh day, not by creating new creatures, but by directing and moving His creatures to the work proper to them, and thus He made some beginning of the *second* perfection. So that, according to our version of the Scripture, the completion of the works is attributed to the seventh day, though according to another it is assigned to the sixth. Either version, however, may stand, since the completion of the universe as to the completeness of its parts belongs to the sixth day, but its completion as regards their operation, to the seventh. It may also be added that in continuous movement, so long as any movement further is possible, movement cannot be called completed till it comes to rest, for rest denotes consummation of movement. Now God might have made many other creatures besides those which He made in the six days, and hence, by the fact that He ceased making them on the seventh day, He is said on that day to have consummated His work.

Reply Obj. 3. Nothing entirely new was afterwards made by God, but all things subsequently made had in a sense been made before in the work of the six days. Some things, indeed, had a previous existence materially, as the rib from the side of Adam out of which God formed Eve; whilst others existed not only in matter but also in their causes, as those individual creatures that are now generated existed in the first of their kind. Species, also, that are new, if any such appear, existed beforehand in various active powers; so that animals, and perhaps even new species of animals, are produced by putrefaction by the power which the stars and elements received at the beginning. Again, animals of new kinds arise occasionally from the connection of individuals belonging to different species, as the mule is the offspring of an ass and a mare; but even these existed previously in their causes, in the works of the six days. Some also existed beforehand by way of similitude, as the souls now created. And the work of the Incarnation itself was thus foreshadowed, for as we read (Philip. ii. 7), *The Son of God was made in the likeness of men.* And again, the glory that is spiritual was anticipated in the angels by way of similitude; and that of the body in the heaven, especially the empyrean. Hence it is written (Eccles. i. 10), *Nothing under the sun is new, for it hath already gone before, in the ages that were before us.*

Second Article.

WHETHER GOD RESTED ON THE SEVENTH DAY FROM ALL HIS WORK?

We proceed thus to the Second Article:—

Objection 1. It would seem that God did not rest on the seventh day from all His work. For it is said (Jo. v. 17), *My Father worketh until now, and I work.* God, then, did not rest on the seventh day from all His works.

Obj. 2. Further, rest is opposed to movement, or to labour, which movement causes. But, as God produced His work without movement and without labour, He cannot be said to have rested on the seventh day from His work.

Obj. 3. Further, should it be said that God rested on the seventh day by causing man to rest; against this it may be argued that rest is set down in contradistinction to His work; now the words *God created* or *made* this thing or the other cannot be explained to mean that He made man create or make these things. Therefore the resting of God cannot be explained as His making man to rest.

On the contrary, It is said (Gen. ii. 2) : *God rested on the seventh day from all the work which He had done.*

I answer that, Rest is, properly speaking, opposed to

movement, and consequently to the labour that arises from movement. But although movement, strictly speaking, is a quality of bodies, yet the word is applied also to spiritual things, and in a twofold sense. On the one hand, every operation may be called a movement, and thus the Divine goodness is said to move and go forth to its object, in communicating itself to that object, as Dionysius says (*De Div. Nom.* ii.). On the other hand, the desire that tends to an object outside itself, is said to move towards it. Hence rest is taken in two senses, in one sense meaning a cessation from work, in the other, the satisfying of desire. Now, in either sense God is said to have rested on the seventh day. First, because He ceased from creating new creatures on that day, for, as said above (A. 1 *ad* 3), He made nothing afterwards that had not existed previously, in some degree, in the first works; secondly, because He Himself had no need of the things that He had made, but was happy in the fruition of Himself. Hence, when all things were made He is not said to have rested *in* His works, as though needing them for His own happiness, but to have rested *from* them, as in fact resting in Himself, as He suffices for Himself and fulfils His own desire. And even though from all eternity He rested in Himself, yet the rest in Himself, which He took after He had finished His works, is that rest which belongs to the seventh day. And this, says Augustine, is the meaning of God's resting from His works on that day (*Gen. ad lit.* iv.).

Reply Obj. 1. God indeed *worketh until now* by preserving and providing for the creatures He has made, but not by the making of new ones.

Reply Obj. 2. Rest is here not opposed to labour or to movement, but to the production of new creatures and to the desire tending to an external object.

Reply Obj. 3. Even as God rests in Himself alone and is happy in the enjoyment of Himself, so our own sole happiness lies in the enjoyment of God. Thus, also, He makes us find rest in Himself both from His works and our own. It is not, then, unreasonable to say that God rested in giving rest to us. Still, this explanation must not be set down as the only one, and the other is the first and principal explanation.

Third Article.

WHETHER BLESSING AND SANCTIFYING ARE DUE TO THE SEVENTH DAY?

We proceed thus to the Third Article:—

Objection 1. It would seem that blessing and sanctifying are not due to the seventh day. For it is usual to call a time blessed or holy for that some good thing has happened in it, or some evil been avoided. But whether God works or ceases from work nothing accrues to Him or is lost to Him. Therefore no special blessing nor sanctifying are due to the seventh day.

Obj. 2. Further, the Latin *benedictio* (blessing) is derived from *bonitas* (goodness). But it is the nature of good to spread and communicate itself, as Dionysius says (*De Div. Nom.* iv.). The days, therefore, in which God produced creatures deserved a blessing rather than the day on which He ceased producing them.

Obj. 3. Further, over each creature a blessing was pronounced, as upon each work it was said, *God saw that it was good.* Therefore it was not necessary that after all had been produced, the seventh day should be blessed.

On the contrary, It is written (Gen. ii. 3), *God blessed the seventh day and sanctified it, because in it He had rested from all His work.*

I answer that, as said above (A. 2), God's rest on the seventh day is understood in two ways. First, in that He ceased from producing new works, though He still preserves and provides for the creatures He has made. Secondly, in that after all His works He rested in Himself. According to the first meaning, then, a blessing befits the seventh day, since, as we explained (Q. LXXII . *ad* 4), the blessing referred to the increase by multiplication; for which reason God said to the creatures which He blessed : *Increase and multiply*. Now, this increase is effected through God's Providence over His creatures, securing the generation of like from like. And according to the second meaning, it is right that the seventh day should have been sanctified, since the special sanctification of every creature consists in resting in God. For this reason things dedicated to God are said to be sanctified.

Reply Obj. 1. The seventh day is said to be sanctified not because anything can accrue to God, or be taken from Him, but because something is added to creatures by their multiplying, and by their resting in God.

Reply Obj. 2. In the first six days creatures were produced in their first causes, but after being thus produced, they are multiplied and preserved, and this work also belongs to the Divine goodness. And the perfection of this goodness is made most clear by the knowledge that in it alone God finds His own rest, and we may find ours in its fruition.

Reply Obj. 3. The good mentioned in the works of each day belongs to the first institution of nature; but the blessing attached to the seventh day, to its propagation.

QUESTION LXXIV.

ON ALL THE SEVEN DAYS IN COMMON.
(In Three Articles.)

WE next consider all the seven days in common: and there are three points of inquiry : (1) As to the sufficiency of these days. (2) Whether they are all one day, or more than one? (3) As to certain modes of speaking which Scripture uses in narrating the works of the six days.

FIRST ARTICLE.

WHETHER THESE DAYS ARE SUFFICIENTLY ENUMERATED?

We proceed thus to the First Article:—

Objection 1. It would seem that these days are not sufficiently enumerated. For the work of creation is no less distinct from the works of distinction and adornment than these two works are from one another. But separate days are assigned to distinction and to adornment, and therefore separate days should be assigned to creation.

Obj. 2. Further, air and fire are nobler elements than earth and water. But one day is assigned to the distinction of water, and another to the distinction of the land. Therefore, other days ought to be devoted to the distinction of fire and air.

Obj. 3. Further, fish differ from birds as much as birds differ from the beasts of the earth, whereas man differs more from other animals than all animals whatsoever differ from each other. But one day is devoted to the production of fishes, and another to that of the beasts of the earth. Another day, then, ought to be assigned to the production of birds, and another to that of man.

Obj. 4. Further, it would seem, on the other hand, that

some of the days are superfluous. Light, for instance, stands to the luminaries in the relation of accident to subject. But the subject is produced at the same time as the accident proper to it. The light and the luminaries, therefore, ought not to have been produced on different days.

Obj. 5. Further, these days are devoted to the first instituting of the world. But as on the seventh day nothing was instituted, that day ought not to be enumerated with the others.

I answer that, The reason of the distinction of these days is made clear by what has been said above (Q. LXX., A. 1), namely, that the parts of the world had first to be distinguished, and then each part adorned and filled, as it were, by the beings that inhabit it. Now the parts into which the corporeal creation is divided are three, according to some holy writers, these parts being the heaven, or highest part, the water, or middle part, and the earth, or lowest part. Thus the Pythagoreans teach that perfection consists in three things, the beginning, the middle, and the end. The first part, then, is distinguished on the first day, and adorned on the fourth, the middle part distinguished on the middle day, and adorned on the fifth, and the third part distinguished on the third day, and adorned on the sixth. But Augustine, while agreeing with the above writers as to the last three days, differs as to the first three, for, according to him, spiritual creatures are formed on the first day, and corporeal on the two others, the higher bodies being formed on the first of these two days, and the lower on the second. Thus, then, the perfection of the Divine works corresponds to the perfection of the number six, which is the sum of its aliquot parts, one, two, three, since one day is assigned to the forming of spiritual creatures, two to that of corporeal creatures, and three to the work of adornment.

Reply Obj. 1. According to Augustine, the work of creation belongs to the production of formless matter, and of the formless spiritual nature, both of which are outside of time, as he himself says (*Conf.* xii. 12). Thus, then, the creation of either is set down before there was any day. But it may also be said, following other holy writers, that the works of distinction and adornment imply certain changes in the creature which are measurable by time; whereas the work of creation lies only in the Divine act producing the substance of beings instantaneously. For this reason, therefore, every work of distinction and adornment is said to take place *in a day*, but creation *in the beginning* which denotes something indivisible.

Reply Obj. 2. Fire and air, as not distinctly known by the unlettered, are not expressly named by Moses among the parts of the world, but reckoned with the intermediate part, or water, especially as regards the lowest part of the air; or with the heaven, to which the higher region of air approaches, as Augustine says (*Gen. ad lit.* ii. 13).

Reply Obj. 3. The production of animals is recorded with reference to their adorning the various parts of the world, and therefore the days of their production are separated or united according as the animals adorn the same parts of the world, or different parts.

Reply Obj. 4. The nature of light, as existing in a subject, was made on the first day; and the making of the luminaries on the fourth day does not mean that their substance was produced anew, but that they then received a form that they had not before, as said above (Q. LXX., A. 1 *ad* 2).

Reply Obj. 5. According to Augustine (*Gen. ad lit.* iv. 15), after all that has been recorded that is assigned to the six days, something distinct is attributed to the seventh,—namely, that on it God rested in Himself from His works: and for this reason it was right that the seventh day should be mentioned after the six. It may also be said, with the other writers, that the world entered on the seventh day upon a new state, in that nothing new was to be added to it, and that therefore the seventh day is mentioned after the six, from its being devoted to cessation from work.

SECOND ARTICLE.

WHETHER ALL THESE DAYS ARE ONE DAY?

We proceed thus to the Second Article:—

Objection 1. It would seem that all these days are one day. For it is written (Gen. ii. 4, 5): *These are the generations of the heaven and the earth, when they were created, in the day that the Lord . . . made the heaven and the earth, and every plant of the field, before it sprung up in the earth.* Therefore the day in which God made *the heaven and the earth, and every plant of the field,* is one and the same day. But He made the heaven and the earth on the first day, or rather before there was any day, but the plant of the field He made on the third day. Therefore the first and third days are but one day, and for a like reason all the rest.

Obj. 2. Further, it is said (Ecclus. xviii. 1): *He that liveth for ever, created all things together.* But this would not be the case if the days of these works were more than one. Therefore they are not many but one only.

Obj. 3. Further, on the seventh day God ceased from all new works. If, then, the seventh day is distinct from the other days, it follows that He did not make that day; which is not admissible.

Obj. 4. Further, the entire work ascribed to one day God perfected in an instant, for with each work are the words *(God) said, . . . and it was . . . done.* If, then, He had kept back His next work to another day, it would follow that for the remainder of a day He would have ceased from working and left it vacant, which would be superfluous. The day, therefore, of the preceding work is one with the day of the work that follows.

On the contrary, It is written (Gen. i.), *The evening and the morning were the second day . . . the third day,* and so on. But where there is second and third there are more than one. There was not, therefore, only one day.

I answer that, On this question Augustine differs from other expositors. His opinion is that all the days that are called seven, are one day represented in a sevenfold aspect (*Gen ad lit.* iv. 22; *De Civ. Dei* xi. 9; *Ad Orosium* xxvi.); while others consider there were seven distinct days, and not one only. Now, these two opinions, taken as explaining the literal text of Genesis, are certainly widely different. For Augustine understands by the word *day,* the knowledge in the mind of the angels, and hence, according to him, the first day denotes their knowledge of the first of the Divine works, the second day their knowledge of the second work, and similarly with the rest. Thus, then, each work is said to have been wrought in some one of these days, inasmuch as God wrought nothing in the universe without impressing the knowledge thereof on the angelic mind; which can know many things at the same time, especially in the Word, in Whom all angelic knowledge is perfected and terminated. So the distinction of days denotes the natural order of the things known, and not a succession in the knowledge acquired, or in the things produced. Moreover, angelic knowledge is appropriately called *day,* since light, the cause of day, is to be found in spiritual things, as Augustine observes (*Gen. ad lit.* iv. 28). In the opinion of the others, however, the days signify a succession both in time, and in the things produced.

If, however, these two explanations are looked at as referring to the mode of production, they will be found not greatly to differ, if the diversity of opinion existing on two points, as already shown (QQ. LXVII., A. 1; LXIX., A. 1), between Augustine and other writers is taken into account. First, because Augustine takes the earth and the water, as first created, to signify matter totally without form; but the making of the firmament, the gathering of the waters, and the appearing of dry land, to denote the impression of forms upon corporeal matter. But other holy writers take the earth and the water, as first created, to signify the elements of the universe themselves existing under their proper forms, and the works that follow to mean some sort of distinction in bodies previously existing, as also has been shown (QQ. LXVII., AA. 1, 4; LXIX., A. 1). Secondly, some writers hold that plants and animals were produced actually in the work of the six days; Augustine, that they were produced potentially. Now the opinion of Augustine, that the works of the six days were simultaneous, is consistent with either view of the mode of production. For the other writers agree with him that in the first production of things matter existed under the substantial form of the elements, and agree with him also that in the first instituting of the world animals and plants did not exist actually. There remains, however, a difference as to four points; since, according to the latter, there was a time, after the production of creatures, in which light did not exist, the firmament had not been formed, and the earth was still covered by the waters, nor had the heavenly bodies been formed, which is the fourth difference, which are not consistent with Augustine's explanation. In order, therefore, to be impartial, we must meet the arguments of either side.

Reply Obj. 1. On the day on which God created the heaven and the earth, He created also every plant of the field, not, indeed, actually, but *before it sprung up in the earth*, that is, potentially. And this work Augustine ascribes to the third day, but other writers to the first instituting of the world.

Reply Obj. 2. God created all things together so far as regards their substance in some measure formless. But He did not create all things together, so far as regards that formation of things which lies in distinction and adornment. Hence the word *creation* is significant.

Reply Obj. 3. On the seventh day God ceased from making new beings, but not from providing for their increase, and to this latter work it belongs that the first day is succeeded by other days.

Reply Obj. 4. All things were not distinguished and adorned together, not from a want of power on God's part, as requiring time in which to work, but that due order might be observed in the instituting of the world. Hence it was fitting that different days should be assigned to the different states of the world, as each succeeding work added to the world a fresh state of perfection.

Reply Obj. 5. According to Augustine, the order of days refers to the natural order of the works attributed to the days.

THIRD ARTICLE.

WHETHER SCRIPTURE USES SUITABLE WORDS TO EXPRESS THE WORK OF THE SIX DAYS?

We proceed thus to the Third Article:—
Objection 1. It would seem that Scripture does not use suitable words to express the works of the six days. For as light, the firmament, and other similar works were made by the Word of God, so were the heaven and the earth. For *all things were made by Him* (Jo. i. 3). Therefore in the creation of heaven and earth, as in the other works, mention should have been made of the Word of God.

Obj. 2. Further, the water was created by God, yet its creation is not mentioned. Therefore the creation of the world is not sufficiently described.

Obj. 3. Further, it is said (Gen. i. 31): *God saw all the things that He had made, and they were very good.* It ought, then, to have been said of each work, *God saw that it was good.* The omission, therefore, of these words in the work of creation and in that of the second day, is not fitting.

Obj. 4. Further, the Spirit of God is God Himself. But it does not befit God to move and to occupy place. Therefore the words, *The Spirit of God moved over the waters,* are unbecoming.

Obj. 5. Further, what is already made is not made over again. Therefore to the words, *God said: Let the firmament be made . . . and it was so,* it is superfluous to add, *God made the firmament.* And the like is to be said of other works.

Obj. 6. Further, evening and morning do not sufficiently divide the day, since the day has many parts. Therefore the words, *The evening and morning were the second day* or, *the third day*, are not suitable.

Obj. 7. Further, *first*, not *one*, corresponds to *second* and *third*. It should therefore have been said that, *The evening and the morning were the first day*, rather than *one day*.

Reply Obj. 1. According to Augustine (*Gen. ad lit.* i. 4), the person of the Son is mentioned both in the first creation of the world, and in its distinction and adornment, but differently in either place. For distinction and adornment belong to the work by which the world receives its form. But as the giving form to a work of art is by means of the form of the art in the mind of the artist, which may be called his intelligible word, so the giving form to every creature is by the word of God; and for this reason in the works of distinction and adornment the Word is mentioned. But in creation the Son is mentioned as the beginning, by the words, *In the beginning God created*, since by creation is understood the production of formless matter. But according to those who hold that the elements were created from the first under their proper forms, another explanation must be given; and therefore Basil says (*Hom.* ii. and iii. *in Hexæm.*) that the words, *God said*, signify a Divine command. Such a command, however, could not have been given before creatures had been produced that could obey it.

Reply Obj. 2. According to Augustine (*De Civ. Dei* ix. 33), by the heaven is understood the formless spiritual nature, and by the earth, the formless matter of all corporeal things, and thus no creature is omitted. But, according to Basil (*Hom.* i. *in Hexæm.*), the heaven and the earth, as the two extremes, are alone mentioned, the intervening things being left to be understood, since all these move heavenwards, if light, or earthwards, if heavy. And others say that under the word, *earth*, Scripture is accustomed to include all the four elements, as

(Ps. cxlviii. 7, 8) after the words, *Praise the Lord from the earth*, is added, *fire, hail, snow, and ice*.

Reply Obj. 3. In the account of the creation there is found something to correspond to the words, *God saw that it was good*, used in the work of distinction and adornment, and this appears from the consideration that the Holy Spirit is Love. Now, *there are two things*, says Augustine (*Gen. ad lit.* i. 8) which came from God's love of His creatures, their existence and their permanence. That they might then exist, and exist permanently, *the Spirit of God*, it is said, *moved over the waters*—that is to say, over that formless matter, signified by water, even as the love of the artist moves over the materials of his art, that out of them he may form his work. And the words, *God saw that it was good*, signify that the things that He had made were to endure, since they express a certain satisfaction taken by God in His works, as of an artist in his art : not as though He knew the creature otherwise, or that the creature was pleasing to Him otherwise, than before He made it. Thus in either work, of creation and of formation, the Trinity of Persons is implied. In creation the Person of the Father is indicated by God the Creator, the Person of the Son by the beginning, in which He created, and the Person of the Holy Ghost by the Spirit that moved over the waters. But in the formation, the Person of the Father is indicated by God that speaks, the Person of the Son by the Word in Which He speaks, and the Person of the Holy Spirit by the satisfaction with which God saw that what was made was good. And if the words, *God saw that it was good*, are not said of the work of the second day, this is because the work of distinguishing the waters was only begun on that day, but perfected on the third. Hence these words, that are said of the third day, refer also to the second. Or it may be that Scripture does not use these words of approval of the second day's work, because this is concerned with the distinction of things not evident to the senses of mankind. Or, again, because by the firmament is simply understood the cloudy region of the air, which is not one of the

273 THE SEVEN DAYS IN COMMON Q. 74 ART. 3

permanent parts of the universe, nor of the principal divisions of the world. The above three reasons are given by Rabbi Moses,* and to these may be added a mystical one derived from numbers and assigned by some writers, according to whom the work of the second day is not marked with approval because the second number is an imperfect number, as receding from the perfection of unity.

Reply Obj. 4. Rabbi Moses (*ibid.*) understands by the *Spirit of the Lord,* the air or the wind, as Plato also did, and says that it is so called according to the custom of Scripture, in which these things are throughout attributed to God. But according to the holy writers, the Spirit of the Lord signifies the Holy Ghost, Who is said to *move over the water*—that is to say, over what Augustine holds to mean formless matter, lest it should be supposed that God loved of necessity the works He was to produce, as though He stood in need of them. For love of that kind is subject to, not superior to, the object of love. Moreover, it is fittingly implied that the Spirit moved over that which was incomplete and unfinished, since that movement is not one of place, but of pre-eminent power, as Augustine says (*Gen. ad lit.* i. 7). It is the opinion, however, of Basil (*Hom.* ii. *in Hexæm.*) that the Spirit moved over the element of water, *fostering and quickening its nature and impressing vital power, as the hen broods over her chickens.* For water has especially a life-giving power, since many animals are generated in water, and the seed of all animals is liquid. Also the life of the soul is given by the water of baptism, according to Jo. iii. 5 : *Unless a man be born again of water and the Holy Ghost, he cannot enter into the kingdom of God.*

Reply Obj. 5. According to Augustine (*Gen. ad lit.* i. 8), these three phrases denote the threefold being of creatures; first, their being in the Word, denoted by the command *Let . . . be made;* secondly, their being in the angelic mind, signified by the words, *It was . . . done;* thirdly, their being in their proper nature, by the words *He made.* And be-

* *Perplex.* ii.

cause the formation of the angels is recorded on the first day, it was not necessary there to add, *He made.* It may also be said, following other writers, that the words, *He said,* and, *Let . . . be made,* denote God's command, and the words, *It was done,* the fulfilment of that command. But as it was necessary, for the sake of those especially who have asserted that all visible things were made by the angels, to mention how things were made, it is added, in order to remove that error, that God Himself made them. Hence, in each work, after the words, *It was done,* some act of God is expressed by some such words as, *He made,* or, *He divided,* or, *He called.*

Reply Obj. 6. According to Augustine (*Gen. ad lit.* iv. 22, 30), by the *evening* and the *morning* are understood the evening and the morning knowledge of the angels, which has been explained (Q. LVIII., A. 6, 7). But, according to Basil (*Hom.* ii. *in Hexæm.*), the entire period takes its name, as is customary, from its more important part, the day. An instance of this is found in the words of Jacob, *The days of my pilgrimage,* where night is not mentioned at all. But the evening and the morning are mentioned as being the ends of the day, since day begins with morning and ends with evening, or because evening denotes the beginning of night, and morning the beginning of day. It seems fitting, also, that where the first distinction of creatures is described, divisions of time should be denoted only by what marks their beginning. And the reason for mentioning the evening first is that as the evening ends the day, which begins with the light, the termination of the light at evening precedes the termination of the darkness, which ends with the morning. But Chrysostom's explanation is that thereby it is intended to show that the natural day does not end with the evening, but with the morning (*Hom.* v. *in Gen.*).

Reply Obj. 7. The words *one day* are used when day is first instituted, to denote that one day is made up of twenty-four hours. Hence, by mentioning *one,* the measure of a natural day is fixed. Another reason may be to signify that a day is completed by the return of the sun to the point from which it commenced its course. And yet another, because at the completion of a week of seven days, the first day returns, which is one with the eighth day. The three reasons assigned above are those given by Basil (*Hom.* ii. *in Hexæm.*).

Milton Keynes UK
Ingram Content Group UK Ltd.
UKHW031421131024
449633UK00006B/42